How this book will help you...

It doesn't matter whether you're heading for mocks in Year 11, or in the final run-up to your GCSE exam – **this book will help you to produce your very best.**

Whichever approach you decide to take to revision, this book will provide everything you need:

1. Total revision support
2. Quick revision check-ups
3. Exam practice

1 Total Revision Support

Everything you need to know

This book contains most of the topics you'll have studied at school. **It covers all the main topics set by all the Exam Boards.**

Short, easy-to-use sections

If, when you're revising, you need to go over something you haven't understood, you'll have no trouble finding it in this book. We've divided each chapter into a number of **short sections with clear headings**. Just look up the topic you want in the contents list or index.

Many of the facts are presented as short, sharp bullet-points so that they're really easy to remember.

Extra points for higher grades

The 'Extra points' boxes contain additional information. **You need to learn these extra facts if you're aiming to gain an A or A* in your exam.**

...Turn over for QUICK REVISION CHECK-UPS and EXAM PRACTICE...→

Quick Revision Check-ups

Check yourself questions

It can be really hard knowing where to start when you're revising. Sitting down and wading through pages of facts isn't easy. You're probably asleep before the third page! This book makes it easy to stay awake – **because it makes revising ACTIVE**.

We came up with the idea of putting **'Check yourself'** questions into each chapter. **The questions test your understanding of all the important facts and ideas** in each section of the chapter. In this way, you can find out quickly and easily just how much you know. You don't need to read through all the text first – just try the questions. If you get all the questions right, you can move straight on to the next section. If you get several of the questions wrong, you know you need to read through the whole section carefully. **This really cuts down on revision time – and helps you focus on where you need to put most effort.**

Answers and Tutorials

If you want the 'Check yourself' questions to be a genuine test of how much you know, then you need to cover up the answers. But, if you'd rather, you can read through a question, then the answer and then the **'tutorial'**. This will still do you a lot of good – and doesn't require quite as much effort!

We've included 'tutorials', as well as answers, to give you even more help with your revision. The tutorials contain extra information, they point out common mistakes that the author knows candidates make, and give you hints on answering similar questions in exams.

3

Exam Practice

Exam technique

Knowing the facts is important. But **it's even more important to know how to use them to answer exam questions properly**. The author sees hundreds of exam scripts a year and students very often lose marks not because they don't know their facts, but because **they haven't understood how to tackle exam questions.**

Questions and sample student's answers

It's often easiest to explain what to do and what not to do by looking at **actual examples of students' answers to exam questions**. This is why we've included sample answers in this book.

These are typical answers, not perfect ones. They highlight the kind of mistakes students often make. **In the examiner's comments, the author runs through these mistakes and shows you clearly what you need to do to score full marks on the questions.**

Questions to Answer

We've also included **lots of past exam questions from different Exam Boards for you to have a go at.** The answers are at the back of the book so it's easy not to cheat. Have a go at the questions yourself and then compare them with the answers. **We've provided comments on most of the answers to give you extra help** – and if you're still unsure you can go back to the relevant section in the book.

Three final tips:

1. Work as consistently as you can during your whole GCSE Modern World History course. If you don't understand something, ask your teacher straight away, or look it up in this book. You'll then find revision much easier.

2. Plan your revision carefully and focus on the areas you know you find hard. The 'Check yourself' questions in this book will help you do this.

3. Try to do some exam questions as though you were in the actual exam. Time yourself and don't cheat by looking at the answers until you've really had a good go at working out the answers.

About your GCSE Modern World History course

Modern World History syllabuses are the most popular GCSE History syllabuses studied. All syllabuses require students to do these three things:

1 **'Recall, select, organise and deploy knowledge of the syllabus content.'**

In other words, you have to know the History you have studied very well. You have to be able to remember names, dates, places and people, and use this knowledge in the right place in the exam. You are more likely to remember these key facts if you have enjoyed studying the topics on your syllabus. This book is written as simply and clearly as possible, with lots of pictures and questions to help you get to grips with the facts you must know.

Fig.3.7 Nazi poster of an 'ideal' family

2 **'Describe, analyse and explain:**
- **the events, changes and issues studied**
- **the key features and characteristics of the periods, people, societies and situations studied.'**

There is more to History than telling a story. You will be asked to explain why things happened the way they did, what the results were, how successful someone or something was, or why they failed. This book emphasises these questions much more than an orthodox school textbook does. There are lists of causes and results, and clear summaries of key events. Most of the thinking has been done for you.

3 **'Comprehend, analyse and evaluate representations and situations of the events, people and issues studied;**
Comprehend, evaluate, interpret and use a range of sources of information of different types.'

Topics covered

All four English GCSE Exam Boards offer Modern World History syllabuses. All their exams ask students to do the things listed opposite. The only differences are in the topics you can study with each. Some boards have a core of topics, with options; others have every topic as an option. Check with your teacher which topics you need to study and revise. This book covers all the popular topics from all of these syllabuses. It is unlikely that you will need to use all of the book, although you may find it useful to read the topics you are not taking for the exam in order to pick up further hints on technique.

Exam requirements

GCSE History exams usually consist of two papers of about 1½ to 2 hours each. There is normally a choice of questions. All students take both papers and answer from the same questions. Marks for both papers, plus coursework marks, are added together and an overall grade awarded. There are no tiered papers or limited grade papers as in most other subjects. The *Check yourself* sections all through this book give worked examples of the different styles of question. The *Examiner's comments* also help prepare you to deal with the different requirements.

The *Check yourself* sections and the exam questions with *Examiner's comments*, will gradually teach you how to deal with all the types of historical sources used in exams: photographs, cartoons, letters, reports, statistics, newspapers and the writings of other historians.

WHAT DO YOU HAVE TO DO IN THE EXAM?

Although the Modern World History syllabuses offered by the four GCSE exam boards are all slightly different in design and content, they all ask candidates to do the same things in their exams. This opening section of the book lists the **different kinds of questions** that are asked and offers some advice on how to tackle them. These various question styles are used throughout the rest of the book, so that you will soon become quite used to their demands and get plenty of practice at answering them.

SOURCE-BASED QUESTIONS

COMPREHENDING SOURCES

Look at this picture. What can you see?

At a glance you can see that there is a queue of black people on the right and some soldiers on the left.

Now read the caption.

Figure 1.1
United Nations soldiers in the Congo, 1961

This information helps a great deal in pinning down what we are actually looking at. But this is not a 'spot-the-ball' competition, it is a historical source. Historians find out about the past by studying sources to obtain evidence. The obvious historical question, in a simple style which often starts off a source paper in a GCSE History exam, is:

What does this source tell us about the United Nations?

Even this very simple opening question needs some thought.

- Look closely at the source.
  Take your time. Go beyond first impressions. For example, in this case most of the people queueing are women or children; they appear to be holding containers – buckets or bowls; the soldiers are armed and there is an armoured car on which some of them are riding. You can just see the olive branch badge of the UN on the front of the armoured car. Most of the soldiers appear to be white. It is all happening on a road, with thick trees in the background. Not all this information may be useful, but it goes far beyond that 'first glance' impression.

- Read the caption carefully.
  In this case it gives three essential bits of information, without which the picture is only a guessing game: the place – the Congo, the time – 1961, and confirmation that these are UN soldiers. The caption gives no information about the people on the right.

- How does the question focus your answer?
  If there is one thing to remember when tackling exams it is to *always answer the question*. In this case, you are asked to act as a historian finding out about the UN. This helps you to focus the bits of information you have put together from your close scrutiny of the picture.

Even this simple question requires two stages of thinking:

1. What is there on view which tells you something about the UN?

2. What can you **infer** from the picture about the UN?

(To *infer* means to work out something which is not actually shown in the picture.)

Under 1, you could say that it shows that the UN took part in active operations in the Congo in 1961. Soldiers were sent, and some were armed.

Under 2, you can infer that these people needed food supplies and that the UN is probably arranging the distribution of food aid. You can tell that the UN was prepared to use armed strength, making up an army with soldiers from member-countries.

Putting these two together, a short answer might read:
This picture tells us that the UN was prepared to use armed force to intervene in crisis areas such as the Congo in 1961. It used soldiers from member-countries, in UN uniform, to keep the peace and look after the basic needs of the people.

Check yourself

QUESTION

Q1 Look at this picture and read the caption.
What does this picture tell us about the effects of the Great Depression on the USA?

Figure 1.2
Unemployed workers in New York queueing for bread, 1930.

REMEMBER! Cover the answer if you want to.

ANSWER

A1 This picture shows how deeply the Depression affected the USA. In just one part of New York several dozen people are queueing for bread handouts. It shows that charities were ready to help the unemployed by handing out free bread and it reminds us that there was no dole or welfare system in the USA, so people who lost their job were utterly dependent on what they had saved, if anything, and on charity.

TUTORIAL

T1 *Quite a good answer – probably enough to get nearly full marks in a question which would only be worth 3 or 4 marks. In these cases examiners are only looking to see if you can provide examples of good observation and inference.*

Other points which are equally valid are: the presence of cars and buses running normally at the top of the picture reminds us that not everyone was ruined by the Depression. The queue is long and orderly: no one is pushing or complaining. The people of the USA nearly all accepted the Depression quietly, often blaming themselves and rarely resorting to violent protest.

COMPREHENDING SOURCES IN CONTEXT

Both the sources used on the previous pages were looked at in isolation – we only considered what you could see and what the caption told you. Historians hardly ever work like that – in complete ignorance of the context of a source. They study sources in the light of what they already know about a topic. In GCSE therefore, questions are set which are more realistic, more like what historians do. Look at the words used in this question and compare it with those on the previous page:

Use this source and your own knowledge to explain why the USA became involved in war in Vietnam.

> 'The threat to the free nations of South-East Asia has long been clear. The North Vietnamese government has constantly sought to take over South Vietnam and Laos .... The USA will continue its basic policy of assisting free nations of the area to defend their freedom.'
> From *President Johnson's message to the* US *Congress*, 1964

This kind of question is asking for two things at once: to comprehend the source in its own right and to use recalled information to explain it further. Because of this double request, it is probably better to tackle the answer in two stages:

1. What does the source say?
   In this case it is telling us what President Johnson put forward in 1964 as his reasons for escalating US forces in Vietnam. He sees it as assistance to free South Vietnam from North Vietnamese invasion. This is an important speech, as the caption tells us: the President speaking to the US Congress.

2. How does our knowledge of the history help us understand this extract better?

There are lots of bits of information we could use: the USA had been determined to halt the advance of Communism as part of its Cold War strategy since the Truman Doctrine of 1947. Johnson was extending this by seeking to prevent South Vietnam from becoming Communist. In fact, Vietnam had been split, supposedly temporarily, at the Peace of Geneva in 1954. The USA had resisted free elections in South Vietnam as they feared the Communists would win. Although Johnson calls South Vietnam 'free' it was not a democratic country. We also know that the date, 1964, is crucial, because in that year Johnson began to increase US presence in Vietnam enormously. This speech gives the justification for this escalation.

A short answer might therefore read:
> *In this speech President Johnson is setting out his reasons for increasing US participation in the Vietnam War. He is explaining to Congress that he sees it as a war to protect free South Vietnam from invasion by North Vietnam. This was part of US Cold War strategy from the Truman Doctrine of 1947 onwards. The US Congress supported him and the number of US soldiers in Vietnam increased dramatically from 1964 onwards.*

Now let's look at another example.

Figure 1.3
A British cartoon from December 1919 called 'The Gap in the Bridge'.

Use this source and your own knowledge to explain one of the problems of the League of Nations.

Cartoons are popular with examiners as they often sum up a situation, covering quite a lot of points in a single picture. However, they are not as easy as they may look!

Start by remembering that this simple drawing has taken the cartoonist many hours of thought and work. Every detail is significant, so the first task, simply observing, is quite demanding.

In this case:

1. The cartoonist has drawn a bridge. We can tell from the noticeboard that it is the League of Nations and that it was designed by the President of the USA. Four nations on the bridge are named: Belgium, France, England and Italy. There is a man sitting nearby, in fact 'Uncle Sam' representing the USA (you will have to learn some of these national symbols: John Bull for Britain, a bear for Russia, etc.). Fortunately Uncle Sam is leaning on a keystone labelled 'USA'. Clearly the keystone is missing from the bridge and the cartoonist draws our attention to it by the title: 'The Gap in the Bridge'.

2. The League of Nations had been designed by US President Woodrow Wilson as a better way of conducting world affairs after the First World War. Its charter was written in to the terms of all the treaties at the end of the war. Unfortunately, the US Senate were reluctant to get entangled with European and world affairs and would not ratify the treaties. In 1919, the year of this cartoon, the USA had not joined the League, and in fact it never did. The organisation was therefore always without its 'keystone', its most important member, the USA.

3. Note that the question does not ask for all of this, but asks us to focus on explaining why the situation shown here was a problem.

As we have seen, not all the details we have listed here need be included in the answer. A good short answer, using the wording of the question to give a sharp focus, would say:

> *One of the problems of the League of Nations was that some important nations were never in it. The USA, whose President, Woodrow Wilson, had given the idea of a League of Nations such prominence, never joined because the US Senate refused to ratify the Treaty setting up the League. The League was therefore always without what was intended to be its most important member.*

IS THE EVIDENCE ENOUGH?

Sometimes the question asks you to use your own knowledge to comment on whether the evidence is **enough** to supply a good answer to some historical question. (These are sometimes called 'sufficiency' questions.)

Look at this example.

Figure 1.4
Map showing parts of the USA within range of missiles based in Cuba, 1962.

Is this map enough to explain why the Cuban missile crisis took place?

You can almost always guarantee that the answer to this kind of question will be 'up to a point only'. Your answer is likely to consist of two paragraphs, first outlining the ways the source *does* fit the question and then laying out the other factors *not* dealt with in the source. The two paragraphs below show a full answer.

> *In this case, the map explains more clearly than any words that missiles based in Cuba would be able to hit almost any part of the USA. The speed of these missiles would mean that these areas would have only a few minutes warning of a nuclear attack. This explains why, when his spy-planes showed photographs of these missile sites being erected, President Kennedy acted fast and strongly. He even considered an attack on Cuba, but decided to blockade the island. He told Soviet leader Khrushchev that he must not install the missiles on Cuba.*
>
> *However (as you will see on p.228 of this book), that is not the whole story – the map only explains the reasons for the crisis 'up to a point'. There were longer-term factors involved. For example, the USA opposed the regime of Cuba's revolutionary leader, Castro, and Kennedy had already tried to remove him wth the 'Bay of Pigs' invasion, 1961. Long-range Soviet missiles could already hit the USA anyway. Khrushchev placed his intermediate range missiles in Cuba by way of retaliation for US missiles on the borders of the USSR in Turkey. And at the most general level, there was an arms race on between the USA and the USSR and Kennedy could not afford to let the USSR get ahead.*

Check yourself

QUESTION

Q1 Use this poster and your own knowledge to explain why the Nazis gained support during the great Depression in Germany.

Figure 1.5
Nazi Election poster, 1932. The wording reads:
'Our Last Hope: Hitler'

REMEMBER! Cover the answer if you want to.

ANSWER

A1 This poster tells the German people that only Hitler can help them now. The people on the poster look desperate, poor and worried and the Nazis are saying that they are the only ones with a solution to their problems. The Depression and unemployment following the Wall Street Crash in 1929 was serious in Germany, whose economy relied on loans from the USA. By 1932, the date of this poster, there were six million unemployed. Before the Depression, support for the Nazis was low and no one seemed to be interested in their remedies. Hitler took advantage of Germany's desperate situation. He told the German people that the Weimar system was bound to fail and only he could solve their problems. He came a good second in the Presidential elections of 1932 and nearly doubled the number of Nazis in the Reichstag.

TUTORIAL

T1 *This answer sticks closely to the question, without wandering off into irrelevant details about Nazism, which is so easy to do on this topic. It also makes very good use of accurate knowledge, particularly in putting the poster in the context of the rise in support for Hitler in 1932.*

It could go even more into the background of Germany in the period up to the time of this poster. In the later 1920s Germany was recovering and people set aside their hostility to the Weimar Republic. They had blamed it for the humiliating Treaty of Versailles and for the crippling inflation of 1923, but this was temporarily forgotten. Then came the crash and what little support democracy had in Germany was lost. President Hindenburg was ruling by decree and many Germans were ready to listen to Hitler's claim that he was 'their last hope' as the poster says:

USEFULNESS OF SOURCES

Historians use sources to find out about the past. It seems fair, then, to ask questions about **how useful** a particular source would be *for finding out about some historical topic.*

Note the last seven words: sources are never useful or useless regardless, they are only useful, or useless, depending what you want to know.

There are a number of issues involved in this idea of **usefulness**:

- **Is it relevant?**
  This means studying the source to see if it is about the topic you are interested in. In an exam it is unlikely that you would be given an irrelevant source. However, you must not forget the **attribution** – the caption or description of the source. This will tell you who said or wrote it, when, where etc.

- **Is it reliable?**
  In other words, is it absolutely accurate and truthful? Here again, study not only the source itself but also the attribution.

  It is important to realise that the *absolutely reliable source is very rare.* It is therefore not very clever to simply dismiss some source as 'unreliable' or 'biased' and leave it at that. You should think about *how* unreliable it is, *why* it is unreliable and *in what ways.*

  You then go on to think about how you could use it *even though it is unreliable in the ways you have described.*

- **How does it increase my understanding of this topic?**
  Even though it may be biased, a source can nevertheless help you find out more about some topic: the important thing is to keep that topic in mind.

It is time to look at an example.

How useful is this source as evidence about the storming of the Winter Palace in 1917?

Figure 1.6
A still picture from the film Oktober, *made by Sergei Eisenstein in 1927.*

This picture shows the storming of the Winter Palace by the Bolsheviks in October 1917 and was made using the actual buildings and streets where the events it shows took place.

Let's use the three checklist points given above:

- It is relevant: it is about the event in question; but, using the attribution, it was made ten years later, and is from a film. But then again, Eisenstein did use the actual buildings and streets where it all happened.

- It may not be very reliable. It is a film and films are made to hold an audience's attention. Events may therefore be altered to make them more dramatic, more interesting. The actual storming of the Winter Palace, for example, took place at night. This still shows a daylight attack because film-cameras at that time could not film at night. Even though Eisenstein used the same buildings and streets, these may have changed in ten years.

  On the positive side, he was quite close in time to these events, so he could easily have spoken to people who were there and so got an accurate impression of events. It may be more accurate than if, for example, we were making the film now, beyond living memory.

- Finally, the film may be accurate, with some care, in showing streets and buildings. It *may* be accurate in terms of what happened, although it will be seen as if it had happened by day. Most of all, however, the film is a better record of how people like Eisenstein, supporters of the Bolshevik Revolution, felt about these events ten years later. It is more accurate in telling us about 1927 than about 1917. (For example, although you cannot see it here and so could not be expected to say this in an exam, Trotsky played a large part in events in 1917, but was becoming disgraced in 1927, so his role was played down in the film.)

Check yourself

QUESTION

Q1 'The Marshall Plan of 1947 led to a reduction in the trade of the USSR... The USA hoped that this would lead to a split among the Communist states and bring them under American influence. It was also clear that much of the Marshall Plan was aimed at rebuilding the military power of Western Germany.'

Written by a Soviet historian in 1968

How useful is this source in finding out about the Marshall Plan?

ANSWER

A1 This source is about the Marshall Plan of 1948, the plan devised by US President Truman's Secretary of State, General George Marshall, to loan $17 billion to help revive European economies.

It is a Soviet view of the Plan. The USSR rejected Marshall Aid and so did all its Eastern European allies. This source helps to explain why they rejected it: they saw it as an attempt to weaken the Communist economies, to split them and particularly to revive Western Germany. The USSR held a deep hatred and fear of Germany because of their experiences in the Second World War, in which fighting off the Nazi invasion cost at least twenty million Soviet lives as well as the destruction of towns, cities, farms and industries. Any revival of Germany was thus regarded with great suspicion.

It is quite useful in explaining the Soviet reactions to the Plan. It is no use in explaining US motives as the writer only assumes the worst of the USA.

TUTORIAL

T1 *A good answer, using the checklist to work through the three considerations: relevance, reliability and use. It also makes good use of the attribution: this is a good example of how absolutely essential the attribution is in answering this kind of question.*

Only two further points could be mentioned: the source is also a view from twenty years later. The writer can look back on events and judge the effects of the Marshall Plan. It may well be true that Soviet trade declined as a result of the Plan, as Western European countries became more self-sufficient, or turned to trade with the USA or each other.

It is also true that the Plan was designed to revive Germany. By 1948 the West had decided that the German people should not be punished any more for the sins of Nazism. It was also better in the long run for everybody if Germany became less dependent on aid and so look after itself. The best way of doing this was by reviving their economy.

These last two points make clear how wrong it is to dismiss a source as 'biased therefore useless' and so write it off completely. The source is biased, and that is what makes it useful. It is also quite accurate in some of the things it says.

COMPARING SOURCES

Further into the paper, you will find comparison questions. These extend the issues raised in the last section, where we looked at the usefulness of a source, to comparing usefulness. For example:

Source A

'Men began slaughtering their cattle every night. Both peasants who had joined the collective and individual farmers killed off their stock. "Kill, it's not ours now", "Kill, the State butchers will take it anyway'", "Kill, they won't give you any meat on the collective'", the rumours spread around.'

From a novel, *Virgin Soil Upturned* by Mikhail Sholokhov, published in 1938

Source B (opposite)

Which of these two sources do you think is more useful for finding out about collectivisation in the USSR in the 1930s?

The most sensible way of tackling this kind of question is to take the sources one at a time and so lead up to the comparison at the end. Source A is about peasants' reactions to collectivisation, but is from a novel. It is therefore a work of fiction, Sholokhov's view of what happened. It was, however published close to the time when Stalin was forcibly collectivising farms in the USSR. It was therefore possible for him to find out about the events he has put in his novel.

Source B

As with any biased source, novels are not necessarily utterly useless; they may not be total fiction, total fantasy, just because the novelist chooses to make a story out of events. You could mention here that other sources would help verify whether the incidents described here actually happened (after all, a historian does not write a book on the basis of one source!). If these incidents did take place (and they did), then *Virgin Soil Upturned* is quite a useful source.

Source B is a photograph. There is a tendency, still, to believe that 'the camera cannot lie'. In fact the camera *can lie*. Photographs can be unreliable evidence because:

- the photo can be cut up, re-made and re-printed.
- the subject can be 'set up' so that the photo shows something that only existed for the camera.
- the camera can select. The photographer can point the camera only at parts of the scene, perhaps untypical parts. We thus see a real photo, but not helpful evidence.

In the twentieth century governments learnt how to use photography to get across the message they wanted, using all of the techniques above. For these reasons, photographs in twentieth-century history should be used with extreme caution.

In this case we are told that the photo is propaganda. The scene it shows did happen but it has been set up to look as if the collectives were full of tractors. The photo, Source B, is therefore relevant, but biased and probaby not what really happened on the average collective. It is, however, *extremely useful* evidence of what the goverment wanted people to think was happening on collectives. One of Stalin's motives for collectivisation was to mechanise Soviet agriculture to make it more efficient. This photo seems to show just what he said was going to happen, and so to prove that collectivisation was a success.

Having analysed each source separately, we can now compare them.

There are two simple golden rules for all sorts of comparison questions:

1. Don't say one is all good and one is all bad.

2. Discuss both.

An answer to the last part of this question could therefore say:
Source A needs checking to see if it is typical, but if it was then it is useful for describing and explaining peasant hostility to collectivisation. Source B is only useful as a propaganda picture of the impression Stalin wanted to create of the success of collectivisation. Both have limited uses, but Source A is probably more useful as we have little evidence of how ordinary Soviet people thought at this time.

(Incidentally, as you will see when you look at mark schemes later in this book, there is no right answer to these comparison questions. The marks go for how you argue your choice.)

Check yourself

QUESTION

Q1 **Source C**

Figure 1.8
New boys join the Hitler Youth at a special swearing-in ceremony.

Source D

'I think one of the worst effects is that our children no longer get any peace and quiet. I dread to think the kind of people they will grow up to be with all this endless propaganda'.

A German woman's comments on the Hitler Youth published in 1945 but made earlier.

Which of Sources C and D is more useful for finding out about the Hitler Youth?

REMEMBER! Cover the answer if you want to.

ANSWER

A1 Source C shows boys lined up in uniform. One boy is giving the Nazi salute as he swears an oath and holds the flag. It is a propaganda photo, but may be quite an accurate record of what happened. It is therefore quite reliable and shows a bit of the ceremony.

Source D is an adult's comment on the Hitler Youth. It is hard to judge its reliability: perhaps she thought this all along, perhaps she only said this in 1945, either just before or just after the end of the war, when Nazism was discredited. If it was not just designed to give an impression of anti-Nazism then it is quite useful as evidence of the propaganda nature of the Hitler Youth.

I think Source C is more useful: it shows that the Hitler Youth went in for ritual, tried to make everyone look alike and be utterly loyal to the Nazis, but Source D does help us understand that some Germans had doubts about it all.

TUTORIAL

T1 *For once we may take the photo at face value. Lots of boys are lined up to join the Hitler Youth in this photo, but then lots of boys did join it. The Nazis did set up scenes like this to be impressive propaganda events, not just in the photographs, but for those present. We can well imagine the effects of this public ceremony on the young boys.*

Source D is useful in reminding us that the real purpose of the Hitler Youth was indoctrination into Nazism. The first comment in the source, that young people had no peace and quiet, is quite important too: it meant that the boys had no time to be on their own, to form their own opinions. Hitler knew that he would never win over all adult Germans, but hoped to win over all young people. By 1939 80 per cent of young people were in one of the Nazi Youth movements. Source D reminds us that total control was what he was after.

ANALYSING INTERPRETATIONS

People make statements about the past all the time: 'Bad King John', 'Good Queen Bess', 'The Roman Empire was the greatest empire the world has ever seen' and so on. Different people make different statements about the same topic. This is because many of these issues are matters of judgement and not matters of fact, because new information comes up which throws new light on old certainties or because different priorities require old judgements to be revised. Beyond a few certain facts, it is impossible to have the last word in History.

These judgements about the past are called **interpretations**. One of the tasks historians is to analyse them, to comment on how accurate they are. Some GCSE questions, usually towards the end of the paper, ask you to comment on interpretations.

For example:

Source E

Figure 1.9
Graph showing the number of people unemployed in the USA 1930–40

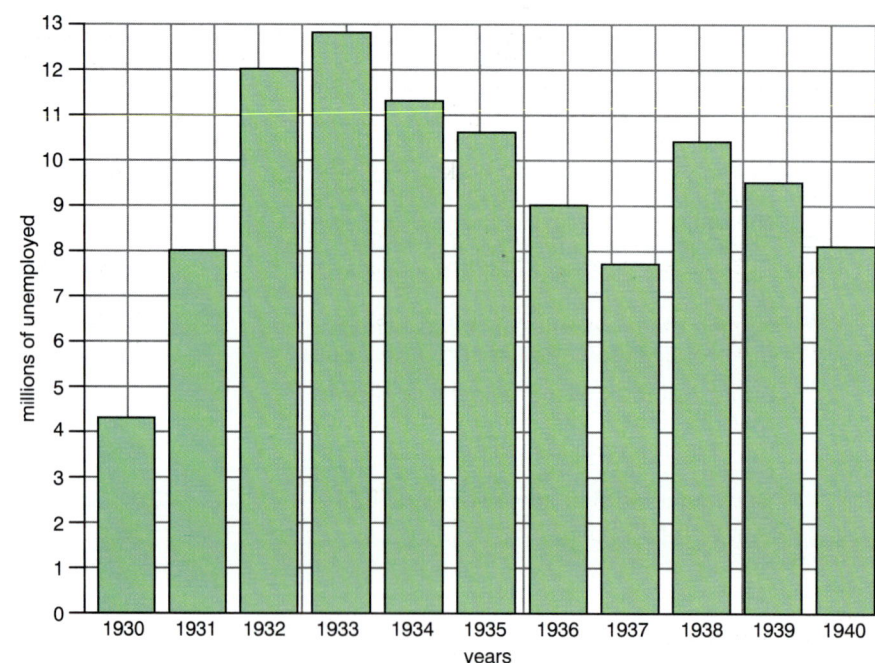

'**The New Deal was a great success.'** Use this source and your own knowledge to comment on this interpretation of the New Deal.

All sorts of thoughts may rush into your mind as you face this question: the graph, the statement, your own views, those you have read. What we need is a plan to sort it all out and put it down:

1. Comment on the source and how far it proves the given judgement.

2. Use your own knowledge to talk about other issues.

3. Come your own conclusion which does not totally agree or totally disagree with the judgement.

The graph shows that unemployment fell during the New Deal period. It was 12.8 million in 1933, when Roosevelt came to power and the New Deal started. It was 7.7 million by 1937.

However, some points need to be made before saying that the graph proves that the judgement is correct:

Graph sources

Don't be frightened by statistical sources like this graph. As you should with any source, take time to come to grips with it. Look first at the 'axes' – the horizontal line along the bottom and the vertical line up the side. These tell you what the graph is about. Try to get an idea of the general trend of the graph – in this case, it shows unemployment rising sharply to a peak and then falling. Don't stop there! Look for the extra bits of information: the extremely low unemployment of 1930, the second rise in 1938. Like any source, a graph can often be 'squeezed' for information beyond what is obvious.

- First, that unemployment never fell to what it was before the Depression: 4.3 million.

- Second, we need to show that it was the New Deal that caused the fall from 1933 to 1937.

- Third, we need to comment on the rise in unemployment in 1938 and 1939, which were when Roosevelt was still in office and most New Deal laws still operative.

In fact, critics of the New Deal had said that many unemployed had simply been removed from the register because they were working on government contracts or directly for one of the 'alphabet agencies', such as the Works Project Administration (WPA), the Tennessee Valley Authority (TVA), the Public Works Administration (PWA), the Civilian Conservation Corps (CCC) and so on. Roosevelt therefore tried to cut government spending in 1937. The result can be seen in the graph. This 'blip' in the graph at least seems to prove that the New Deal was the cause of the fall from 1933 to 1937. The fall in unemployment after 1937 was mainly due to growth in industry to make weapons for the US armed forces or to sell to Britain and other Allies. (Although the USA did not join the war until the end of 1941, it was heavily involved from 1939 onwards.)

In making our own judgement on the New Deal, we need to judge it by what it intended to do. From our own knowledge we know that solving unemployment was one of the main aims of the New Deal, but not the only one. Roosevelt also set about restoring faith in the USA, improving the environment, protecting workers' rights, establishing a sound banking system, and so on. Some would say that he also wanted to preserve the capitalist system and avoid revolution. If we are going to make a judgement on the New Deal, we need to look at these points too.

In conclusion, we can say that the New Deal was successful in many of its aims. In cutting unemployment it was only partially successful as there were still 10.4 million unemployed in 1937 and the fall in the years after that are more due to military contracts for armaments for the Second World War than to New Deal measures.

Check yourself

QUESTION

Q1 **Source F**

'The situation in Petrograd is serious. The government can do nothing. Food and fuel are running out. Troops are firing at each other. Someone who is trusted by the country must form a new government.'

Telegram from Rodzianko, President of the Duma (Parliament) to Tsar Nicholas II, who was away at the Front, 11 March 1917

Source G

'That fat Rodzianko has sent me some nonsense. I shall not even reply.'

Letter from the Tsar to a friend, 12 March 1917

'Tsar Nicholas II was responsible for his own downfall.'
Use Sources F and G and your own knowledge to comment on the accuracy of this statement.

ANSWER

A1 Source F describes the situation in Petrograd. Rodzianko describes food and fuel shortages leading to riots. The troops were unreliable. There was a feeling that a new government was needed. Source G shows Tsar Nicholas' reply, ignoring Source F and showing his contempt for Rodzianko. Nicholas disliked the Duma and all it stood for, even though it was far from fully democratic.

In fact Rodzianko was right: within days there was a revolution, Nicholas was deposed and a Provisional Government set up.

Nicholas had brought this on himself, not only by his ignoring good advice in 1917, but ever since he had become Tsar in 1896. He was out of touch with his people, so had little idea of the hardships of the workers, the difficulties of the peasants. He despised democracy and used his power to weaken the Duma set up after the 1905 revolution. His secret police suppressed all opposition.

It is therefore largely true that Nicholas was responsible for his own downfall. However, it was the First World War which pushed Russia over the edge. Nicholas must take the blame for the defeats and the problems which it caused in Russia which led to the revolution, but he was not responsible for the war.

TUTORIAL

T1 *This shows the planned approach outlined above used well in quite a short, but strongly argued, answer.*

Rodzianko's letter, Source F, shows a good grasp of what was going on. The coup which happened a few days later was intended to find a government which was more acceptable than Nicholas. The actual revolution, with soldiers mutinying, peasants seizing land and workers seizing factories, was later in the year.

The only criticism of the conclusion is the wider one: what could anyone have done in Russia in the early twentieth century? Nicholas was not on his own in rejecting democracy and the social structure of Russia meant that it would have shallow roots. His mixture of mild reform and economic growth after 1905 might have allowed Tsarism to continue, some think, if it had not been for the war.

For more details on this interpretation, see chapter 5; however, you can see here how interpretation questions require you pull in information as well as deal with the sources.

WRITING ESSAYS

The majority of the marks in a GCSE History exam – normally about 60 per cent – are awarded for recalling, selecting and organising knowledge in answer to questions which ask you to describe, explain or analyse historical events. That is why the bulk of this book is given over to laying out the History you have to know in a way that will make it easy for you to recall it for the exam.

Shorter questions, with anything from 3 to 6 marks, usually require a paragraph of information. Here is an example:

Choose two items from this list:
> **Hotline between Washington and Moscow**
> **Strategic Arms Limitation Talks**
> **Helsinki Agreements**
and show how they contributed to better relations between the superpowers.

To answer this, you will have to do only two, quite simple, things:

- **describe** two of the items;
- **explain** how it made relations between the superpowers better.

More demanding, however, are questions which:

- cover a wider range of History;
- ask you to think about a more serious question;
- carry more marks;
- require a longer answer.

This book is written so as to help you tackle these big questions. When you get into the chapters you will see that they are:

- organised around questions, so that you are used to the idea of History being about answering questions.
- laid out in lists of points. These give the basis of an essay-plan.

An essay is:

- extended writing. In an exam you will be expected to write two to three sides.
- organised so as to answer a question. You will never be asked to 'write all you know about...' You will always have to organise your answer. Hence the need for a plan.

Think about this example:

Why were the people of Germany angry about the Treaty of Versailles?

If you know this topic well, this is an easy question. Lots of ideas will rush into your mind: loss of colonies, war-guilt, reparations – and should I mention the Rhineland?

Stop! Don't start the essay yet!

Take a piece of scrap paper and jot down all these ideas. Where is the pattern? Is an order emerging?

Note that this essay does *not* say: Write all you know about the terms of the Treaty of Versailles. It has a clear question: Why were the German people angry? History is full of 'why?' questions: they are the most common kind of GCSE essay question.

Here are three tips to help you form your plan:

- Make a list. Very few historical events had only one cause. You will get yourself above the 'ground floor' of marks at once if you can present several reasons.

- Think of a logical pattern for your list; it shouldn't just be one thing after another. Often 'why?' questions divide into long-term/short-term causes. Another possible distinction is more important/less important causes. When you have done this, number the items on your list – it is unlikely that the final essay will deal with items in the order you first thought of.

- Make up your mind what you think about the whole question. In this case: were the German people justified in feeling angry? Be ready to make comments to support your general view as you write the essay, both in an opening statement, and as comments on the items on the list/plan as you go through it.

You will find the details for this question on p.52, but a plan might look like this:

- **Para 1**   Introduction (brief) Germans v. angry when terms of T of V announced: had expected negotiated peace between near-equals. Despite German anger terms not in fact that bad.

- **Para 2**   Diktat: a dictated peace. Describe situation of 1918: German army surrenders on basis of Fourteen Points, expecting lenient settlement. German people unaware of depth of defeat. Terms actually worked out by WW, LLoyd G, & Cl. Last two much more revengeful.

- **Para 3** Territorial terms: loss of land (give as many details as you can remember). Colonies.
- **Para 4** Other restrictions: armed forces; Rhineland.
- **Para 5** War guilt clause, leading to reparations
- **Para 6** Seen as unfair – e.g. self-determination applied to others, not Germans, many left living under non-German governments. Reparations punished the German people, not their rulers, and carried on well into future. Failure of Allies to disarm as promised.
- **Para 7** Conclusion Up to you: could mention harsh German treatment of Russia at Brest–Litovsk; could point out rapid German recovery as evidence of underlying strength. Probably need to repeat German people's ignorance of events of 1918.

Some essay questions are double questions, the first usually being quite straightforward but moving on to a judgement in the second. For example:

How did Hitler try to solve Germany's unemployment problems between 1933 and 1939? How successful was he?

The simplest plan deals with these two questions in the order given, although you might like to refer to the second question in your introduction, as below. (Details of this topic are on p.82)

- **Para 1** Introduction Situation in Germany in 1933: 6m unemployed. Hitler's election promises to cure unemployment. By 1939 a labour shortage. Apparently his greatest success.
- **Para 2** National Labour Service (started before he came to power) Forced labour for six months from 1935.
- **Para 3** Big public schemes: e.g. autobahns. Good propaganda. Some of Hitler's policies, e.g. road building, began under Weimar.
- **Para 4** Rearmament. Growth of armed forces + contracts to rebuild armaments against terms of T of V.
- **Para 5** Conclusion. A success and source of popularity. Unemployment was cured, unlike many other countries. In a dictatorship workers are tools of the state: cost to workers – loss of freedoms, low wages, etc.

Check yourself

QUESTION

Q1 Write a plan for an essay to answer this question:

In September 1938 Britain and France were ready to make an agreement with Germany. In September 1939 Britain and France declared war on Germany. Explain why this change came about.

ANSWER

A1

Para 1 Introduction. Appeasement policy of 1938: to give Hitler his 'reasonable demands'. Failed as Hitler broke his word. Hence declaration of war when Germans invaded Poland.

Para 2 Reasons for appeasement – determination to avoid war; British unpreparedness; British feelings that Versailles was too harsh so Germany had legitimate demands.

Para 3 Sudetenland crisis. Chamberlain meets Hitler. Munich meeting, with France & Italy. Terms of agreement. Hitler's promises.

Para 4 March 1939 Ger. invasion of Czechoslovakia. British & French reactions.

Para 5 Hitler's reactions to Munich. Nazi–Soviet Pact. Invasion of Poland, September 1939.

Para 6 Conclusion. Br & Fr apparently turned round in a year. In fact circumstances of September '38 and September '39 changed utterly.

TUTORIAL

T1

This is really a double 'Why?' question: Why agree with Hitler in 1938? Why go to war in 1939? There is also an apparent complete inconsistency to justify.

The plan above works quite well. It hinges on para 2 where the reasons for appeasement are given. Chamberlain was praised at the time and vilified afterwards for his policy, but he certainly carried most of the British people with him when he proclaimed that the Munich Agreement was 'Peace in our time'. Perhaps it was wishful thinking: everyone wanted it to be lasting peace.

A large part of this essay consists of the details of events, but merely supplying a record of what happened is not enough. You have to tie in the story of these twelve months, as they unfold, to the explanation of British and French motives.

SPELLING, PUNCTUATION AND GRAMMAR

Five marks in History GCSE are awarded for spelling, punctuation and grammar (SPG), over and above the 100 marks for the History. In case you think this is not worth bothering about, look at the results of the two candidates below:

	Candidate A	Candidate B
History marks	53	51
SPG marks	1	5
Total	54	56
Cut-off mark for Grade C	56	56
Grade achieved	D	C

So although Candidate A did better in the History exam than Candidate B, Candidate B gets the better grade.

Note that these five marks are awarded for punctuation and grammar as well as spelling. This means things like using full stops correctly, writing in proper sentences, dividing your answer into paragraphs, avoiding slang, etc. If you know you are a poor speller, or do not write accurately, it is worth your while making an effort to improve these aspects of your writing so as not to let yourself down to the extent unlucky Candidate A did, in the scenario above.

COURSEWORK

You will normally be asked to do two pieces of coursework, each targeted on one objective. These objectives are the same as those on which the examination is based. The only differences, therefore, are:

- that you will not be writing them against the clock
- that you do not have to commit all the information to memory but will be writing with access to whatever books you need.

The temptation, given these circumstances, is to spend too much time telling the story and not enough on analysis. Here is some simple advice to think about before tackling coursework:

- Are you clear which objective is being targeted?
- When you are, read about that objective in the appropriate section of this chapter.
- Plan your answer.

  Normally each piece of coursework consists of between three and six questions. Each one will need some planning.

- Make sure you answer the question.

  This advice applies, of course, to exam questions too, but in coursework you must produce a well-focused answer. Do not be led astray by the fact that you have ready access to all kinds of resources into writing a long story. When you have finished your answer, read the question again and then read your answer again. This is a luxury you will not have time for in the exam, but will be a check that you answered the question.

- Write enough to answer the question properly, but not so much that you exceed the word-limit.

  Word-limits are not absolute rules – you won't fail if you go over it – but the moderator won't be very pleased. If you have writtten too much, chances are you have not answered the question and not met the analytical requirements of the objective.

THE WAR BEGINS

When the First World War actually broke out in August 1914, the people of Europe had been expecting a war for some time. Now it had started, young men rushed to join their country's armies. They expected a short war, all over by Christmas. In fact, the war went on for over four years (August 1914 to November 1918), nine million people were killed and many millions more were mutilated, orphaned or widowed.

The heaviest fighting and the greatest loss of life was on the **Western Front**. Here, millions of men dug into trenches from which they hardly moved for most of the war.

> The Western Front is the line of trenches marked in Figure 2.2. It is called *Western* because there was also an Eastern Front (see p.28).

THE SCHLIEFFEN PLAN

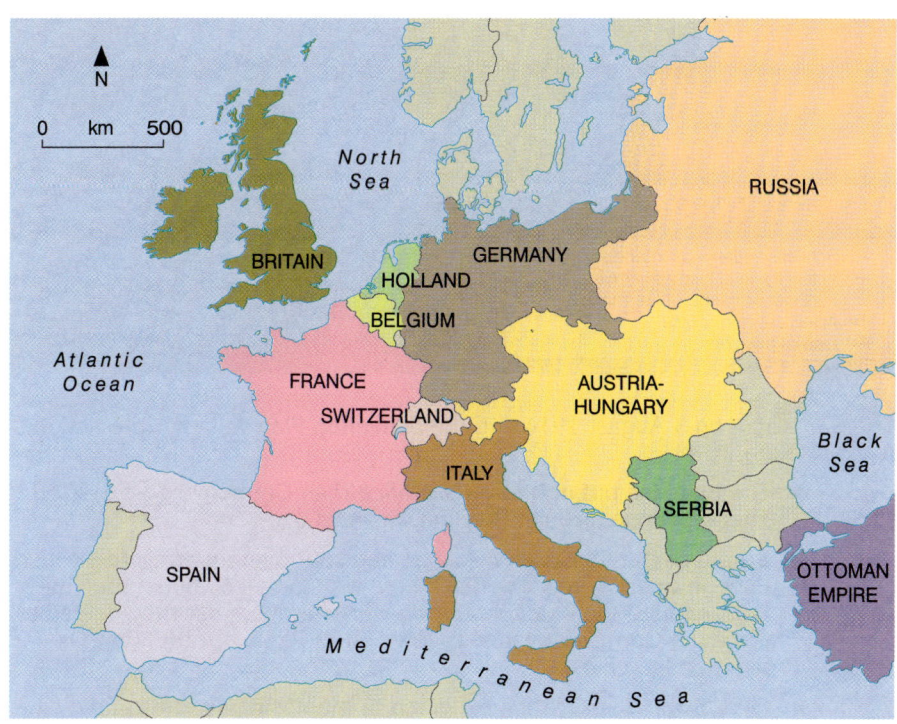

Figure 2.1
Europe in 1914

As you can see in Figure 2.1, Germany had a problem. It had enemies on two sides: Russia to the east and France to the west. Germany had a very powerful army, but it looked as if it would have to split its forces. To meet this problem, General von Schlieffen had worked out a plan, as long ago as 1895 (see the two large arrows in Figure 2.2). He calculated:

- Russia was a vast country and poorly organised. The Russian army would be large, but slow to get ready.
- The German left would keep the main French army busy.
- The German right would invade France through Belgium, cross northern France and capture Paris. France would be defeated in three weeks and the German forces would then turn to deal with Russia.
- Britain would not take part, even when Germany invaded Belgium. Britain had a treaty promising to protect Belgium, but this dated back to 1839 and Germany calculated that Britain would not fight for 'a scrap of paper' as the German ruler, the Kaiser, called it.

WHY DID THE SCHLIEFFEN PLAN FAIL?

Figure 2.2
The beginning of the war

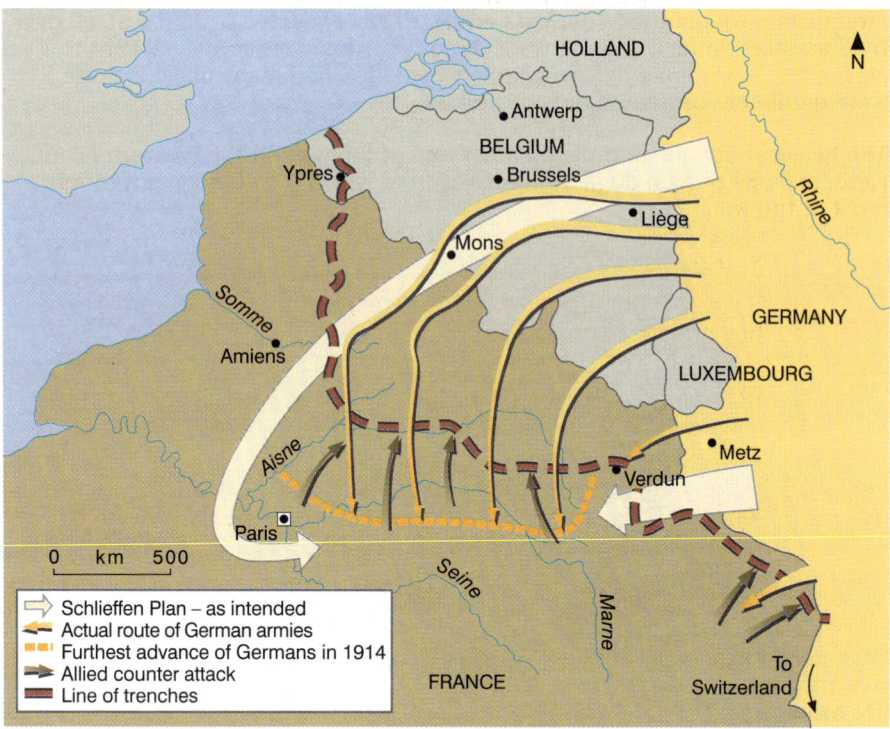

The war began on 3 August 1914 and the Schlieffen Plan was put into action. It didn't quite work.

- The Belgians put up more resistance than Germany had expected. Their advance through Belgium was held up.

- Britain declared war on 4 August and sent over an army, the British Expeditionary Force, the BEF. There were only 160,000 men – the Kaiser called them 'a contemptibly little army' – but they helped to force the German advance to the east of Paris, not the west, as planned (see Fig. 2.2).

- Russia was quicker than expected at mobilising its army and invaded Germany. 100,000 German soldiers had to be moved to the Eastern Front.

- After three weeks the German army was only 30 kilometres from Paris, along the River Marne, but exhausted.

THE BATTLE OF THE MARNE AND THE TRENCHES

The Allies then counter-attacked at the Battle of the Marne, in early September 1914. They were so close to Paris that the city's taxis were used to take men into battle. The Germans were forced to retreat to a line of trenches they had prepared.

Some German forces were rushed north to try to get round the Allied lines. The Allies moved to stop them in a 'rush to the sea'. By November both sides had dug into trenches which stretched from the sea to the Swiss Alps.

WHY WASN'T IT A SHORT WAR?

- Both sides had enormous armies, but they were more or less evenly balanced. By 1918 the total numbers of millions of men mobilised by each side in the war was:

Central Powers		Allies	
Germany	13.25	France	8.2
Austria–Hungary:	9	Russia	13
		Britain & British Empire	9.5

- Both sides could get these huge armies into battle using modern means of transport: railways and motor lorries. They could also keep up the supply of food and ammunition these huge armies needed.

- Both sides had heavy industry. Their factories could produce huge quantities of powerful modern weapons: artillery, rifles, machine guns.

- But these were mainly defensive weapons. Machine-guns, for example, were superb at defending a position, but they could not be used on the move.

- The generals on both sides were stumped by this new situation. They had planned for a war of movement, using cavalry. Now they had to develop new tactics for this new kind of war: this would take time.

◄ **EXTRA POINTS**

1. Most people expected a short, fast-moving war because the last big European war, the Franco–Prussian War, had been all over in a few months in 1870. A better lesson would have been the long-drawn out slugging of the American Civil War, 1861–5, or the Boer War in South Africa, 1899–1902.

2. The war would last as long as the balance between the two sides was roughly equal. Once the Schlieffen Plan had failed, Germany was likely to lose, but it would take years for a real imbalance between the two sides to develop.

Check yourself

QUESTIONS

Q1 Use the two big arrows on Figure 2.2 to describe how the Schlieffen Plan was supposed to work.

Q2 Use the smaller arrows on Figure 2.2 to describe what actually happened in 1914.

Q3 Use these points to explain why the war was not 'over by Christmas'.

(a) Balance of forces (b) Weapons (c) Tactics

REMEMBER! Cover the answers if you want to.

ANSWERS

A1 On the left, south of Metz, German forces would keep the French army occupied. North of Metz, the German right would advance into northern France, through Belgium. Moving fast, they would capture Paris from the west and south. France would surrender and Germany could then attack Russia.

A2 The German army invaded Belgium as planned. The Belgians and the British held up the German advance a bit. Some German forces had to be diverted to the East to deal with an unexpected Russian invasion. The German forces arrived near Paris in an exhausted condition. The Allies counter-attacked at the Battle of the Marne and the Schlieffen Plan had failed.

A3
a) There was little to choose between the two sides: neither had the edge over the other.
b) The weapons of 1914 were better in defensive fighting than in attacking.
c) It was a new kind of warfare and the generals did not how to win victories in this situation.

TUTORIALS

T1 *The French expected the Germans to advance south of Metz, not to strike through Belgium. Remember that the planned German advance had to be fast as they calculated they only had three to four weeks before the huge Russian army ('the Russian steamroller') was ready. As far as possible, they used railway trains to carry their troops.*

T2 *Try not to give the impression that the Schlieffen plan was bound to fail: it nearly succeeded. On the other hand, try not to give the impression that the German army was as good as it was in spring 1940, in the Second World War, when they really did defeat France in six weeks. Back in 1914 it still depended on horse-drawn wagons for its food supply, and hundreds of tonnes of fodder for the horses.*

T3
a) *Once the Schlieffen Plan had failed, the war could not be over by Christmas. A quick victory comes when one side is far superior to the other in numbers or weapons or tactics. This was not the case in 1914.*
b) *The machine-gun, for example, was the big killer of the Western Front. With this new, industrial weapon a few men could mow down much larger numbers of attacking soldiers.*
c) *It is common to criticise the generals for this. For more on this issue, see p.26.*

Stalemate is a word used in the game of chess. It means that whatever move either player makes, no one can win.

STALEMATE ON THE WESTERN FRONT

By the end of 1914 the two huge armies were dug into their trenches on the Western Front. There they stayed until mid-1918. Neither side could break through the enemy lines. This situation is often called **stalemate**.

WHY WERE THE ARMIES IN TRENCHES?

The way a war is fought is decided by the weapons used.

- **Machine-guns**   A machine-gun was operated by two men. It could fire eight bullets a second and so was deadly in breaking up attacks. You were only safe below ground level in a trench.
- **Artillery**   Heavy guns pounded enemy lines, destroying the landscape (see Fig. 2.3). You were safe in a trench against all but a direct hit.

Figure 2.3
Landscape on the Western Front in 1917

LIFE IN THE TRENCHES

The diagram, Figure 2.4, shows what a trench was like. Soldiers took turns in the trenches, spending three or four days in the front line, followed by time in support trenches, or resting.

Figure 2.4
Diagram of a trench

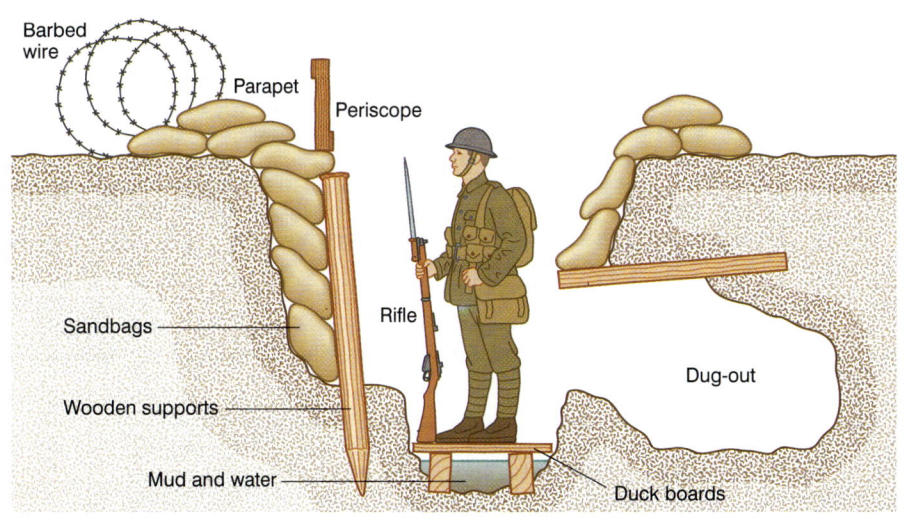

In the trenches, the day started just before dawn, as this was the most likely time for an enemy attack. Everyone waited, with their rifles at the ready. After this, one man would stay on sentry duty while the others rested or did necessary jobs. There was another alert at dusk. At night, patrols would go out over 'No Man's Land' to spy on the enemy.

Apart from the dangers from artillery fire and 'snipers' (marksmen who shot at anything that they could see), life in the trenches was unpleasant in other ways too:

- They were infested with lice and rats.
- They were often waterlogged.
- This led to a painful condition called 'trench feet', in which the soldiers' permanently wet feet swelled and rotted.
- Food was poor and monotonous.

Tremendous comradeship grew up among the men as a result of enduring these conditions together.

BREAKING OUT OF STALEMATE

The generals tried to find ways of breaking through the enemy lines.

- **Artillery barrages**
  Many generals, on both sides, thought that if only they could get enough heavy guns, with enough shells, to keep pounding the enemy line, they would break through. Pressure was put on industry at home. Factories frantically turned over to making guns and shells. In fact, as the British discovered at the Battle of the Somme in 1916 (see below), it was possible for the enemy to survive tremendous artillery barrages by digging into deep bunkers. The barrage also gave the enemy warning that an attack was about to start.

- **Over the top**
  For most of the war the only way the generals thought enemy trenches could be captured was by sending their men 'over the top' (of the trench). They would then run, carrying rifle, kit and trench-digging tools, towards the enemy lines. Generals hoped that enough would survive this charge to capture the trench. As you would expect, this led to millions of deaths. As the war went on the generals demanded more and more men.

- **Gas**
  Both sides used poison gas – chlorine or mustard gas – to try to clear the enemy line of soldiers. It was not very reliable and not used much in the later part of the war, but soldiers feared it.

- **Tanks**
  Tanks are an example of the new technology invented in the war. They were first used in 1916. They carried machine-guns and moved across No Man's Land, crushing barbed wire barriers. However, many broke down. They were also used on their own, in small numbers, so were not very successful. Only late in the war did commanders learn how to use them successfully.

EXTRA POINTS ▶

1. Gas actually killed only about 3,000 men in the whole war. But soldiers were terrified of it, perhaps because it was silent and caused a slow, painful death.

2. Even if soldiers advancing across No Man's Land did capture an enemy trench, it was very hard to follow this up. The group of successful soldiers had to be supplied, across No Man's Land. Enemy counter-attacks were often successful. This helps to explain the tiny territorial gains made from enormous attacks involving huge loss of life.

KEY BATTLES

Verdun, 1916

Verdun was a massive French fortress (see Fig. 2.5). The German commander calculated that if he attacked Verdun, the French would defend it to the last man. If two Frenchmen died for every German, France would be 'bled white' and have to surrender.

The German bombardment of Verdun began in February 1916. There were enormous casualties on both sides: by August 1916 315,000 French and 282,000 German soldiers had been killed.

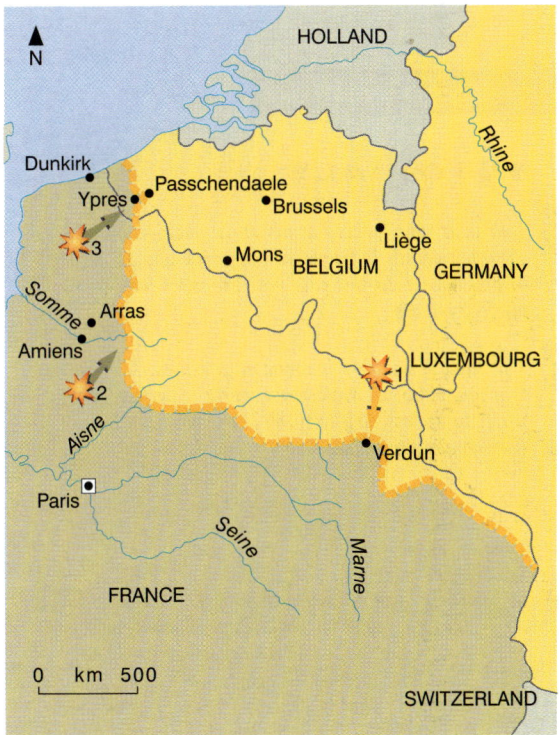

Figure 2.5
The Western Front

Legend:
- Approximate line as at 1915–17
- Allied offensives
- German offensives
- ❈ 1 Battle of Verdun 1916
- ❈ 2 Battle of the Somme 1916
- ❈ 3 Battle of Ypres (Passchendaele) 1917

The Somme, 1916

To relieve pressure on Verdun, the French asked the British commander, General Douglas Haig, to attack further along the line. Haig ordered a five-day artillery barrage and on 1 July 1916 100,000 British soldiers went 'over the top'. They had been told they would be able to walk into the German trenches. Unfortunately, the massive barrage had failed to destroy the German barbed wire entanglements. Haig was also unaware that the Germans had spent the last two years digging deep bunkers, so they had survived the artillery barrage. By the end of the first day 20,000 British soldiers were dead. By the time the battle was called off, in November, total British losses were 420,000 and German losses were almost as many.

Ypres (often called Passchendaele), 1917

This battle began in July but the British advance was soon bogged down in deep mud. By November 265,000 men had been killed for a gain of about eight kilometres.

Check yourself

QUESTIONS

Q1 Describe three things you can see in the photograph, Figure 2.3.

Q2 Compare the photograph, Figure 2.3 and the diagram of the trench, Figure 2.4. Which do you think tells you more about life on the Western Front?

Q3 Make a list of all the reasons you can think of why the numbers killed on the Western Front were so large.

REMEMBER! Cover the answers if you want to.

ANSWERS

A1 Horses used for carrying supplies. Trees with their branches shot away by artillery fire. Mud. Pools of water. Shell-craters. Soldiers. A rough track.

A2 The diagram gives you more factual information, more details. However, it looks quite clean and organised.

The photograph gives you a better idea of what it was really like. However, it does not give precise information.

A3
a) The weapons – machine-guns and heavy artillery – were very efficient.
b) The armies were very large – lots of people to kill.
c) The generals seemed prepared to throw lots of men into battle, knowing that many would be killed.

TUTORIALS

T1 *Take your time looking at historical photographs. There are often details to be picked out which you do not see at first glance. In this case note the ropes used to mark off deep craters.*

T2 *This kind of question is common in exams. Always try to give a balanced answer: no source is perfect, or perfectly useless. Try to think of the pros and cons of each as you have done here.*

T3
a) *The British estimated that, of the 20,000 killed on the first day of the battle of the Somme, most had been killed by just 100 machine-gun positions.*
b)&c) *Some have accused the generals of waging 'a war of attrition'. That is, expecting lots of your own men to be killed in return for lots of the enemy, hoping that you can last out longest – see, for example, German tactics at Verdun. Haig never admitted that he was waging a war of attrition, saying that he always fought to win outright.*

THE EASTERN FRONT

- The Russian army attacked Germany in August 1914 but were soon defeated in two battles, Tannenberg and the Masurian Lakes, in September.

- The war on the Eastern Front never became bogged down in trenches. There was more space and more movement.

- Russia did quite well against Austria–Hungary. Germany sent troops to support her ally and drove the Russians back. Russian soldiers fought bravely, but suffered from poor leaders, poor transport, lack of weapons and medical supplies.

- There was a successful Russian counter-attack in 1916, the Brusilov offensive.

- However, this could not be followed up. By winter 1916 German forces were 400 kilometres into Russia. Russia was in chaos and the country on the verge of revolution.

As long as Russia was fighting on the Eastern Front, Germany had to fight on two fronts at once and could not put all her efforts into the Western Front.

THE WAR ON OTHER FRONTS

Figure 2.6 *Other fronts in the First World War*

GALLIPOLI

The British government looked for a way of breaking out of the stalemate on the Western Front. Winston Churchill suggested an attack on Turkey, Germany's ally, at Gallipoli. He said this would:

- Knock Turkey out of the war.
- Open up a supply route to Britain's hard-pressed ally, Russia.
- Open up another front by advancing through the Balkans to attack Austria–Hungary.

In March 1915, British and French warships attacked but suffered heavy losses from Turkish guns and mines.

In April, British, French and ANZAC (Australia and New Zealand Army Corps) soldiers were landed. The Turks resisted hard, helped by German advisers. The Allies were barely able to get beyond the beach. There they stayed, unable to advance inland, suffering from extreme heat in summer and extreme cold in winter, until they were taken off in December 1915.

THE MIDDLE EAST

Turkish forces with German advisers threatened British oil supplies in Persia (now called Iran). Combined forces of 600,000 British, ANZAC and Indian troops drove the Turks out of Palestine and Iraq from 1916 to 1918. In Palestine they were helped by Arab guerrilla forces led by T.E.Lawrence, Lawrence of Arabia.

Conclusion

The tough resistance of the Turks surprised everyone. It meant that the war in the Middle East took time and lots of men to win. There was never a breakthrough which might have affected the rest of the war.

THE WAR AT SEA

- The British navy was the most powerful in the world, but the large, modern German fleet was the Kaiser's pride and joy.

- This was going to be a long war. Victory would come to the side which could survive, and fight, longest. European countries could not feed themselves: they had to have supplies from overseas. The British navy therefore blockaded Germany, preventing vital food and war supplies from getting in. It was boring but vitally important to victory in the end.

- Germany retaliated with submarine (U-boat) attacks on Britain's supply ships. A new weapon, the torpedo, made these very successful. In 1915 the liner *Lusitania* was sunk, with the loss of 1,198 passengers, including 128 US citizens. It looked as if the USA might come into the war against Germany and the U-boat war was called off.

- There was only one big naval battle: in 1916 at Jutland. Fourteen British ships were sunk to eleven German, but both fleets returned to port where they stayed for the rest of the war.

- In 1917, suffering from the blockade and desperate to break the stalemate, Germany began unrestricted U-boat warfare again. Six hundred British ships were sunk in March and April 1917. Only the introduction of the convoy system (grouping large numbers of ships together and giving them an armed escort) prevented a serious crisis.

THE WAR IN THE AIR

- German Zeppelins (airships) bombed British cities. However, as defences improved more and more of them were shot down.

- Aeroplanes were a new invention (the first powered flight was only in 1903), so the first aeroplanes used in the war were quite basic. They were used to observe and photograph enemy trenches and troop movements.

- Pilots began to take weapons up with them and have 'dogfights' (one-to-one combats). Soon aeroplanes were being designed with mounted machine-guns. The only popular heroes of the war were pilots, like Baron von Richthofen of Germany and Albert Ball of Britain.

- By the end of the war enormous developments had taken place. Britain began the war with thirty-seven aeroplanes and ended it with 20,000. The Royal Air Force was founded in 1918. Aeroplanes did not affect the course of the war, but they were bigger, faster and better made by the end. A new age of warfare was about to begin.

 **EXTRA POINT**

The Italian Front

Italy stayed out of the war at first. Then she declared war on Austria–Hungary in 1915. Germany sent support to Austria–Hungary and Italy was defeated at the battle of Caporetto in 1917.

Check yourself

QUESTIONS

Q1 Why would the Allies be worried if Russia was defeated?

Q2 What did they do in 1915 to help Russia?

Q3 Why was the British naval blockade 'boring but important'?

Q4 Why did the British and German fleets avoid a pitched battle for most of the war?

Q5 Make a list of all the inventions described in this section which were either new or greatly improved during the war.

REMEMBER! Cover the answers if you want to.

ANSWERS

A1 The Eastern Front kept German forces split. Germany could not put all her effort into the Western Front.

A2 They tried to capture Gallipoli. This would enable the Allies to send supplies to Russia.

A3 It was more boring than big battles fought between impressive battleships. It was important because it was gradually starving Germany of essential food and other supplies.

A4 Because it was risky: a whole fleet could be lost in a day. Also it was unnecessary: Britain and Germany were fighting a war of blockades and U-boats.

A5 Tanks. Poison gas. Torpedoes. Aeroplanes. Motor lorries. Mines. Submarines.

TUTORIALS

T1 Look at p.39 for what did happen when Russia dropped out of the war in 1917.

T2 The other supply route was round northern Norway, and closed by ice for several months a year.

T3 Before the war both Britain and Germany had been building up their navies with the latest battleships. Popular opinion in both countries expected there to be exciting naval battles, using these new ships.

T4 As on the Western Front, the stalemate was caused by the near equality of the two sides.

T5 The first three were invented in the war. The other four were improved. All except gas played an important part in the Second World War.

THE HOME FRONT: THE GOVERNMENT

RECRUITING

For many years Britain had relied on her powerful navy for defence and kept only a small army. When it became clear that this was going to be a long land war, the Minister for War, Lord Kitchener, began to build up a mass British Army.

- **Volunteers** At first the government relied on persuading men to volunteer. There was a massive recruitment campaign, with posters and recruiting offices in every town. A million men had joined up by early 1915, sooner than Kitchener expected.

- **Conscription** However by 1916 conscription had to be introduced:
  - The army needed more and more men as the casualties on the Western Front grew.
  - Volunteering was seen as unfair.
  - Volunteering left some factories and mines short of skilled workers. Better planning was needed.

  In January 1916 all unmarried men between 18 and 40 were called up. In May 1916 this was extended to married men.

- **Conscientious objectors** Some people refused to be called up: they were called Conscientious Objectors (COs or 'conchies') because they objected to the war on grounds of conscience (their beliefs). Each CO had to appear before a tribunal to state his case. Many of these tribunals were hostile to COs and 6,500 were put into the army anyway. In the army they were treated harshly. Later the army realised they were wasting their time and COs were put in prison.

DEFENCE OF THE REALM ACT (DORA), 8 AUGUST 1914

This Act, passed just after the war began, gave the government sweeping powers:

- To take over businesses, factories and land. The government used this power at once to take over the important coalmining industry.

- To censor what the public was told about the war.

PROPAGANDA

The government used propaganda for several reasons:

- To persuade men to join the army (up to 1916) (see Fig. 2.7).

- To keep up the morale of people at home. This was important: everyone was involved in the war effort, see p.35. One way of doing this was to make people hate the Germans (see Fig. 2.8).

- To persuade people to do what the government needed, such as getting women to work in munitions factories (see Fig. 2.9).

Figures 2.7, 2.8, 2.9
First World War posters

NEWS

DORA was used to restrict news of the war. Only victories and stories of heroism were published. No journalists were allowed near the Front. The numbers killed in battle were only released over several months, so the impact was weakened.

The Battle of the Somme in 1916 was a turning-point. Casualties were so huge that it was impossible to hide the figures. The government also made a film about the battle, much of it taken at the Front. Millions of people flocked to cinemas to see it. The film was quite realistic and included shots of dead soldiers. Some were deeply shocked, but many felt that the truth, however grim, was better than lies.

GOVERNMENTS

In the first wave of patriotism everyone supported the Liberal government led by Asquith.

- **The 'shell shortage'** By 1915 generals were blaming the government for not supplying them with enough shells to win the war. Asquith reacted by forming a coalition government, that is, he included leaders from all parties in his Cabinet. Lloyd George, a Liberal, was made Minister for Munitions to try to solve the 'shell shortage'.

- In December 1916 Lloyd George pushed Asquith out and became Prime Minister.

- **Women workers** It was clear by 1915 that if Britain was to have both a large army and the industry to keep it going for a long war, there would not be enough male workers. The government began to persuade women to take jobs in industry previously closed to them (see Fig. 2.9). They met resistance from trade unions who were worried that women would do the same jobs as men for less pay. Lloyd George promised the unions that women would be paid the same as men, but that their jobs were only temporary – until the men returned from the war. He also employed thousands of women in the government's own munitions (weapons) factories. (For more on women's roles in the war, see p.36.)

● **Food shortages**   By 1917 unrestricted U-boat warfare (see p.39) was creating a serious shortage of food. The government response was:

■ Women's Land Army formed, February 1917.

■ 2.5 million acres of land taken over by the government under DORA, to grow food.

■ November 1917: early voluntary rationing schemes failed. Food prices rose, queues formed, foodshops closed early when they ran out. There were strikes in some areas as the lack of rationing seemed to favour the rich.

■ February 1918: Rationing of sugar, butter, meat and beer in London. Extended to rest of Britain in April.

EXTRA POINTS ▶

1. Conscientious Objectors were mainly pacifists, who believed that all war was wrong, and socialists, who believed that this was a capitalists' war so workers in different countries ought not to fight each other. COs were very unpopular. After the war they lost the right to vote for five years.

2. Lloyd George split the Liberal Party by pushing Asquith out. The Liberal Party never recovered from the split. The Labour Party, on the other hand, increased its support. Arthur Henderson, the leader, was a minister in the wartime coalition and trade unionists worked in close partnership with the government. Labour got two million more votes in 1918 than they had had before the war.

Check yourself

QUESTIONS

Q1 Look at the three posters on p.33. How does each get its message across?

Q2
a) What attitudes did people at home in Britain have to the war at the beginning?
b) How did these change during the war?

Q3 DORA gave the government special wartime powers. Pick out some examples of these powers from these pages.

REMEMBER! Cover the answers if you want to.

ANSWERS

A1 The poster Figure 2.7 tells men that women wanted them to join the army. Men would feel ashamed if they didn't.

The poster Figure 2.8 stirs up hatred against the Germans.

The poster Figure 2.9 is intended to make women feel that if they were not working in a munitions factory they were not 'doing their bit' for Britain.

TUTORIALS

T1 *With an army dependent on volunteers, as the British army was up to 1916, all kinds of propaganda skills were used. You will study different kinds of propaganda in this period of History. Analysis of propaganda often forms part of an exam question.*

Figure 2.7 claims to speak for women. Certainly many women, including suffragette leaders, encouraged volunteers to join up. However, not all women relished the thought of their menfolk going off, perhaps to be killed. Figure 2.8 seems to be directed at women, but in fact the message is aimed just as much at men. Figure 2.9 appeals to women's patriotism.

A2
a) At first most people were enthusiastic about the war and felt very patriotic. Very little criticism was heard.
b) In 1915 the government was criticised over the 'shell shortage'. COs refused to fight after conscription was introduced in 1916. People became more realistic from about 1916: they knew millions were being killed and that the war wasn't going to be an easy victory.

A3
Censorship of the news; taking over control of the mines; taking over land for food production; directing women into factory jobs.

T2
a) Some of the Labour Party, including its leader, Ramsay MacDonald, were against the war from the start.
b) The simple patriotism of the early years faded from about 1916. Some say that the child-like optimism of the pre-war years died too. Life was now more realistic, more of a struggle, both in the war and in the years afterwards.

T3
People accepted that the government was going to have more control over your life as they began to realise that this was total war and needed special measures.

THE HOME FRONT: THE PEOPLE

TOTAL WAR

Wars in previous ages had involved only the fighters or those unlucky enough to be nearby. Everyone else could get on with their lives as normal. The First World War was Britain's first **total war**. This means a war in which everyone in the country was involved, whether they liked it or not:

- Britain was no longer a safe island haven. East-coast towns were shelled by German battleships in December 1914. Air-raids on British cities started in January 1915. Fifteen hundred civilians were killed by enemy action in the war.

- The soldiers depended on industry at home to supply them with weapons and ammunition. Factory workers were therefore as important as soldiers in this war.

- Almost everyone lost a relative, killed in the war, or knew someone who had.

- Food shortages eventually led to rationing which affected everybody.

Total war brought great changes to the Britain of 1914.

BRITAIN IN 1914

- **Men and women**
  Women did not have equality with men. They were not expected to work, but to stay at home and look after their families. For working-class women this was not possible, but still many jobs were closed to them, leaving only low-paid work. Women did not have the vote, despite the efforts of the suffragettes in the years before the war.

● **Rich and poor**
  There was a huge difference between the lives of the rich and the poor. The well-off ran the country. They owned land and businesses. They had houses in London, the country and abroad. They had lots of servants. There was a growing middle class and increasing numbers of better-off workers, but still millions of poor, earning under £1 a week. They suffered from low standards of housing, health and education. Only about 75 per cent of men had the vote.

WOMEN AND THE WAR

● From the beginning, women supported the war as keenly as the men. They encouraged recruitment. They collected books and clothing for the troops. Many became nurses in the VAD (Voluntary Aid Detachments).

● When, in 1915, the government called on women to volunteer to work in industry, many responded. Once the opposition of male employers and trade unionists had been overcome (see p.33), they took on all kinds of jobs. They worked on the land, in transport, as nurses, in factories and offices. They worked in government munitions factories, amid the dangers of explosives and chemical poisoning. Table 2.1 shows the most important changes:

Table 2.1 **Women's employment in Britain, 1914 and 1918**

	1914	1918
Munitions	212,000	947,000
Transport	18,000	117,000
Business	505,000	935,000
Agriculture	190,000	228,000
Government and teaching	262,000	460,000
Hotels and catering	181,000	220,000
Industry	2,179,000	2,971,000
Servants	1,658,000	1,250,000
Self-employed	430,000	470,000
Nursing and secretarial	542,000	652,000

In all, there were over two million more women working in 1918 than in 1914.

BRITAIN IN 1918

Men and women

● **No change**   Nearly all women gave up their jobs, willingly or unwillingly, when the men came back from the war. There were actually fewer women working in 1920 than in 1914.

● **Men's attitudes had changed**   Men had been forced to recognise that women could do virtually any job as well as men could. The door never quite closed again.

- **Women's attitudes changed**   Even if they had to give up their job, women had gained confidence. Family relationships were never quite the same again.
- **Politics**   In 1918 some women over 30 got the vote, about 60 per cent of women. In 1928 all women got the vote.

Rich and poor

After the sacrifices the common soldiers had made in the war there was a feeling that the country had to pay more attention to everyone's needs.

Lloyd George promised 'a country fit for heroes to live in'. All men were given the vote in 1918. A start was made on improving housing and education, although many of these hopes were shelved by the economic depression of the 1920s and 1930s.

The old upper classes began to lose their hold on power. The bullets had struck down young aristocrats as well as young workers. Old titles began to die out for lack of heirs. It became hard to get people to work as servants.

◀ **EXTRA POINTS**

1. Britain was financially ruined by the war. The National Debt (the money the country owed) had risen by 1200 per cent. Britain owed the USA £1,000 million.

   Some old industries – coal, iron, steel, shipbuilding, textiles – had done well on government contracts during the war. They now had to wind down, struggling to find customers in a new and competitive world. Some new industries were given a boost by the war: electric goods, aeroplanes and motor-lorries.

2. From 1917 women also joined the forces: 57,000 joined the Women's Auxiliary Army Corps, 3,000 the Women's Royal Naval Service and 32,000 the Women's Royal Air Force. They were in the forces, with military uniforms, and learnt to march, but the work they were given was mainly in the kitchens and offices.

Check yourself

QUESTIONS

Q1 Why did the war open up more jobs for women?

Q2 Use Table 2.1 to make three statements about how the war changed the position of women at work.

Q3 Why did trade unions resist these changes?

Q4 What changes did the war make to attitudes in Britain concerning (a) gender roles? (b) class differences?

REMEMBER! Cover the answers if you want to.

ANSWERS

A1 With so many men in the armed forces, the government had to persuade industry to take women workers on.

A2 The biggest increase was in industry. Munitions also employed lots of women. The number of servants actually fell.

A3 Trade unions feared that if women did skilled men's work for lower pay, men's wages would fall. They also feared that employers would keep women on after the war ended.

A4
a) It showed men that women were not weak, or incapable of working hard, or unable to do skilled work.
b) It made everyone think that if every citizen, whatever class they belonged to, could be called up to fight and die for Britain, then the country owed them something in peace too.

TUTORIALS

T1 The government had to break down the resistance of trade unions and employers to taking on women to do jobs which they had not been allowed to do in peace.

T2 Don't be frightened of statistics. You don't have to do complicated maths with them. Start by making some simple comparisons like those given here.

T3 Women did do the same work for less pay. Trade unions allowed what they called 'dilution'. This meant that a skilled job was broken down into smaller tasks that women did. Trade unions would not have agreed to this in peacetime.

T4 In both cases the change was not dramatic. Women were discriminated against from the end of the war until it was made illegal fifty years later; class differences were still great. But the absolute barriers which existed before 1914 were broken. The war was the turning-point.

THE END OF THE WAR

The USA entered the war on the Allied side in April 1917. Although it was some months before many US troops fought on the Western Front, the might of US industry and the promise of more men were a great boost to the Allies.

WHY DID THE USA ENTER THE WAR?

- Germany returned to unrestricted U-boat warfare in early 1917. This angered the Americans as it led to the loss of American lives and goods.
  (Note that the sinking of the *Lusitania* in 1915 (see p.30) did *not* bring the USA into the war immediately. Germany abandoned unrestricted U-boat warfare for a while. US President Woodrow Wilson won the 1916 presidential election on the promise of keeping the USA out of the war.)

- Germany made secret suggestions to Mexico to declare war on the USA. British intelligence found out about this and made sure Woodrow Wilson was told.

THE RUSSIAN REVOLUTION, 1917
(see Chapter 5 for a full account)

The Russian Revolution of March 1917 threw out the Tsar and set up a democratic Provisional Government. They decided to continue the war. However the revolution of November 1917 brought Lenin and the Bolsheviks to power. They made peace with Germany at the Treaty of Brest–Litovsk in March 1918.

THE GERMAN SPRING OFFENSIVE 1918 (also called the Ludendorff Offensive)

Germany was desperate by early 1918. The blockade had brought terrible food shortages, affecting everyone, both soldiers and the civilians. Many of their best soldiers had been killed. Morale was low. The entry of the USA looked like the last straw.

However, peace on the Eastern Front gave them one last chance. Soldiers were moved to the west. New tactics were worked out. The attack began in March and was at first successful in breaking out of the stalemate.

- General Ludendorff, the German commander, used heavy guns and gas attacks to start with.
- Then small groups of well-armed, well-trained, fast-moving soldiers called 'storm troops' broke through at many points in the Allied line. For the first time in over three years they saw open country in front of them.

- But it did not lead to victory:
  - They had no overall plan: where did they go once they had broken through?
  - The Allies retreated and re-grouped.
  - The Germans were short of supplies and could not keep up the effort. They had no reserves. As they advanced further, their supply-lines became longer.
  - German soldiers had been told the Allies were just as hungry as they were. When they reached Allied food and wine stores they were amazed and stopped to loot.

THE ALLIED COUNTER-ATTACK

In August the Allies counter-attacked. They had plenty of food, supplies and soldiers. They had learnt how to use accurate artillery, gas, tanks and aircraft. The demoralised German army began to retreat and could not hold the lines they had had in early 1918. Their commanders asked for a ceasefire (armistice) and the war ended on 11 November 1918.

WHY DID GERMANY LOSE THE WAR?

- Once the Schlieffen Plan had failed, Germany had to fight a two-front war. They could not keep this up over a long war, with limited population and resources. The peace of 1918 with Russia came too late.

- The naval blockade prevented supplies getting through to German industry and food getting through to the German people. By 1918 their morale was almost broken.

- The entry of the Americans was decisive. By mid-1918 American troops and supplies made a difference, but even before that the knowledge that they were coming helped the Allies to hang on.

- By 1918 the Allied commanders had learnt how to break the stalemate of trench warfare, particularly by using tanks. The German army did not develop an effective tank.

EXTRA POINT ▶

US President Woodrow Wilson did not just throw in his lot with the Allies. If the USA was going to enter the war, they would do so in order to create a better world after it was over. Woodrow Wilson called it 'a war to end wars'. In January 1918 he listed Fourteen Points for a fair and lasting peace as the war aims of the USA. (For more on the Fourteen Points, see p.46.)

Check yourself

QUESTIONS

Q1 Why was US entry into the war so helpful to the Allies?

Q2 Why was Germany's spring 1918 offensive their 'last chance'?

Q3 Was it obvious by the end of 1917 that the Allies would win the war? Answer this from this section, then look back over pages 27–31 as well.
Start by listing the events which support the idea that things looked good for them by the end of 1917. Then list anything which pointed in the other direction.

Then write your own opinion in answer to this question in one sentence. Then write an essay answer, using the following sentences to start each paragraph:
'By the end of 1917 the USA had joined the war on the Allied side. This was good news because ...'

'However, the prospects for the next year were not all good. Russia ...'

'Further, fighting on the Western Front was ...'

'In conclusion, I think that at the end of 1917 it was/was not obvious that the Allies would win the war. I think this because ...'

REMEMBER! Cover the answers if you want to.

ANSWERS

A1 By April 1917 the Allies had been fighting for over two and a half years. They had lost millions of men. Their industries were running at bursting-point. The USA offered industrial supplies and fighting men in almost limitless quantities.

A2 By early 1918 Germany was in a bad way. They had lost millions of soldiers. The blockade had brought their people to the edge of starvation and morale was falling. By the middle of 1918 US support for the Allies would begin to make a difference. On the other hand, Lenin's determination to take Russia out of the war closed the Eastern Front and permitted Germany to do what it had not been able to do since August 1914: fight on one front only. They only had a few months to take advantage of this before the odds against them increased again.

A3 By the end of 1917 the USA had joined the war on the Allied side. This was good news because of the huge reserves of men and resources which the USA possessed. Germany could not bring such resources to the war.

However, the prospects for the next year were not all good. Russia had pulled out of the war following the Russian Revolution in October and was now seeking peace. This meant that the Germans could concentrate all their efforts on the Western Front.

Further, fighting on the Western Front was still in deadlock. The Allies seemed as unable as ever to break out of the stalemate and thousands more soldiers had died at the battle of Passchendaele.

In conclusion, I think that at the end of 1917 it was not obvious that the Allies would win the war. I think this because Germany was now freed to put all their efforts into the Western Front. The Allies had not found a way of breaking out of the deadlock. The advantage of US support was a long-term thing and the Allies could be defeated before it could make a difference.

TUTORIALS

T1 *By 1917 it had become a war of attrition: who could last out longest? US support meant that the Allies could now go on, if necessary for years more.*

T2&3 *It is worth remembering that we always know how the story ends, but people at the time did not. We know that 1918 was the last year of the war and that it was over by November; in January 1918 they did not know that. They certainly could not be sure that Germany would be defeated.*

1917 was not a good year for the Allies at all. A further cause of concern was a serious mutiny in the French army which, miraculously, Germany did not seem to know about.

EXAM PRACTICE

Sample Student's Answers & Examiner's Comments

1 a) Write a sentence to explain the term 'conscription'. (2)

The British government introduced conscription in 1916, which meant that everyone between the ages of 18 and 40 had to join the armed forces.

2/2

EXAMINER'S COMMENTS

MARK SCHEME

Level 1	Defines conscription	**1 mark**
Level 2	Puts this definition in the context of this topic	**2 marks**

Exam papers sometimes start with this kind of question. The examiner is trying to find an easy question to get you started, on a subject which you will have heard of. As you can see from the mark-scheme, you should try and include some factual information about the topic as the answer above does, as well as offering a kind of dictionary definition.

The other important thing to remember is to note the number of marks available: only 2. Don't get carried away and write for ten minutes, covering a page. The most you can get is 2 marks and you will have wasted valuable time which you might need for more high-scoring questions later on in the exam.

· ·

b) Write a paragraph explaining why the British government issued recruiting posters like this one. (4)

The British army for the first part of the War was made up of volunteers. They needed lots of men to replace those killed and, in order to persuade them to join up, they issued posters. They used all kinds of methods to get men to feel they had to join up. Some tried to make them hate the Germans, some appealed to patriotism and some, like this one, tried to make men feel guilty or ashamed in front of their children.

3/4

Daddy, what did YOU do in the Great War?

MARK SCHEME

Level 1   Explains need to persuade men
to volunteer.   **1–2 marks**

Level 2   Puts this in context of why there
was a need for lots of volunteers.   **3–4 marks**

Note the clear guidance in the question about how much to write. Not all exam questions say this: you may have to use the clues provided by the number of marks, in this case 4. This means that short paragraph is required.

This answer is good on the way such posters work, but more could have been said on why so many volunteers were needed. Many people were against conscription in 1914. They preferred to keep with the tradition of a volunteer army. At the beginning of the war the army was quite small and the government decided to build up a mass army. There were heavy casualties to be replaced too. They did not introduce conscription until 1916 and so all the techniques of advertising had to be used to pressurise men into joining up.

2   **SOURCE A:** Part of a report by Field Marshal Sir John French, Commander-in-Chief of British forces, written in February 1915:

'The deadly accuracy of the modern machine-gun means that No Man's Land must be crossed in the shortest possible time. If men are held up by mud, attacks like this become impossible because of the losses which they suffer.'

Read Source A. What can you learn from this source about problems facing soldiers on the Western Front in the First World War?   (4)

The problem was that the only tactic the commanders had for attacking enemy lines was to order their soldiers to charge straight at them across No Man's Land, the strip of territory between the trenches. While they were running, they could easily be shot down by machine-guns, which were extremely accurate. There was huge loss of life and this source explains that any hold-up, such as mud, produced terrible casualties.

4/4

MARK SCHEME

Level 1   Picks items from the source   **1 mark**

Level 2   Uses source to explain some
of the aspects of the problem   **2–3 marks**

Level 3   Answer focuses on the issue
of problem   **4 marks**

This is a good answer. There are other things the student could have written, but it is not necessary to produce the perfect answer to get 4 out of 4. The strength of the answer is that it does take up the main point of the question, which is about 'the problem' of the soldier.

Note that this question does not ask you to bring any other information into your answer – unlike question 3 below. In these cases you should go through the source phrase by phrase, picking up any point which is relevant to the question.

Questions to Answer

The answers to Questions 3 and 4 can be found on p.267

3 SOURCE B: British troops advancing across No Man's Land at the Battle of
the Somme, June 1916.

Source A was written over a year before the picture in Source B was taken.
Use the sources and your own knowledge to explain why attacks like these
were still being carried out over a year later

(6)

4 What impact did the First World War have on the social and economic
position of women in Britain?

(15)

WHAT PROBLEMS FACED THE PEACEMAKERS IN 1919?

Many people have criticised the Treaties at the end of the First World War, both at the time and since. But, for several reasons, it was hard for the peacemakers to do a good job.

EUROPE IN 1919

- In large parts of Europe people were suffering from near-starvation because of the Allied naval blockade of Germany, which continued while the Conference was going on. Then a terrible 'flu epidemic in 1919 caused over a million deaths.

- Many countries were in chaos. In Germany the Kaiser had abdicated and fled to Holland. A new government had taken over, but was having difficulty controlling the country. Spurred on by the Russian Revolution of 1917, there were Communist uprisings in Berlin and Munich. Communists had seized power in Budapest. There were nationalist risings all over eastern Europe. It looked as if changes would be made whatever the peacemakers decided.

- Many people in the Allied countries were angry and wanted revenge:
  - They had lost over nine million dead.
  - Their economies were in ruins.
  - The areas of France and Belgium which had been fought over were devastated (see Fig. 3.1). Houses, villages, whole towns were destroyed. Some of France's best farmland had been made useless and her industries disrupted.
  - They believed Germany had been to blame for starting the war and so should be made to pay for it.

- The desire for revenge was all the stronger when people saw the harsh terms of the Treaty of Brest–Litovsk between Germany and Russia, signed in 1918. Germany had made Russia give up huge amounts of land see chapter 5, p.107.

Figure 3.1
The desolate landscape of 1918

Figure 3.2 *The three leaders at Versailles in 1919: Lloyd George (top), Clemenceau (middle), Wilson (bottom)*

The Allies met at Versailles, just outside Paris. Holding the Conference in the heart of the country most deeply affected by the war influenced the peacemakers. Thirty-two nations took part, but none of the defeated countries, Germany, Austria–Hungary, Turkey and Bulgaria. Russia was left out because of its Communist government and because it had broken its alliance with the Allies by making its own peace. In fact, the terms of the most important Treaty, affecting Germany, were worked out by the representatives of Britain, France and the USA.

Britain: Lloyd George

Lloyd George won a sweeping election victory in 1918. Many successful candidates had promised to punish Germany, 'To squeeze her until the pips squeaked' as one put it. Lloyd George had to listen to these views, but he felt that severe terms would probably only lead to another war as Germany looked for revenge. He wanted Germany back on her feet quickly, in order to restore trade with Britain, which would help British industry. He also wanted increase the British Empire by taking some of Germany's overseas colonies.

France: Clemenceau

Clemenceau was twenty-nine years old when Germany had invaded France in 1870 and seventy-three when Germany had done it again in 1914. He wanted to cripple Germany so that it could never happen again by imposing a huge fine and by permanently disarming her.

USA: Woodrow Wilson

The USA had obviously suffered less death and destruction than her European Allies. Wilson put forward very idealistic reasons for coming into the war. In a speech in January 1918 laid down Fourteen Points for a better world after the war:

1. No secret treaties: all diplomacy should be open.
2. Freedom of the seas in peace and war.
3. Free trade between all countries: no customs barriers.
4. Disarmament by all nations.
5. The wishes of people in colonies should be listened to when deciding their future.
6. German forces to leave Russia.
7. Belgium should be independent.
8. Alsace–Lorraine, taken by Germany in 1871, to be returned to France.
9. Italy's frontier with Austria to be changed to avoid further disputes.
10. Self-determination for the peoples of eastern Europe. This meant that the nationalities living in each area should rule themselves.
11. Serbia should have access to the sea.
12. Self-determination for the peoples of the Turkish Empire.
13. Poland should become an independent country, with access to the sea.
14. An international organisation should be set up to settle disputes between countries, called the League of Nations.

Woodrow Wilson's allies were far from happy about the Fourteen Points when he announced them, but they were eager to get the USA into the war. Disagreements began to emerge between the three of them at the Conference:

- Clemenceau felt that Wilson was being far too soft on Germany and did not understand how much France had suffered and lost.
- Lloyd George could not agree with Wilson over point 2. The British blockade of Germany had contributed to the Allied victory.
- Clemenceau felt Lloyd George was prepared to be lenient with Germany in Europe only to be greedy for Germany's colonies.

1. Wilson beieved that the war had been caused by national frustration at being ruled by people of a different nationality. He did not know much about eastern Europe or understand the tangle of nationalities in some areas. Complete self-determination was impossible: there would always be some people living as a minority under different rulers.

2. He was increasingly ill as the Conference went on and was losing the support of the American people back home, see chapter 7, p.134.

 **EXTRA POINTS**

Check yourself

QUESTIONS

Q1 Look at the Fourteen Points. Put them into three groups:

    a) Those which dealt with certain named bits of territory;

    b) Those which laid down ideas for deciding what should happen to certain areas;

    c) Those which laid out plans for a better way of running the world and keeping peace in the future.

Q2 Why did the people of Britain want revenge on Germany?

Q3 Why didn't Lloyd George entirely support this desire?

REMEMBER! Cover the answers if you want to.

ANSWERS

A1
a) Numbers 6, 7, 8, 9, 11, 13
b) Numbers 5, 10, 12
c) Numbers 1, 2, 3, 4, 14.

A2 Britain had lost over a million dead. Most families had lost somebody. Fifteen hundred civilians had been killed and property destroyed in air raids. The British had had to sell off foreign investments and borrow money. As a result her economy was in ruins.

A3 Lloyd George could see the dangers of revenge. He feared that a shattered Germany would not rest content until she had put things right in another war. He also knew that for Britain's economy to pick up there would have to a revival of trade and that included trade with Germany.

TUTORIALS

T1 *These were quite mild terms compared to what Clemenceau and even Lloyd George wanted. It was on the understanding that the Fourteen Points would form the basis of the peace settlement that Germany asked for a ceasefire in 1918.*

T2 *Four years of anti-German propaganda had also had an effect. Most British people believed that Germany had caused the war and many actively hated Germans.*

T3 *Politicians in democratic countries have to pay attention to public opinion. But they do not necessarily have to follow it. Lloyd George could perhaps see further than the immediate desire for revenge, and events proved him right.*

THE TERMS OF THE TREATIES

The Treaty of Versailles is often used as the name for all the peace treaties at the end of the First World War. In fact there were five treaties. The Treaty of Versailles was the most important. It was signed in June 1919 and dealt with Germany.

THE TREATY OF VERSAILLES

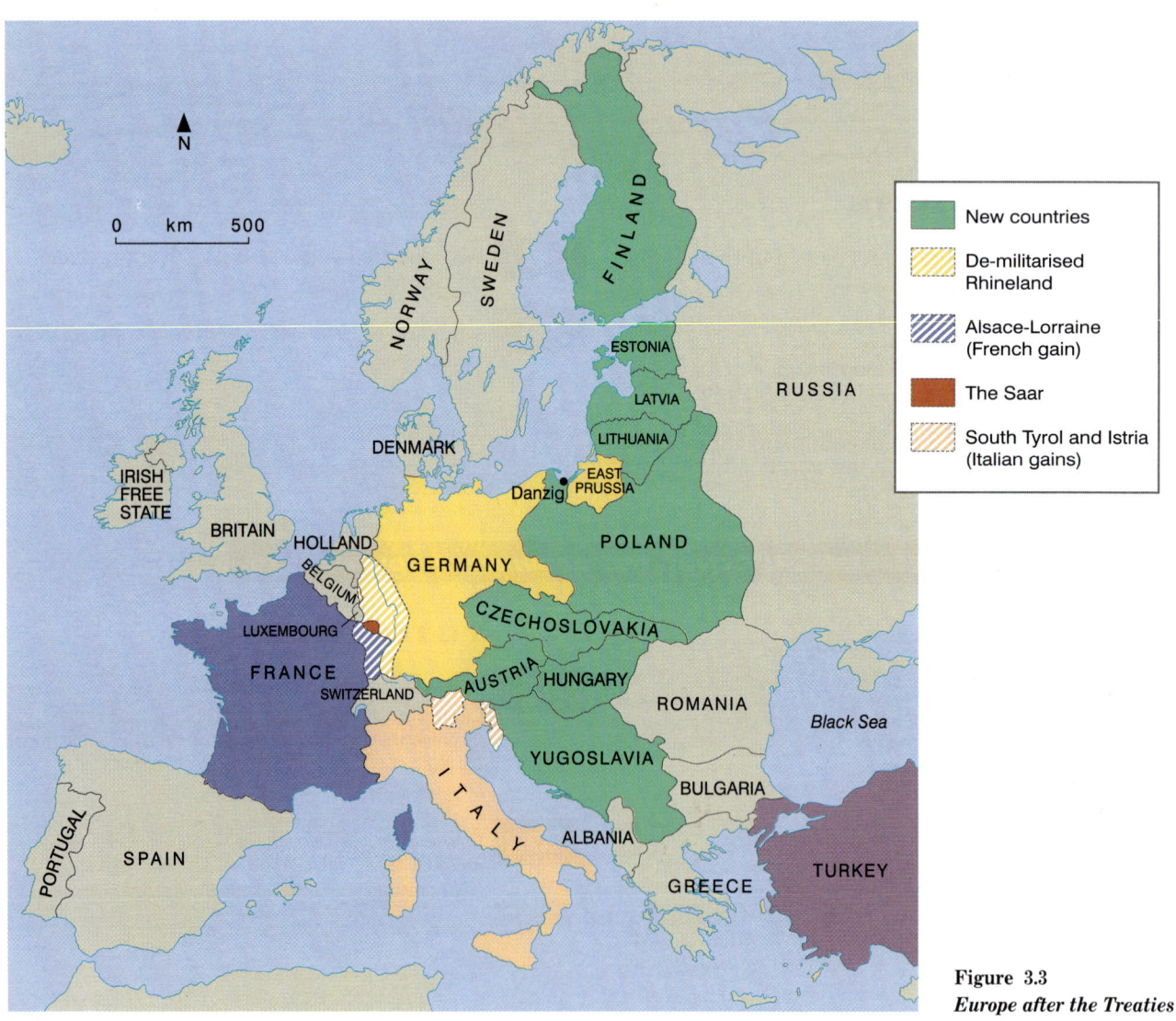

🟩	New countries
▨	De-militarised Rhineland
▨	Alsace-Lorraine (French gain)
🟫	The Saar
▨	South Tyrol and Istria (Italian gains)

Figure 3.3
Europe after the Treaties

● **Territory** (see Fig. 3.3)
- Alsace–Lorraine was returned to France.
- The left bank of the River Rhine was to be occupied by the Allies. A strip 50 kilometres wide on the right bank was to be de-militarised (no German bases or soldiers would be allowed in it).
- The Saar, with its important coalfield, was to be handed over to France for fifteen years. After that time its people would be asked to vote, in a **plebiscite**, whether they wanted to stay French or return to Germany.

■ Poland became an independent country. Most of Poland was Russian in 1914 but the new country also took land from Germany, including the coalfield of Upper Silesia, and a 'corridor' of land to the sea. This split off the German province of East Prussia from the rest of Germany, as the map shows. The former German port of Danzig was made a free city so as to give Poland access to the sea.

■ Finland, Estonia, Latvia and Lithuania became independent countries. Virtually all of these countries had been Russian territory in 1914.

■ Denmark and Belgium also received small bits of land from Germany.

● **Colonies**

Germany lost all her empire. The former colonies were not simply handed over but became **mandates** of the League of Nations. The League made sure that the country taking them over looked after the well-being of people of the colony.

■ Tanganyika became a British mandate.

■ Cameroons became a French mandate.

■ South-West Africa became a South African mandate.

■ The German Pacific islands became a Japanese mandate.

● **Armed forces**

■ The German army was to be cut down to 100,000 men. They were all to be volunteers – no conscription.

■ The German navy was to be cut down to thirty-six ships, of which only six could be battleships.

■ Germany was not allowed to have any tanks, submarines or aircraft at all.

■ Germany could not make an alliance or unite with Austria.

● **War-guilt**

By article 231 of the Treaty Germany had to accept all blame for starting the war.

● **Reparations**

Having established that Germany was to blame for the war, she then had to pay the Allies the cost of all the damage caused by the war. This was assessed later (in 1921) as £6,600 million.

● **The League of Nations**

An international peace-keeping organisation, the League of Nations, was set up as part of the Treaty.

Once the Treaty of Versailles had been signed, Clemenceau, Lloyd George and Woodrow Wilson went home. The four remaining treaties dealt with Germany's four allies and were worked out by diplomats on the same basis as the Treaty of Versailles.

AUSTRIA: TREATY OF ST GERMAIN, 1919

● Two new countries were set up out of the old Austria–Hungary: Czechoslovakia and Yugoslavia.

● Austria handed over land to Italy.

● Austria had to reduce her army and was forbidden to ally with Germany.

It became a small, second-rate power. It had severe problems re-adjusting to the new boundaries as much of its former industrial areas were now in different countries.

HUNGARY: TREATY OF TRIANON, 1920

- Hungary also lost teritory to Czechoslovakia and Yugoslavia.
- Hungary lost territory to Romania.

Hungary also had to disarm and lost land and people as well as industrial raw materials.

BULGARIA: TREATY OF NEUILLY, 1919

- Bulgaria lost land to Greece, Romania and Yugoslavia. As a result it had no access to the Mediterranean Sea.
- Bulgaria also had to disarm.

TURKEY: TREATY OF SÈVRES, 1920

- Turkey lost what was left of its empire.
  - Britain took over Palestine, Iraq and Jordan as mandates.
  - France took over Syria and Lebanon as mandates.
  - Greece took Smyrna (Izmir).

EXTRA POINT ▶

These treaties mark an important moment on European and world history. They re-organised the boundaries of Europe. They altered the lives of millions of people all over the world. They provide a baseline for the rest of the twentieth century. There had been nothing like it since the Congress of Vienna in 1815. The end of the Second World War in 1945 did not bring anything like so many changes, but rather re-established most of the boundaries laid out in 1919–20.

Check yourself

QUESTIONS

Q1 What were:
a) the de-militarised Rhineland;
b) mandates; c) war-guilt; d) reparations;
e) the League of Nations?

Q2 a) Which new countries were set up by the Treaties?
b) Do they still exist?

REMEMBER! Cover the answers if you want to.

ANSWERS

A1 a) This is the strip of land running 50 kilometres east of the River Rhine in which Germany was not allowed to have anything military – no soldiers, weapons, bases or forts.
b) These were the former German and Turkish colonies, taken over by the League of Nations and then handed to victorious Allied powers. The mandated power was responsible to the League of Nations for looking after the colony on behalf of its people.
c) This said that Germany was solely and entirely to blame for the war.
d) This is the money that Germany was ordered to pay to the Allies for all the damage caused by the war.
e) This was the new international peace-keeping organisation which Woodrow Wilson hoped would prevent future wars by settling disputes before they got as far as fighting.

A2 a) Finland, Estonia, Latvia, Lithuania, Poland, Czechoslovakia, Yugoslavia.
b) They all existed until 1990, when Czechoslovakia split into two parts and Yugoslavia collapsed into civil war.

TUTORIALS

T1 a) *The purpose of this was, with the Allied troops on the left bank of the Rhine, to keep German armed forces at least 100 kilometres away from the French frontier.*
b) *This did mean that the mandated powers had to make some moves towards independence for the colony by providing, for example, education for its people. Much later there was a real clash over South Africa's rule over South-West Africa (Namibia).*
c) *This article was the basis for reparations: only if Germany was solely and entirely to blame could reparations be justified.*
d) *Germany never paid anything like all the £6,600 million demanded.*
e) *See chapter 8 for how effective the League actually was.*

T2 a) *With Austria and Hungary, both effectively new countries created out of the former Austro–Hungarian Empire, they make a continuous strip of countries down the centre of Europe from the Arctic to the Mediterranean.*
b) *Austria was in fact taken over by Germany and ceased to exist from 1938 to 1945 (see chapter 4). Estonia, Latvia and Lithuania were part of the USSR from 1940 to 1990 (see chapters 6 and 10). Poland, Czechoslovakia and Hungary were satellites of the USSR from 1945 to 1989 (see chapters 6 and 10).*

HOW DID THE PEOPLE OF EUROPE REACT TO THE TREATIES?

Figure 3.4
Street soup kitchen for poor people in Germany at the end of the First World War

GERMANY

When the terms of the Treaty of Versailles were revealed in May 1919 the German people were angry:

- The terms had not been negotiated. They were simply told to sign or the war would re-start.
- They thought the terms were harsh.
  - They had to lose 13 per cent of their land, 12 per cent of their population, 16 per cent of their coalfields, 48 per cent of their iron industry and 10 per cent of their manufacturing industry.
  - They had to lose all their colonies.
  - They had to lose most of their proud army and navy.
  - They had to accept total blame for the war.
  - They would be crippled by reparations for years to come.
- They thought the terms were unfair:
  - Although the Fourteen Points said that every nation should disarm, the Allies were not doing so.
  - Self-determination did not seem to apply to Germans. The new countries set up by the Treaties left 3.5 million Germans in Czechoslovakia and one million in Poland.
  - Germany was treated as some kind of outcast by not being allowed to join the League of Nations.

Historians' Comments

- Germany had opened neogotiations with the Allies on the basis of Wilson's Fourteen Points. The eventual terms of the Treaty were far removed from the Fourteen Points.

- The German people under the Kaiser were even more subject to propaganda about the war than the British people. They had been told that they were fighting a defensive war against attacking nations. They did not know that in autumn 1918 the German Army was in retreat and almost defeated. The tough, dictated terms therefore came as a surprise and were even harder to swallow.

- Reparations payments punished the people of Germany and their new Weimar government, not the Kaiser and the old rulers.

However:

- Germany did not, in fact, lose that much by the Treaty of Versailles. It was still the largest country in western Europe. Its economy was still powerful. As you will see in chapter 4, Germany experienced an economic revival in the 1920s despite all that the Treaty had done.

- The complaints about not being fair, and not in line with the Fourteen Points, are a bit weak. Germany had ignored Wilson's Fourteen Points when he first produced them. Only when defeat was staring them in the face did they appeal to the USA for peace. Their own treatment of Russia at the Treaty of Brest–Litovsk in March 1918 (see chapter 5) was extremely harsh. Their plans for the Allies, if Germany had won the war, were very tough.

Whatever historians now say about the Treaty of Versailles, the German people thought it was very unfair and were angry.

Figure 3.5
Bayern, *a ship in the German High Seas Fleet, scuttles at Scapa Flow*

In protest, the German High Seas Fleet, captive in Scapa Flow in the Shetlands, scuttled their ships rather than let them fall into British hands.

The Kaiser, whose government had taken Germany into the war, had fled. Germany was now run by his arch-enemies, the democratically-elected politicians. Ebert, the new Prime Minister, thought about fighting on, but was told by his generals that Germany would only be crushed, with more loss of life. He decided that the German people were suffering enough and agreed to sign the treaty.

THE OCCUPATION OF THE RUHR, 1923

The reparations payments were fixed in 1921 at £6,600 million, to be paid in instalments. The German economy was in a poor state after the war. In 1922 the government said they could not pay that year's instalment, pointing out that people were starving in Germany. France and Belgium did not believe them. In 1923, as agreed in the terms of the Treaty of Versailles, they sent troops into the Ruhr, Germany's main industrial area. They took over every mine, factory, railway and shop in the Ruhr.

The German response was 'passive resistance': everyone refused to work or co-operate in any way with the occupying forces. The French were furious. They deported 150,000 people for disobeying orders and 132 Germans were killed.

German resistance to the occupation cost the country dearly. Its currency collapsed completely and hyper-inflation resulted: by November a dollar was worth 4 billion marks (see chapter 4, p.61). This was no use to France either and talks began which led eventually to the Dawes Plan (see chapter 4, p.63).

ALLIED REACTIONS

Britain

The British soon began to have second thoughts about the peace terms. In his book *The Economic Consequences of the Peace* J.M.Keynes showed that the treaties were bad for everyone.

USA (see chapter 7)

When Woodrow Wilson returned to the USA he found that the mood had changed there, too. The US public and politicians wanted nothing to do with Europe. They refused to agree the Treaties and did not join the League of Nations.

France

France had wanted a tougher treaty for Germany. They still feared Germany and needed reparations payments to pay off their huge debts. But the alliance of 1917, already crumbling in 1919, was over. The USA had pulled out. Britain was lukewarm. After the failure of the Ruhr invasion, France looked for allies elsewhere.

OTHER REACTIONS FROM DEFEATED POWERS

Hungary

Hungary had lost two-thirds of its pre-war territory by the Treaty of Trianon. Anger fuelled a Communist uprising and then a right-wing dictatorship.

Turkey

The other country to protest loudly at the terms of the Treaty (of Sèvres) was Turkey. An nationalist army under Mustafa Kemal drove the Greeks out of Smyrna. A new treaty, the Treaty of Lausanne, 1923, was signed to recognise this.

EXTRA POINTS

1. Italy had expected to do better from the Treaties and felt aggrieved.

2. The Chinese were furious that German ports in China were not handed back in 1919, but became Japanese mandates. There were huge protests: one of the key stages in the growth of Chinese nationalism.

3. The Arabs were deeply disappointed by the Treaties. They had helped the British against Turkey expecting to gain independent Arab countries. Instead their lands became British or French mandates.

4. The peacemakers have been criticised for setting up small, weak nations in eastern Europe and for failure to achieve real self-determination: for example 30 per cent of the people in Poland in 1919 were non-Poles. It is also true that most of these new nations fell easy prey to Hitler in 1939–41 and to the USSR in 1945. But their nationhood was an important factor in throwing off Communism in 1989. Only two have completely disappeared: Czechoslovakia peacefully, and Yugoslavia in a terrible civil war. It remains to be seen how successful the new small nations of eastern Europe will be in the immediate future.

Check yourself

QUESTIONS

Q1 Why did the Germans call the Treaty a 'Diktat' – a dictated peace?

Q2 If they were so angry about it, why did Germany sign the Treaty of Versailles?

Q3 Why did France occupy the Ruhr in 1923?

REMEMBER! Cover the answers if you want to.

ANSWERS

A1 It was a dictated peace because they were not present at the Versailles peace talks and could not negotiate any of it.

A2 The Allies gave Germany only two alternatives: sign or renew the war. Although the truth was hidden from the people, the generals knew that a renewal of the fighting would lead to further defeats and casualties.

A3 Hatred of Germany did not subside in France as it did in Britain as life returned to normal after the war. They expected to enforce the terms of 1919 to the letter. They were also in deep financial trouble and needed reparations to pay off their war-debts. When Germany tried to stop payments, they sent in troops to seize German economic assets.

TUTORIALS

T1 *A starting-point in answering many questions about Hitler is his criticism of the Treaty of Versailles. Some of the things he said were untrue (for example, that the German Army was 'stabbed in the back' by the politicians in 1918). However, it is true that this was not a negotiated peace. The terms were worked out by the victors and handed to the Germans as the defeated power.*

T2 *Germany was in a terrible state in 1919. The Kaiser had built up huge debts expecting winning the war. The British naval blockade had reduced the entire population to near-starvation. Some generals wanted to go down fighting but Ebert decided to sign the Treaty.*

T3 *By 1923 the differences between the former Allies were enormous. With the USA uninvolved and Britain wanting to get on a better footing with Germany, France was isolated. The failure of the French occupation of the Ruhr showed that, only four years later, the mood of Versailles was over.*

EXAM PRACTICE

Sample Student's Answers & Examiner's Comments

1 When the terms of the Treaty of Versailles were announced, one German newspaper described them as 'disgraceful'.

Choose one of the terms of the Treaty and explain why they disliked it. (4)

They disliked losing territory to other countries: the Polish corridor and Danzig to Poland, Alsace Lorraine and the Saar to France. Also smaller territories to Belgium and Denmark. It amounted to about 10 per cent of their land.

3/4

EXAMINER'S COMMENTS

MARK SCHEME

Level 1 Chooses one aspect of the Treaty and describes it. **1 mark**

Level 2 Describes briefly why Germany was angry over the item chosen. **2–3 marks**

Level 3 Sets item chosen in wider context of German history. **4 marks**

Note that there is no right answer to this question: no one item from the terms which the examiner thinks was more resented than others. It all depends how well you argue your point.

In this case the explanation is good. For full marks you could have said that Germany was very sensitive about territory: they had only united their country quite recently, in 1870. To lose territory now was bitterly resented.

Historians would argue that Germans made too much of this: after 1919 Germany was still a large and powerful country, as chapter 4 will show.

2 Why didn't Woodrow Wilson get all that he wanted from the peace negotiations at Versailles?

(12)

Woodrow Wilson came to Versailles with certain aims which he had set out in his Fourteen Points in January 1918. Some of these were to do with quite specific pieces of land: Serbia to have a seacoast, for example. Some were clear principles for deciding disputed areas, such as self-determination, which means the right of people of the same nationality to rule themselves. Some were plans for creating a better world in the future, such as the League of Nations. He got all of his specific aims, because they did not conflict with those of his allies, Britain and France.

Self-determination was all very well in principle but in many parts of Eastern Europe there were large minorities of different nationalities. In this case the situation was more complicated than he had bargained for. Nor were Britain and France prepared to ask colonial people what they wanted. His 'big idea', the League of Nations was agreed, but Britain was not prepared to agree to freedom of the seas and hardly anyone was prepared to agree to free trade.

8/12

EXAMINER'S COMMENTS

MARK SCHEME

Level 1 Describes Woodrow Wilson's aims

1–2 marks

Level 2 Describes aims and shows how far these were achieved **3–6 marks**

Level 3 Shows how far Woodrow Wilson's aims were achieved and explains reasons why some were not met **7–9 marks**

Level 4 Puts Woodrow Wilson's aims in context of all the terms of the peace treaties. **10–12 marks**

This answer is good at checking off what Woodrow Wilson wanted against what happened. It also offers some explanation of why he failed in some areas, so is in the middle of Level 3.

However, the other two great power leaders at Versailles, Lloyd George and Clemenceau came to Versailles with their own agendas. Woodrow Wilson had to negotiate with them, often in bitter wrangles. He often backed down in order to retain their support for his League of Nations. In this way he was forced to go along with the terms which so enraged the Germans, like war guilt (article 231), reparations and de-militarising the Rhineland.

Note that he was in favour of reducing the German armed forces, but only as a step to everyone disarming, which they never did.

Question to Answer

The answer to question 3 can be found on p.268

3 Look at this cartoon. It shows Woodrow Wilson *(right)*,
Clemenceau *(centre, with walking stick)* and Lloyd George *(far left)*
leaving Versailles after the Treaty was worked out. Clemenceau is saying:

'Curious, I seem to hear a child weeping.'

The young child is labelled '1940 class', that is, those who
would have to fight another war in 1940.
The cartoon was published in Britain in 1919.

PEACE AND FUTURE CANNON FODDER

The Tiger: "Curious! I seem to hear a child weeping!"

a) What does this cartoon tell us about British attitudes in 1919? (4)

b) Use the cartoon and your own knowledge to explain why
people in Britain felt like this. (6)

GERMANY AFTER THE WAR 1918–1923

HOW DID GERMANY BECOME A DEMOCRATIC COUNTRY?

By late 1918 Germany was in a terrible state:

- The country's pride and joy, the great German army, was on the verge of defeat.
- The German people were nearly starving, living on handouts of potatoes, turnips and sawdusty bread.
- The Kaiser and his advisers had lost the support of many of the German people.
- Germany was in financial ruin as a result of the cost of the war.

In late October 1918, in a last, desperate throw, the Navy commanders ordered their ships to sea to attack the British Navy. The sailors in the port of Kiel mutinied. This was followed by risings of workers and soldiers all over the country. The Kaiser fled to Holland, leaving Germany as a republic in the hands of the men he most hated, the democratically-elected politicians. The leader of the biggest party, the Social Democrats, was Ebert. He made an armistice – a ceasefire – on 11 November 1918 and called an election for January 1919.

Figure 4.1
Striking workers and soldiers on the streets of Berlin, 1918

A smaller group of socialists, called **Spartacists**, were admirers of the revolution which had taken place in Russia only a year earlier. They wanted a similar revolution in Germany, based on the soviets of mutinying soldiers and striking workers (see Fig. 4.1) which had sprung up across Germany. Led by Rosa Luxemburg and Karl Liebknecht, they could see that elections would put power back into the hands of more moderate, middle-class politicians. Armed Spartacists took to the streets of Berlin.

Ebert and the Social Democrats now also turned to violence. They formed groups of armed anti-Socialist ex-soldiers, called the **Freikorps**, to crush the Spartacists. Luxemburg and Liebknecht were brutally murdered and hundreds of Spartacists killed.

Results

- The Spartacists called themselves Communists and began to take part in democratic politics. They were always the bitter enemies of the Social Democrats.
- Many Germans remained deeply afraid of the Communists.

The Weimar Republic

Because Berlin, the capital of Germany, was still in chaos, the new democratic government met in the town of Weimar and so was called the Weimar Republic. The new constitution said:

- Everyone over twenty, men and women, had the vote.
- Freedom of speech, of travel, of religious belief were all guaranteed.
- The elected Parliament was called the Reichstag. There was also an elected upper chamber, called the Reichsrat. The Chancellor (or Prime Minister) had to have the support of a majority of members of the Reichstag.
- The President was to be the elected head of the country. It was expected that the President would be merely a figurehead, although with the power to rule without the Reichstag's support in emergencies.
- Elections were held by **proportional representation**, so a party with 25 per cent of the votes cast all over Germany would get 25 per cent of the members of the Reichstag.

> Proportional representation means that each party gets members according to its proportion of the vote.

> A coalition is where two or more parties agree to work together and form a government.

This system leads to the growth of small parties. No party, throughout the life of the Weimar Republic, ever got more than 50 per cent of the votes cast, so all governments had to be **coalitions**. It was rare for these coalitions to last very long, so governments were always changing.

PROBLEMS OF THE EARLY YEARS OF THE WEIMAR REPUBLIC

The Treaty of Versailles

The angry reaction of the German people to the Treaty of Versailles, and the reasons for it, can be found on page 52. The Weimar government was faced with the choice of signing the Treaty or resuming the war. The latter would have brought the destruction of Germany, so they signed.

But the anger of many Germans was transferred to the Weimar politicians. They were called, by Hitler, but also by others, 'November Criminals', for making the Armistice of November 1918. They were accused of 'stabbing the army in the back' (when, in fact, the army was quite incapable of fighting on).

Right-wing violence

Many Germans remained loyal to the old system of rule by the Kaiser. They hated democracy and the Weimar politicians. These years were full of violence:

- The Kapp putsch, 1920. This was an attempt by the Freikorps to seize power in Berlin. They were defeated when the workers held a general strike.
- Murders. There were nearly 400 political murders between 1919 and 1923, including two government ministers.
- Hitler's Beer-Hall putsch, 1923 (see p.68).

The French occupation of the Ruhr (see p.54)

Hyper-inflation

The French occupation of the Ruhr was met by passive resistance. Postal, telegraph and telephone services stopped, trains and boats didn't run, production of factories came to a halt. This was effective in resisting the French, but the workers and those expelled from the Ruhr had to be fed. However, the country was not making anything to sell. So the government printed more money. Soon this got out of control.

Prices in a restaurant changed while you were eating a meal. Wages were paid in basketfuls of paper notes. A loaf of bread which cost 29 pfennigs in 1913, cost 1,200 marks in summer 1923 and 428,000,000,000 marks by November 1923. People in debt were able to pay them off easily, but those with savings found they had become worthless and people on fixed incomes were in real distress.

Result

Middle-class Germans who had lost their savings never forgave the Weimar government.

EXTRA POINTS

Here are the main parties in the Weimar Republic in the 1920s:

1. The Nazis (see p.67)
2. The German Nationalist Party: a right-wing party of the landowners and industrialists who had supported the Kaiser.
3. The German People's Party: not quite as right wing as the Nationalists; a party of business.
4. The Centre Party: a party for Roman Catholics.
5. The Democratic Party: a middle-of-the-road party with support from the German Jewish community.
6. The Social Democratic Party.
7. The Communist Party.

Parties (1), (2) and (7) were all utterly opposed to the Weimar system of government.

Check yourself

QUESTIONS

Q1 Why did: (a) the Communists, and (b) many patriotic Germans, hate the Social Democrats and the Weimar Republic?

Q2
a)   What is a coalition?
b)   Why were coalitions in the Weimar Republic difficult to operate?

Q3 Why did the massive inflation of 1923 cause chaos and distress?

REMEMBER! Cover the answers if you want to.

ANSWERS

A1
a)   The Communists hated the Social Democrats because the Social Democrats had formed the Freikorps, which had ruthlessly crushed their attempted revolution of January 1919.
b)   Many patriotic Germans hated the Social Democrats for making the armistice of November 1918 and for signing the Treaty of Versailles. They regarded the armistice as 'stabbing the army in the back' and the Treaty as a humiliation for Germany.

A2
a)   A coalition is a government made up of more than one party.
b)   Coalitions were hard to operate partly because there was so much hatred between parties. Coalitions also need experienced politicians to make them work. The Weimar Republic was Germany's first experience of real democracy.

A3 People could not run their daily lives with prices rising by the hour. Even wage-earners could not keep up: at the height of the inflation in autumn 1923, a good wage in one week would not buy a loaf of bread the next. The world seemed topsy-turvy: respectable people on fixed incomes were really starving. People who had spent a lifetime saving up their money, found it was all suddenly worth virtually nothing. Debtors, normally looked down on, were the only ones to benefit.

TUTORIALS

T1 *The Communists also hated the Weimar Republic because they did not believe in parliamentary democracy. Many patriotic Germans did not believe in democracy either and wanted the return of the Kaiser. You need to remember both groups' hatred of Weimar in general and their hatred of the Social Democrats in particular for later. When the Nazis threatened the end of democracy in Germany (see p.74) too few Germans cared enough to stop them.*

T2 *Unlike the Weimar Republic, Britain does not have proportional representation. This usually brings single party governments. Coalitions have only been formed in wartime and in the crisis of the 1930s Depression. All the governments of the Weimar Republic, from 1919 to 1933 were coalitions.*

T3 *Paper money is based on trust: people expect to be able to exchange a note for what it cost them. During the inflation, the paper money carried enormous values, like '100 billion marks', but was actually worthless. In some areas people stopped using money and bartered for goods. Germany's trade, and international banking system failed too.*

THE WEIMAR REPUBLIC 1923–1930

WHAT DID STRESEMANN ACHIEVE FOR GERMANY?

The problems of Germany in 1923 were:

- economic – the massive inflation;
- but underlying that was diplomacy – Germany's bad relations with her ex-enemies.

From 1923 until his death in 1929, German politics was dominated by Gustav Stresemann. He was Chancellor briefly in 1923 and then Foreign Minister until his death in 1929. He dealt effectively with both these problems.

Economic recovery

- He called off passive resistance to the French invasion of the Ruhr.
- He introduced a new currency, the *rentenmark*, cancelling the old, inflated, mark.
- Inflation stopped; industry began to pick up, unemployment began to fall.
- He negotiated the Dawes Plan, 1924, named after the US banker, Charles Dawes.

Figure 4.2
The Dawes Plan

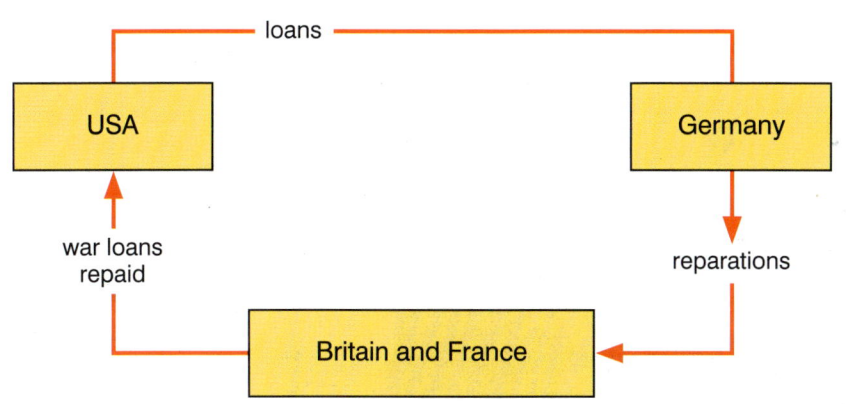

- The Dawes Plan agreed that Germany should pay a lower amount of reparations. It also arranged loans to German industry from US bankers. With Germany beginning to recover, some reparations could be paid to the Allies, who could then pay off some of their wartime debts to the USA (see Fig. 4.2).
- The Young Plan, 1929. This was a further negotiated reduction of the amount of reparations to one-third of the 1921 figure.

Diplomatic recovery

- The French could see that the invasion of the Ruhr had not got them what they wanted. In 1923 they withdrew. They also agreed to the Dawes Plan, 1924: better to receive some reparations than none at all.

- Locarno Pact, 1925. Stresemann increased this new mood of co-operation by agreeing to respect the boundaries with France and Belgium agreed at Versailles. He agreed not to re-militarise the Rhineland, from which Allied troops were gradually withdrawn. In turn, France agreed not to invade Germany.

- In this new atmosphere of trust, sometimes called the 'Locarno Honeymoon' Germany was admitted to the League of Nations, 1926.

Results

- The diplomatic recovery helped Germany's economic recovery: now that she was behaving normally, investors poured money into Germany, which prospered (see below).

- Stresemann showed that Germany could be trusted to behave like any other democratic nation.

- Parties which fed on desperate conditions in Germany declined: votes for the Nazis fell. In 1928 they were reduced to just thirteen members of the Reichstag.

THE GOLDEN YEARS

Economic prosperity

Germany prospered in these years. 25,000 million marks of foreign loans were invested. New industries sprang up. Cars, telephones, radios, airships, ocean liners were built. After the USA, Germany in the 1920s was the most up-to-date country in the world.

The arts

Censorship had been tough under the Kaiser. Under the Weimar Republic there was freedom and the arts flourished. New techniques in film-making were developed by Fritz Lang, in drama by Bertold Brecht, in song by Kurt Weill, in architecture by Walter Gropius and the Bauhaus school (see Fig. 4.3)

Figure 4.3
Bauhaus building, 1932. This may not look very new to us. Buildings like this are all around us now. But look at the date: 1932. This was one of the first buildings to use modern techniques and materials to devise a new style.

Entertainment

Berlin became a 'good time' city, with hundreds of night clubs and jazz bands. Sexual freedom, for some at least, replaced the repression of the Kaiser's Germany. Many Germans, and stuffy puritans like Hitler, hated this aspect of Weimar too. They thought it was decadent.

THE GREAT DEPRESSION

Stresemann died in 1929 and in October of that year the bubble of German prosperity burst. The Wall Street Crash (see chapter 7) brought disaster for US financiers. They called in their loans. German companies closed down. Unemployment rose fast. By 1932 one worker in three was out of work, including clerks and teachers, as well as manual workers. With their dependents, this meant that 23 million people had no wages to live on. The government paid unemployment benefit for 26 weeks. After that there was a handout, not really enough to survive on. Many could not afford to pay their rents and became homeless. Even those in work suffered pay reductions and shortened hours. Germany was deep in crisis again.

 **EXTRA POINT**

Stresemann had, by negotiation:

- lowered the amount of reparations.
- by agreeing only Germany's western boundaries there was a suggestion that the eastern boundaries were not so fixed.
- foreign troops had left German soil.

He thus achieved, peacefully, a good deal of what right-wing Germans wanted. Recent research has shown his aims were the same as theirs: to improve on the terms made at Versailles, but by negotiation rather than defiance. Nevertheless, they hated him. For Hitler, and others, nothing less than total defiance of the Versailles Treaty would do.

Check yourself

QUESTIONS

Q1 What was the 'Locarno Honeymoon'?

Q2 Why did the Depression hit Germany so hard?

Q3 Was the Weimar Republic doomed to failure?

REMEMBER! Cover the answers if you want to.

ANSWERS

A1 This was the period when Stresemann built up good relations with other countries, following the Locarno Conference of 1925.

A2 Because the German economy was so dependent on loans from abroad. When these were called in, the boom collapsed and millions were thrown out of work.

TUTORIALS

T1 *The good mood of the Locarno Honeymoon also reflects a change in the attitudes of the Allies too: France had seen that invading the Ruhr had achieved nothing. She now turned to other tactics to preserve her security.*

T2 *The precarious nature of Germany's economy meant that the depression, when it came, was more severe than in other countries.*

ANSWER

A3 It may seem that it was doomed from the start. The Kaiser's Germany had not been democratic, so people and politicians lacked experience in making real democracy work. The Weimar constitution led to coalition government. Coalition governments tend to be weak governments, unable to act decisively in a crisis. The Weimar Republic was created in a crisis and faced several serious crises, in 1918–23 and again in 1929-33. Furthermore, several parties and people did not want democracy and hated all that the Weimar Republic stood for.

However, the Weimar constitution was a brave attempt to set up real democracy in Germany and might have worked. The achievements of Weimar in the 1920s, in industry and the arts, showed what German democracy was capable of. If it had not been for the Wall Street Crash, which was not Germany's fault, Weimar could have survived. Also, it eventually fell because of Hitler. No one could have foreseen Hitler, so it was not inevitable that Weimar would fail.

TUTORIAL

T3 *This is a good balanced answer. The two paragraphs sum up the arguments on each side. It is important to remember that nothing in History is inevitable: just because we know that that the Weimar Republic was rapidly dismantled by Hitler in 1933–34 does not mean it was doomed.*

Another prejudice we have is to see things from a British point of view: Britain does not like coalitions, but that does not mean they are automatically a bad thing. From 1923 to 1930, the 'golden years', coalition governments ran Germany.

However, it is important to note that, in fact, proper parliamentary government was already dead by the time Hitler had become Chancellor. Ministers had ruled by presidential decree, by-passing the Reichstag, for some time (see p.70). The ageing President Hindenberg had spent most of his life under the undemocratic government of the Kaisers. Most of the people around him had little belief in democracy. Weimar collapsed because not enough people believed in making democracy work.

One further point: Weimar was important training for the democratic politicians who were to run the Federal Republic of Germany so effectively after it was set up in 1949.

HITLER AND THE NAZIS, 1918–1930

WHO WAS HITLER? AND WHO WERE THE NAZIS?

Adolf Hitler was born in 1889. He did not get on with his elderly father, a minor Austrian customs official on the German border, but loved his mother. He failed to get into art school in Vienna in 1907, and barely scraped a living as an artist.

When war broke out in 1914 he joined the German Army, the 16th Bavarian Infantry Regiment, and served on the Western Front. He loved army life. He was a messenger and twice won the Iron Cross for bravery. When the war ended, he was in hospital recovering from a gas attack. Like many Germans, he could not believe that the war was over and Germany had lost.

He was still in the army in 1919 when he was sent to investigate the German Workers Party, one of the many tiny political parties which had sprung up after the war. Although Hitler did not ask to join, he was sent a membership card. He decided he could mould this little party into his own organisation.

THE NAZIS

In 1920 the party changed its name to the National Socialist German Workers Party (National Sozialistische Deutsche Arbeiter Partei, NSDAP, or Nazis). The Nazis' 25-point programme of 1920 contained elements of nationalism, socialism and anti-Semitism:

- **Nationalism**
  Union with Austria, abolition of the Treaty of Versailles, seizure of land from Poland and Russia.

- **Socialism**
  Old age pensions, profit-sharing in industry, abolition of big business, protection for small shopkeepers.

- **Anti-Semitism**
  Jews to lose their right to German citizenship.

In 1921 Hitler became leader of the Nazi Party. It adopted the swastika symbol he had designed. The party became quite successful in Bavaria, in southern Germany, with 50,000 members by 1923.

REASONS FOR EARLY SUCCESS:

- Hitler was a powerful speaker. In packed meetings in Munich beer-halls, he was able to play on the anger felt by many Germans over their defeat in the war and the hardship they were suffering. Many leading Nazis were moved to join at this time: Roehm, Goering, Hess, Himmler, Streicher, Rosenberg.

- Violence. Hitler formed the SA (Sturm Abteilung, stormtroopers, also called brownshirts, from their uniforms). Many were unemployed ex-soldiers (see Fig. 4.4). They kept order at Hitler's meetings and broke up other parties' meetings. By their violence they demonstrated their rejection of democratic and peaceful methods and, supposedly, their determination to take action to solve Germany's problems.

Figure 4.4
SA – Sturm Abteilung (stormtroopers)

THE BEER-HALL PUTSCH, 1923

By 1923 Hitler's 35,000 brownshirts were pressing him to seize power. When Stresemann ended passive resistance to the French invasion of the Ruhr all nationalist Germans were furious. Hitler decided the moment was ripe to take power in Bavaria and then launch a 'March on Berlin'. For this he needed the support of the Bavarian leader and local army and police chiefs.

All three were at a meeting at a beer-hall in November 1923. Hitler surrounded it with armed brownshirts, marched in, fired his pistol at the ceiling and called on the leaders to support his seizure of power. The German war hero, Ludendorff, arrived and declared his support. The local leaders were forced to agree, but Hitler let them get away. The next morning they went back on their promises.

Nevertheless, Hitler and Ludendorff decided to march into Munich with their armed brownshirts. They hoped that the people would rise in support and that the police would not shoot at the war hero. They were wrong on both counts. The police opened fire. Sixteen Nazis were killed. Hitler was arrested and put on trial.

Hitler was allowed to give a long speech in his own defence, which was fully reported in the papers, giving him national publicity. It is a sign of conditions in Weimar Germany that he was sentenced to only three years in prison, of which he served only nine months (April–December 1924), in comfort in the Landsberg Prison. He used the time to write a book, *Mein Kampf* (*My Struggle*). It is a long-winded, badly-written account of his life and beliefs.

HITLER'S BELIEFS

- Racism. The German people belonged to a superior race, the Aryans. They were the master-race, the *herrenvolk*, while other races, like Slavs, Jews and black people, were inferior.

- Germany must be great again. The Treaty of Versailles should be overthrown. Germany should seize more land in the east, by war if necessary.

- Communism was evil because it was international.

- Democracy was feeble. Germany needed a dictator to lead it to the great future Hitler had promised.

THE NAZIS 1924–30

On his release Hitler fought off a challenge to his leadership from Gregor Strasser, who emphasised the more socialist aspects of Nazism. Hitler then began re-organising the party:

- The Nazis, having failed to seize power by violent means, would win it democratically, through the Reichstag.

- Local Nazi party branches were started.

- A youth organisation, the Hitler Youth, was set up.

- The black uniformed SS (Shutz Staffel) was set up in 1925, personally loyal to Hitler.

- Goebbels was put in charge of propaganda.

However, this change of policy did not bring Hitler immediate success. Nazi Party support fell in the 'Golden Years'. In 1928 they gained the votes of just 2 per cent of Germans. Hitler seemed to be offering desperate remedies to problems which the German people did not have any more.

1. The founder of the German Workers Party was a railwayman, Anton Drexler. It was intended to appeal to working-class patriotism. Its nationalist, socialist amd anti-Semitic policies contained nothing new, but the combination of all three in one party was new.

2. Hitler seems to have picked up anti-Semitic ideas before the war. Such ideas were common in Europe at the time and, indeed, for centuries beforehand.

Check yourself

QUESTIONS

Q1 How did the Nazis get their name?

Q2 'Instead of working to achieve power by armed conspiracy, we shall have to hold our noses and enter the Reichstag. Sooner or later we shall have a majority and after that we shall have Germany.' (Hitler, in the Landsberg prison in 1924)

a) What change in policy for the Nazis does Hitler describe in this source?
b) Why do you think he was making this change?
c) What does this source tell you about Hitler's attitude to democracy?

REMEMBER! Cover the answers if you want to.

ANSWERS

A1 The Nazis were the National Socialist German Workers Party. Nazi takes two letters from NAtional and (in German) SoZIalist.

A2
a) He has abandoned the idea of seizing power by force and is going to concentrate on elections to the Reichstag.
b) Because the Beer-Hall Putsch had failed.
c) Hitler hates democracy: he says 'we will have to hold our noses' as if democracy and the democratic parties smell.

TUTORIALS

T1 *For many early Nazis, like Drexler and Roehm, Socialism was as important as Nationalism. Hitler was not really interested in socialism: he believed in the German people, but as a racist, not as a socialist.*

T2 *a)&b) The idea of seizing power by force was widespread in Germany and Europe in these years. The Bolsheviks had taken power in Russia. In Germany there had been the Spartacists and the Kapp putsch and in 1922 Mussolini had seized power in Italy.*

However, the armed forces in Munich had not supported his Beer-Hall Putsch.

c) It is a good idea in source questions to quote from the source to support your answer. Be sure to make it a short, selected, quote - don't write out most of the source. Note Hitler's last words in the Source: going into the Reichstag is, for him, just a better way of seizing power, as you will see on the next page. After he has won the election he will 'have Germany'. Notice also his supreme confidence that one day he will be successful. This is what carried him and his followers through the next six years.

HOW DID HITLER WIN POWER IN GERMANY IN 1933?

THE EFFECTS OF THE DEPRESSION

The single most important factor is the Depression, see p.65. By 1932 there were six million Germans out of work.

Reaction of the Weimar governments

The Weimar government, like most governments in the world, seemed unable to deal with the Depression. However, in Germany democracy itself began to crumble.

It was difficult to take decisive action with coalitions of several parties. When bankers and financiers wanted to cut the dole, the Social Democrats, the largest party, left the coalition. This made successful coalitions hard to keep together. Under the Weimar constitution, the President had the power to rule by decree (without the agreement of the Reichstag) in an emergency. From 1930 President Hindenburg, with the advice of his friends in the army, began to use these powers on a regular basis.

Reaction of the German people

For many Germans the Depression was the last straw. They blamed Weimar for the defeat and humiliation at the end of the war in 1918–19, for the inflation of 1923, and now this. In the 1930 elections the Nazis increased their support to 107 seats and Communist support went up from 54 to 77 seats. People were turning to two parties both utterly committed to overthrowing Weimar. The 1932 Presidential elections gave Hitler a tremendous opportunity for publicity. He won 13 million votes to Hindenburg's 19 million.

In the 1932 Reichstag elections the Nazis won 230 seats and were the biggest party.

WHY DID THE NAZIS WIN SUPPORT AT ELECTIONS?

Violence

The SA (brownshirts) grew in size, from 30,000 in 1929 to over 440,000 in 1932. Many were full-time members, living in SA hostels and paid out of Nazi funds. They continued to use violence, breaking up opponents' meetings and beating people up. This had three results:

- It increased the impression of lawlessness and the Weimar government's inability to keep law and order.
- It increased the impression that the Nazis were ready to take tough action.
- Many middle-class and rich business people were scared stiff at the increase in support for the Communists. They liked the Nazis' hostility to Communists and gave them lots of money for their campaigns.

Law and order

Nazi uniforms and processions gave an impression of order and purpose, and reminded older Germans of the great days of the Kaiser.

Nazi policies

Nazi policies began to appeal to people who had lost faith in Weimar:

- They gave you someone to blame: Jews and Weimar politicians.
- They offered strong leadership and strong government instead of the deals and incompetence of Weimar.
- They promised to make Germany great again by rejecting the Versailles peace terms.
- They offered an end to unemployment by putting men into the army (see Fig. 4.5).

Figure 4.5
Nazi election poster, 1928. It says 'Work, Freedom and Bread. Vote for the National Socialists!'

Propaganda

Nazi propaganda, especially at election times, was far ahead of their opponents. Goebbels organised torchlight processions, huge rallies, radio broadcasts, films, records, concerts, sports days, theatre groups. Hitler used aeroplanes to travel about. It was all exciting, impressive, modern, purposeful.

Hitler's oratory

Many Germans were won over to the Nazis by hearing Hitler speak. They began to think only he could save Germany.

EVENTS 1932–33

Although the Nazis were the biggest party after the July 1932 elections, Hindenburg refused to make Hitler Chancellor. Instead he chose his friend von Papen and ruled on his own, by decree, when von Papen could not get support in the Reichstag.

In the November 1932 elections the Nazis lost some support, but were still the biggest party. Still Hindenburg refused to appoint Hitler. Then, in January 1933, von Papen came up with the idea of making Hitler Chancellor, but in a coalition with only three Nazi ministers and nine from other parties. Von Papen thought he could control Hitler, while Hitler supplied him with the votes in the Reichstag.

New elections were called for March 1933, the third in nine months. Goering was now in charge of much of the police and simply enrolled SA members as special constables. There was massive Nazi violence: at least fifty anti-Nazis were killed and many injured. A week before the election the Reichstag building was set on fire and a Communist was found inside. (It may be that the Nazis set it on fire in order to blame the Communists.) Four thousand Communists were arrested. Hindenburg was persuaded to suspend basic rights and in the last week before the election only Nazi candidates were heard or seen. In this undemocratic situation, the Nazis won 17.3 million votes and with 288 seats were the biggest party, but still 22 million Germans voted for other parties. However, by outlawing the Communists, Hitler got a majority in the Reichstag.

EXTRA POINTS ▶

Was the Weimar Republic doomed from the start?

1. The Weimar Republic came into existence out of defeat and hardship and carried the blame for them to the end.

2. Germany had little experience of democracy and how to make it work. Many Germans never supported it. Although the Kaiser fled in 1918, leading figures from his government and army remained in power under Weimar. Even President Hindenburg, who should have upheld democracy, was quite ready to rule undemocratically. Democracy really ended in Germany in 1930.

3. The constitution led to coalition governments. These demanded a high level of agreement and willingness to work together. This was never achieved.

However:

4. Weimar worked quite well under Stresemann and the country prospered.

5. No one could have foreseen the Wall Street Crash and Depression.

6. No one could have foreseen Hitler. He was determined to overthrow Weimar and very successful at turning events to his advantage.

Check yourself

QUESTIONS

Q1 Why did the Depression help the Nazis?

This looks a big question at first sight: there is the Depression itself, the Nazis, and the country as a whole. Use this plan to sort out your answer.

'The worldwide Depression hit Germany hard. Its effects were ...'

'The Nazi Party had little support when the Depression started. But ...'
'People rejected Weimar because ...'
'People turned to the Nazis because ...'

Q2 How did the Nazis appeal to:
(a) the unemployed; (b) ex-soldiers;
(c) business people?

REMEMBER! Cover the answers if you want to.

ANSWERS

A1 The worldwide Depression hit Germany hard. Its effects were a massive increase in unemployment, which reached six million in 1933. The economy had been dependent on US loans. When these were called in business collapsed.

The Nazi Party had little support when the Depression started. But in the 1930 elections it won 107 seats. By 1933 Hitler was in power.

People rejected Weimar because they blamed it for all that had gone wrong in 1919–23. Its coalition governments now seemed unable to deal with the crisis. From 1930 President Hindenburg ceased to work through the Reichstag, which was deadlocked, but instead ruled by decree. Democracy was therefore already in difficulties.

People turned to the Nazis because they looked impressive and businesslike. They offered solutions to the problems of the country – powerful leadership by Hitler to replace the weak compromises of Weimar leaders; full employment by building up the army; scapegoats to blame for the mess they were in. These messages were forcefully put across by skilled propaganda and exciting political meetings.

A2
a) They offered jobs in the army or a revived armaments industry.
b) They wanted to see Versailles rejected and the army re-built.
c) They were worried by the increasing support for the Communists and the Nazis were violently anti-Communist.

TUTORIALS

T1 *Many Germans were desperate, and desperate times led people to consider the desperate remedies Hitler was offering. Don't forget, however, that not all Germans thought like this: Hitler never got a majority of the votes of the German people in a free election.*

T2 *Although these divisions help us understand the appeal of Nazism, people are more complicated than this: there were, for example, patriotic unemployed people, or anti-Semitic ex-soldiers.*

HITLER'S DICTATORSHIP

Hitler had plans to change Germany completely and build a new Reich (Empire). This Third Reich (the others were the Kaiser's rule and the Weimar Republic) would last for a thousand years. These plans were sometimes called the Nazi revolution.

WHAT WERE HITLER'S PLANS FOR GERMANY?

- To take over complete control of the country, see below.
- To build a community in which everyone had a place, which Hitler had decided for them. If people agreed they would benefit, see p.78.
- To make Germany strong, economically and militarily, see p.82.
- To make Germany racially pure, see p.86.

> Totalitarian means the total control of the lives of everyone in the state. Dictatorship means rule by one person.

These four aims overlap, but they are mainly dealt with in the pages shown. In this section we shall see how Hitler took over complete control of Germany. After the March 1933 elections Hitler rapidly went about making himself **totalitarian dictator** of Germany.

REMOVAL OF OPPOSITION

- Enabling Act, March 1933 gave Hitler the right to pass laws without consulting the Reichstag. It was passed with the agreement of some other parties while SA and SS members surrounded the building. President Hindenburg was thus sidelined and democracy ended.
- Local government was brought under Nazi control. In April 1933 each of the eighteen provinces of Germany was given a Nazi Governor appointed by Hitler, with the power to make state laws. In January 1934 state parliaments were abolished.
- Trade unions were abolished, May 1933.
- Other parties' leaders were attacked, their offices raided. In July 1933 all parties apart from the Nazi Party were banned.
- Opponents fled abroad or were arrested. They were beaten up or put in concentration camps, the first of which, at Dachau, was opened in 1933. Concentration camps were run by the SS. Inmates did hard labour, with poor food and harsh discipline.

RIVALS TO HITLER

By early 1934 the only rival to Hitler's personal power over the German people was the SA:

- There were now three million of them.
- They thought Hitler owed them a debt for having helped him to power. They wanted jobs and rewards.
- They were more left-wing than Hitler and wanted to carry out some of the Socialist points of the Nazis' 25-point programme (see p.67).
- Their leader, Ernst Roehm, had a plan to merge the SA and the army. As head of both he would be more powerful than Hitler.

Hitler had to act. The army was horrified at the idea of being swallowed up in the SA. One weekend in June 1934 Hitler ordered his SS to execute four hundred SA leaders, including Roehm. This was called the Night of the Long Knives.

Then, a few weeks later, Hindenburg died. Hitler combined the jobs of President and Chancellor, calling himself simply *Der Führer* (*the Leader*). The Army now swore its loyalty oath to Hitler. In return for their support Hitler had removed the SA and now promised to increase the size of the army to half a million men, contrary to the Treaty of Versailles.

THE CHURCHES

The other big organisations in Germany to which lots of people belonged were the Churches. Hitler and many leading Nazis were hostile to Christianity, but about two-thirds of Germans were Protestants and one-third were Roman Catholics. Hitler did not feel strong enough to attack the Churches at first. Many church members, particularly Protestants, supported the Nazis.

Roman Catholics

Hitler made a 'concordat' (agreement) with the Pope in 1933 not to interfere in the life of the Roman Catholic Church. However, his drive to establish totalitarian control led to shutting down monasteries and Catholic Youth groups. The Pope protested but it did no good. Several Catholic bishops were imprisoned.

Protestants

Hitler attempted to set up a 'Reich Church' of Nazi supporters, 'with the swastika on our chests and the cross in our hearts' as they said. Many Protestants could not agree to this and left the Reich Church. Many were arrested and put in concentration camps, including their leader, Martin Niemöller.

Other groups

Some smaller religious groups had firmly-held beliefs which were completely contrary to Nazism. Jehovah's Witnesses, for example, did not believe in serving in the army. Thousands of them were arrested and died in concentration camps.

POLICE CONTROL

Germany became a country where it was unsafe to do or say anything against the government.

The **Gestapo** was the secret police. After 1936 they were under the control of Himmler, who also ran the SS. They could arrest and imprison anyone without trial. A network of informers ensured that no one dared to step out of line. People were encouraged to inform the police about neighbours or even their own family.

They were helped by the members of the Nazi Party, grown to five million by 1938. Every block, every village street, had its Block Leader, 400,000 of them, to report on suspicious behaviour. 'Suspicious behaviour' could mean simply not giving the 'Heil Hitler' salute, or not letting your children join the Hitler Youth. There was an atmosphere of fear. Local police were run by Nazis. Judges swore an oath of loyalty to the Nazis.

THOUGHT CONTROL

Once Hitler was dictator of Germany, Goebbels turned his skill at propaganda to controlling the German people. Books, plays, films, newspapers, art and music, so free under the Weimar Republic, were now strictly controlled. In 1933 Nazi students held huge bonfires of books by authors of which the Nazis disapproved. No rival newspapers, magazines, radio stations were allowed. No material criticising Hitler or the Nazis was allowed to be published.

Cheap radios were made and radio ownership went up four times in the 1930s. On their radios German people only heard what Goebbels wanted them to hear: how Hitler and the Nazis were making Germany great again. The message was even broadcast from loudspeakers in the streets.

Hitler was almost worshipped. His picture was everywhere: in schools, offices, law-courts. He was portrayed as Germany's saviour from all her enemies.

Huge rallies were held at the specially-built stadium at Nuremberg (see Fig. 4.6). Thousands of uniformed Nazis lined up, focused on the rostrum from which Hitler spoke. Whether seen in person, or on film, these rallies:

- showed the power of the Nazis
- gave a sense of discipline and order
- made people feel that everyone thought the same.

Figure 4.6
Nazi rally at Nuremberg

EXTRA POINTS ▶

1. Hitler's other rival for power in Germany was the army. He settled this in 1938, when he sacked his War Minister, the Chief of Staff and sixty other generals for opposing his war plans.

2. Do not think that Hitler's Germany was efficiently run: many historians have pointed out that it was in fact quite chaotic. All power, in theory, lay with Hitler, but he only worked in the afternoons and did not try to know everything that was going on. His close colleagues could take their own decisions, and spent most of their time building up their own positions. Himmler, for example, built up the SS to be the biggest organisation in Germany. By 1945, he controlled the Gestapo, the 'Death's Head Units', which ran the concentration camps, the Waffen SS, fighting units which rivalled the army during the war years and some 150 factories using slave labour.

Check yourself

QUESTIONS

Q1 What were: (a) the Enabling Act; (b) the Night of the Long Knives; (c) the Reich Church?

Q2 'Hitler became dictator of Germany quite legally.'

(a) When did Hitler become dictator?
(b) Is the statement above true?

Q3 How did the Gestapo and propaganda work together to crush opposition in Germany?

REMEMBER! Cover the answers if you want to.

ANSWERS

A1
a) The Enabling Act was passed in 1933 and gave Hitler the power to pass laws without consulting the Reichstag.
b) The Night of the Long Knives, 1934, was Hitler's attack on the SA, killing their leaders and removing their threat to his supremacy.
c) The Reich Church was a Nazi church of Protestants who supported the Nazis.

A2
a) Hitler had become dictator by removing all democratic opposition by July 1933 – only five months after winning the election.
b) Hitler did use legal methods: the Acts abolishing trade unions and other parties and local elections were all legally passed. The judges agreed to swear a Nazi oath. The only major act of illegal force, the Night of the Long Knives, was used against his own supporters.

A3 People were frightened of the Gestapo, because they could arrest and punish you without a proper trial. You could not trust anyone because police and Nazi Party informers were all around and would pass on even a casual remark. Nazi propaganda made it look as if everyone supported them. People therefore felt isolated, afraid to confide in others and afraid that they were the only ones who doubted that the Nazis were a good thing.

TUTORIALS

T1
a) *The Enabling Act carried out just what Hitler had promised back in 1924: to use democratic methods to take over Germany and then destroy democracy (see p.74). At a stroke it made both President Hindenburg and the elected Reichstag powerless.*
b) *The Night of the Long Knives – as opposed to the Enabling Act – shows Hitler's readiness to use brute force.*

T2
a) *The speed with which democracy collapsed in Germany is quite shocking, but Hitler was helped by the widespread disillusionment with Weimar and Hindenburg's use of dictator-like powers since 1930.*
b) *This kind of question – putting up a sentence and asking if you agree with it – is often used. It is better to try to find a way of partly agreeing and partly disagreeing.*

In this case, although Hitler won elections and passed laws, these were not done fairly. The elections were carried out with massive violence and intimidation of opponents; the Enabling Act, ending the power of the Reichstag, was passed after elected members had been jostled by Nazis outside and with SA and SS members all over the building. This kind of intimidation is not democratic.

T3 *The Nazis were very successful at suppressing opposition by this mixture of fear and propaganda. The two factors help to explain why there was so little opposition to them (see p.83).*

WOMEN AND CHILDREN

WHAT WERE NAZI PLANS FOR WOMEN AND CHILDREN?

Hitler and the Nazis had very clear ideas about what they wanted from women and from children in the Third Reich. In both cases, they used both 'the stick' – passing laws, and 'the carrot' – encouragement and propaganda, to achieve what they wanted. In both cases they were not completely successful.

WOMEN

The Nazis were in many ways quite old-fashioned in their views. The Nazi Party was a man's party, with no women in any senior positions. They did not like the idea of women's equality in jobs. Instead, they believed that women should stay at home, support their husbands and have lots of children:

- For racial reasons, to build up the numbers of German people by increasing the birth-rate;
- For economic reasons, to free jobs for unemployed men.

The Nazis started by passing laws:

- Women were removed from state employment. This meant they could not be employed as civil servants, lawyers, judges or doctors. Many women teachers and all Germany's 3,000 women doctors were sacked. Women could not serve on juries.

Women were also encouraged to follow Nazi policy:

- Jobs: sex discrimination was encouraged.
- Marriage and child-breeding: Couples received a loan of 1,000 marks on getting married. Less and less of this loan had to be paid back the more children you had. They also gave medals for child-bearing: bronze for four children, silver for six and gold for eight. In 1938 childlessness was made grounds for divorce.
- 'Racial purity' was ensured by sterilising women with hereditary diseases, or mental illness, even colour blindness (because soldiers need to be able to recognise colour). Unmarried women could also volunteer to have a child by a guaranteed 'Aryan' SS member.
- Fashion: Nazi propaganda discouraged wearing make-up, dyeing or perming your hair, wearing high heels, smoking in public. Posters encouraged peasant styles of fashion, flat shoes, hair in plaits or buns.

The propaganda image of women (see Fig. 4.7) was thus one of the devoted wife, mother and home-builder. The traditional German '3Ks': *Kinder, Kirche, Küche* (children, church, cooking), summed up the Nazi ideal.

Problems

There were problems with the Nazi ideal. By 1937 Germany was short of workers. When the war got under way and men were called up into the armed forces, the shortage was even greater. So women were encouraged to take jobs. However, even at the height of the war, German women were never mobilised as much as women in Britain and German industry relied on slave labour from all over Europe.

Figure 4.7
Nazi poster of an 'ideal' family

CHILDREN

Young people were particularly important to the Nazis. They knew that they could never win over all Germans, but a new generation was growing up who would not know anything but the Third Reich. The lives of young people, especially boys, were controlled both in school and out of it.

In school

- Schools were taken out of the hands of local government and put under central government control. All teachers had to swear an oath of loyalty to Hitler and join the Nazi Teachers League. Jewish teachers were sacked.

- The curriculum was changed. The key subjects were History, Biology and PE.
  - In History all the pre-Nazi textbooks were banned. Pupils were to be taught only about the greatness of the German race. The Nazi version of events since 1918 was taught, including the so-called 'stab in the back' of 1918 and Hitler's great mission to restore Germany.

- In Biology they were taught a false 'race science', concerned with the supposed superiority of the Aryans and the inferiority of races such as Jews, Slavs and black people.
- The amount of PE in the timetable was tripled and boxing was made compulsory for boys. Hitler wanted fit people much more than clever people, the boys to become soldiers and the girls to breed lots of Aryan babies.

Out of school

Young people were expected to join one of the Nazi youth movements. From the age of six they could join the 'Pimpfen'. Then, from ten to fourteen they joined the Young Girls or the Young German Folk. Girls then joined the League of German Girls and boys joined the Hitler Youth. They went camping, learnt Nazi songs and played games. They also had lots of Nazi political talks and films. The girls were given lectures on health, racial purity and child-rearing. The emphasis for boys was much more military: they learnt to clean and fire rifles, read maps, go on long marches and throw hand grenades. In both cases it was clear how the Nazis saw their future.

There were 2.3 million youngsters in the Nazi Youth movements in 1933, about 30 per cent of all young people in Germany. Only about half as many girls had joined their organisations as boys. Hitler appointed Baldur von Schirach to build up the numbers. From 1936 it became almost impossible not to join. Many young people were fanatical supporters of the Nazis. By 1939 there were eight million members, about 82 per cent of German young people.

Problems

By the late 1930s, when membership was virtually compulsory, still nearly one in five young Germans had avoided joining. Those who were members were often fed up with the long boring talks and readings from *Mein Kampf*, which they had heard many times before, in school as well, about the Nazis and how Hitler was saving Germany. Many young people simply wanted to be left alone to lead their own lives. It was now more exciting to join rebel groups like the Swing or the Edelweiss Pirates (see p.84).

EXTRA POINTS ▶

1. The position of women in Nazi Germany contrasted with the relative freedom women had had in the Weimar Republic and were having in Britain and the USA at this time.

2. At school, Nazi ideology got into every part of the curriculum, even maths, as this problem shows:

   'It costs 4 marks a day to keep a mentally ill person in care. There are 300,000 mentally ill people in Germany. How much, in total, do these people cost the country per year? How many marriage loans at 1,000 marks each could be granted from this money?'

Check yourself

QUESTIONS

Q1 How were German women under the Nazis encouraged to get married and have lots of children?

Q2 Hitler, speaking about young people:

'Weakness has to be knocked out of them. The world will shrink in alarm from the youngsters who grow up in my schools: a violent, masterful, dauntless, cruel, younger generation. They shall learn to overcome the fear of death by the severest tests. Then I shall have in front of me the pure and noble natural material. With that I can create the new order.'

Use this source and the information in this book to describe Hitler's educational aims.

REMEMBER! Cover the answers if you want to.

ANSWERS

A1 Women in Nazi Germany were directly encouraged to get married by marriage loans. There were also medals for having lots of children. Indirectly, Nazi propaganda at school, in youth movements (which young people had little choice about joining) and everywhere on posters, books, art, films did the same. It always showed desirable images of women at home, with children.

A2 Hitler was more concerned to develop fit young people than well-educated ones. Education included lots of PE. The other main purpose of Nazi education policy was to turn out young people who supported the Nazis unquestioningly. This source describes how he wants them to be fit, but says nothing about the rest of their education. He also wants them to be rather nasty: 'violent, cruel etc.' He wanted to develop these qualities because the most important role he had for young Germans was as soldiers.

TUTORIALS

T1 It was almost impossible for women to develop a career. Women state employees (doctors, civil servants etc.), were sacked and job discrimination encouraged.
There was also pressure from Nazi busybodies: women in make-up, or smoking in public would be told off in public and your local Block Leader would speak to you if you were of marriageable age and unmarried or married with no children.

T2 This is a good answer to the 'Use the source and your own knowledge' type of question. It starts from the wider information in the text and uses it as a context for the ideas in the source. The quotes are well-chosen and short.

Hitler in this source seems only to be talking about boys: clearly, when he thought about young people he thought about boys. It is quite revealing about his view of the unimportance of women. The mention of them overcoming the 'fear of death' is another item proving that war is his ultimate aim for German boys. Boys in the Hitler Youth learnt to overcome their fear by doing slightly dangerous things like jumping over fires and out of first-floor windows.

THE NAZI ECONOMY

Hitler had three aims for the German economy under 'the Nazi revolution':

- To reduce unemployment – this had been one of his main election promises.

- To re-arm Germany – he had always said he would do this, despite the restrictions in the Treaty of Versailles.

- To make Germany more self-sufficient – he knew that Germany was dependent on imported goods like rubber, textiles and petrol and so could be strangled in a wartime blockade, as the Allies had done in the First World War.

HOW WAS UNEMPLOYMENT REDUCED?

Before the Nazis came to power a National Labour Service had been set up. This used government money to pay unemployed men to do public works, like planting forests, building houses and schools. Hitler expanded these schemes. He was especially keen on building motorways, 'autobahnen'. 80,000 men worked on these. These had great propaganda value, as well as military value, transporting motorised armies rapidly around the country.

From 1935 all 18 to 25 year olds had to spend six months in the National Labour Service. They were paid only pocket money, wore uniforms and did drill, like soldiers. The scheme took millions off the unemployment figures.

RE-ARMAMENT

As soon as he came to power Hitler ordered the building of aircraft, tanks, battleships and submarines, at first secretly and then, from 1935, openly. All this military build-up provided work in factories, ironworks, coalmines and other industries. He also increased the size of the army, from 100,000 in 1933 to 1,400,000 by 1939.

The re-armament campaign also helped to reduce unemployment. It was down to one million by 1936 and by 1938 Germany needed more workers. However, quite a number of people had disappeared from the list of unemployed but were not actually in paid work: Jews, many women, soldiers, many 18 to 25 year olds.

Self-sufficiency

Tough controls were put on imports. Industry was told to try to find substitutes for imported rubber, petrol, cotton and coffee. Agriculture was stepped up to try to feed all Germans without food imports. There were often shortages of some foods as a result, even before the war. It soon became clear that this was impossible unless Germany seized more land from other countries.

Workers' lives

Nazi policies for workers, like those for women and children see p.78, were that they should do as they were told, shut up, not complain, and the Nazis would make them happy. All workers had to join the Labour Front. There were no trade unions, so no way of negotiating better wages or conditions. Businesses and employers liked this, of course. Wages were low and hours long, but at least workers now had secure jobs. The standard of living of German workers remained quite low.

The Nazis organised 'Strength through Joy'. This campaign gave workers cheap holidays, foreign cruises, theatre trips, concerts, sporting facilities.

The Nazis also promised workers a cheap 'workers' car', the Volkswagen. This was designed, and many workers began to pay for theirs, but none were delivered.

 EXTRA POINTS

1. Hitler did not know much about economics. He appointed Schacht as Minister of the Economy. Schacht did very well, fulfilling all three of Hitler's economic aims, see p.82. However, he fell out with Hitler in 1937 because Hitler wanted to re-arm Germany faster than Schacht said he could afford. He was sacked and sent to a concentration camp.

2. Goering took over the economy. He was also head of the *Luftwaffe* (the air force), but not an economist. Goering introduced a Four-Year Plan in 1937 to build up the economy so that Germany would be ready for war in four years.

DID MOST GERMANS SUPPORT HITLER?

In a country with no free elections and no free media it is very difficult to tell what public opinion is. Until the middle of the war, however, when rationing, bombing and high casualties brought increasing disillusionment, many Germans were quite happy with Hitler. He had carried out many of his promises; most people had jobs, Germany was strong and successful. Unless you were Jewish, or a convinced Socialist or Communist, or a strong believer in personal freedom (and most Germans were none of these), you had little to complain about. People grumbled about the endless propaganda and the interference in their private lives. They attended the parades and meetings if their job depended on it. Anti-Nazi jokes were as far as most people dared to go.

RESISTANCE

Caught between the fear of the Gestapo and the pressure of propaganda, resistance to Hitler was very difficult.

- The Communists and Social Democrats set up underground organisations. They published secret newsletters and sent information to friends abroad. Some workers sabotaged factories or railway lines. But they would not work together.

- The churches. Several priests and bishops spoke out against the Nazis. They managed to have the euthanasia campaign (see p.86) stopped. Some hid Jews or helped them get out of the country. Some were imprisoned or executed. Martin Niemöller, for example, spent from 1938 to 1945 in a concentration camp. Some resisted more actively: Dietrich Bonhöffer was executed in 1945.

- The army. Later, in the war years, some people in the army could see that, far from making Germany great, Hitler was leading their country to destruction. By this time upper-class Germans who had earlier supported Hitler as the best defence against the Communists now turned against the Nazis, disgusted by their brutality and greed. In 1944 an attempt was made to assassinate Hitler: the Bomb Plot. It failed and 5,000 people were executed in retaliation.

- Young people
  - Swing groups and Edelweiss Pirates
    Some young people rejected the boring, restricted life in Nazi Germany. Swing groups were mainly middle class and admired British clothes and American jazz. Working-class young people joined a variety of groups all of which the Nazis called Edelweiss Pirates. They hung around together, drew anti-Nazi graffiti on walls and mocked the Hitler Youth.
  - The White Rose group
    This was a small group of students at Munich University around Hans and Sophie Scholl and Christoph Probst. They published anti-Nazi leaflets and posters. They were arrested and executed in 1944.
- Upper-class Germans. They despised Hitler at first, but agreed with his nationalist policies. Later they became disgusted with the Nazis' corruption and greed. Although this class was not firmly committed to democracy under Weimar, many came to see that strong democracy was a better system than dictatorship.

THE GERMAN PEOPLE IN THE WAR YEARS

Shortages

Rationing was introduced right from the start of the war in 1939. It gradually got more severe until most Germans were living on a monotonous diet of potatoes, vegetables and cheap bread. Clothes were rationed too. The German people had been promised that they would get food from the lands they had conquered, but most of the loot from these territories went to Nazi Party members and the black market.

Total war

Germany was prepared for a short war, not a long one. Goebbels' wish for total war was only implemented from 1943. The German people, faced the choice of fighting on or being overrun by their enemies, could only fall in with this. All non-essential shops and industries were closed. All sporting events stopped. Slave labourers were brought in from all over Europe to work in the factories.

Bombing

Germany was bombed by the Allies with increasing intensity after 1942. Huge raids towards the end of the war devastated large parts of German cities. 150,000 people were killed in one night's raid on Dresden in 1945 – more than in Hiroshima. Millions of people were made homeless.

Hardship

The hardship of the German people got worse as the war went on. There were almost no doctors, as Jewish doctors and women doctors had been sacked and then most of the rest had been sent into the army. There were hardly any left for civilians. So many men were called up that there were not enough left to work the land. In the towns and cities there was often no water, no power, no light, no food. From 1944 refugees began to pour into Germany from the East, fleeing from the Soviet Army. By 1945 there were 16 million refugees, of which two million died. When Hitler committed suicide on 30 April 1945 Germany and its people were in a state of total devastation.

Check yourself

QUESTIONS

Q1 List the ways in which Hitler solved the unemployment problem.

Q2 Look at this picture of men in the Labour Front. Use this source to describe the Labour Front.

Q3 What were the motives of the various groups opposing Hitler?

Figure 4.8
Men in the Labour Front

REMEMBER! Cover the answers if you want to.

ANSWERS

A1 Young men aged 18–25 had to join the National Labour Service, working on public works schemes, like building autobahns, planting forests, building houses etc.
Re-armament of Germany created jobs in factories building battleships, aeroplanes etc and all the supply industries they needed.
Increasing the size of the army took many men came off the unemployed register.
Women had to give up their jobs.
Jews were not allowed to claim unemployment benefit so disappeared from the figures.

A2 Men in the Labour Front were treated a bit like soldiers. As you can see, they are wearing a uniform and carrying their shovels like rifles.

TUTORIALS

T1 *The public works schemes were strikingly like the New Deal being carried out by President Roosevelt in the USA at the same time, see p.150. Hitler took all the credit for them, but they were started under the Weimar government, not the Nazis.*

T2 *Much of the work they did was deliberately done with simple hand tools like shovels, rather than using machines, in order to employ as many men as possible*

ANSWER

A3 Communists and Social Democrats were Hitler's old enemies. The Communists hated him because the Nazis were nationalist, not international. The Social Democrats hated him for destroying democracy.

Some Church leaders hated Hitler because he cut down the power of their Church. But many hated him because his ideas were anti-Christian.

Army officers and upper-class Germans may have looked down their noses at Hitler at first for having risen from the streets, but he pleased them by getting rid of the SA in the Night of the Long Knives and by expanding the armed forces. Only when his interference in the army and his determination to fight to the bitter end looked like ruining Germany did many people in the army turn against him. Young people disliked the endless propaganda, which, by the late 1930s had lost the excitement of the early days. The White Rose Group was quite different and were supporters of proper democracy in Germany.

TUTORIAL

T3 *Both Communists and Social Democrats hated Hitler for removing workers' rights, but they would not work together against him. Nor were any of these groups in contact with one another. You can see they all had very different motives: the splits which had dogged Germany before 1933 continued to make the opposition to Hitler weak.*

HITLER AND RACISM

We have seen that Hitler was, in many ways a clever politician, realistic and clear-thinking. When it came to racism, however, he was obsessive, with an unthinking hatred. Racism, particularly anti-Semitism, was something which Hitler had picked up quite early in his life, when he was down and out in Vienna, and carried with him to the end. He did not start anti-Semitism, it had been present in Europe for centuries, but he had the power and technology to take it to extremes.

WHAT WERE THE RESULTS OF NAZI RACIAL BELIEFS?

Racial purity

We have seen that the Nazis believed in the superiority of the 'Aryan' race. They encouraged women to breed more 'Aryan' babies, see p.78. They also prevented certain people from having children: handicapped people, prostitutes and habitual thieves were sterilised. Euthanasia was secretly introduced for the mentally ill: 72,000 patients in mental hospitals were gassed between 1939 and 1941, until a campaign led by the church led to its being called off.

HITLER AND THE JEWS

About 1 per cent of the population of Germany were Jews. Their ancestors had lived there for centuries and they were full German citizens.

Hitler's attack on them began in his first few weeks in power. It was, like many of Hitler's measures, haphazard and unsystematic, but it became increasingly violent. As in other campaigns, he combined law-making and propaganda.

Propaganda

- In schools, 'race-science' was put on the curriculum. Pupils were encouraged to identify and despise Jews.
- A campaign of hate was waged in Goebbels' propaganda newspapers, posters and films, with crude and vicious stereotyping of Jews.

Laws

- April 1933, a boycott of Jewish-owned shops. Shop windows were scrawled with Jewish symbols, SA and SS stood outside and intimidated anyone trying to go in.
- April 1933, Jews banned from all state jobs, as civil servants, broadcasters, teachers, journalists, lawyers.
- Nuremberg Laws, 1935. Jews could not be German citizens. Jews could not marry or have sexual relations with a German citizen.
- Over the next few years many other laws were passed. Some took away basic civil rights, like the right to vote, attend a state school, go to university, own a shop or business or travel. Others affected small but important aspects of everyday life, like not being allowed to own a radio or a pet, not being allowed to go to the theatre, the cinema or a sporting event.
- In 1939 all Jews had to add the name 'Sara' (for women), or 'Israel' (for men), to their own names. From 1941 every Jew had to wear the Star of David badge.

Kristallnacht, 1938 ('The Night of Broken Glass')

Angry at the treatment of Jews in Germany, a young Jewish student assassinated a German diplomat in Paris. This was made the excuse for a vicious attack by SS and other Nazis on Jews, their homes, businesses and synagogues all over the country. The police did nothing. Ninety-one Jews were killed, 20,000 put in concentration camps. Jews in Germany were forced to pay the government a fine of one billion marks.

The 'Final Solution'

Hitler and the Nazis had various plans for German Jews. One idea they considered was to transport them all to the African island of Madagascar. The war, and the huge conquests of land Germany had made by 1941, changed the situation. To the half million German Jews under Nazi rule were now added four million more in Poland and Russia. There were also the Slav populations of these areas, whom Hitler considered to be 'inferior'.

At first, the Nazis treated these people with casual violence. Jews were forced to live together, separately from the rest of the population in ghettoes. These were desperately overcrowded: the Warsaw ghetto, for example, held 400,000 people in an area where 100,000 people used to live.

Then, in July 1941, came the proposal for the 'Final Solution'. This was probably proposed by Goering and agreed by Hitler. Himmler was responsible for carrying it out. It was for killing all eleven million Jews in Europe. It is a sign of the racist views at the heart of the Nazi Party that such an evil plan was talked of as a 'solution' to a 'problem'.

Figure 4.9
*Jews being shot and put
in a mass grave.*

It is not easy to kill millions of people one by one. At first they were shot by special units of the SS called Einsatzgrüppen (see Fig. 4.9). Then the Nazis turned to twentieth-century technology to find a way of killing as many people as possible at once. The result was the gas chambers built at Auschwitz in 1941, which could kill 2,000 people at a time. Five other death camps were built, all in Poland. Auschwitz was the largest because of its position on the railway network.

So, from all over Europe, Jews were collected, put on trains (where many died), and taken to these camps. This went on right to the end of the war, even taking up fuel and trains which might have been put into the war effort. By then six million Jews and five million others, including Slavs, gypsies and homosexuals, had been killed.

EXTRA POINTS

1. On arrival at the death camps, families were separated. Most women, children, the elderly and the ill, about 80 per cent of arrivals, were sent at once to the gas chambers. It took up to twenty minutes for them to die. The doors were then opened and special prisoners took out the bodies and burnt them. Those who were selected as fit to work toiled at the SS-run factories attached to the camps. With poor food and harsh treatment, they lasted about two months on average. At some camps gruesome 'medical' experiments were carried out on inmates.

2. It was difficult, almost impossible, for Jews to resist what was happening, but some did. In April 1943 there was a rising in the Warsaw ghetto which held out for forty-two days. There were rebellions and escapes at several camps, including Treblinka.

Check yourself

QUESTION

Q1 What were: (a) Kristallnacht? (b) Nazi euthanasia policies? (c) The Final Solution?

REMEMBER! Cover the answers if you want to.

ANSWER

A1

a) Kristallnacht means the 'night of broken glass' and took place in 1938. It was a Nazi attack on Jews, their homes, property, businesses and synagogues, following the murder of a German diplomat in France by a young Jew.

b) Euthanasia was the policy of killing off mentally ill Germans. About 72,000 were killed between 1939 and 1941. The Nazis believed that people who were not physically and psychologically fit Germans were a burden on the state and should not be kept alive.

c) The Final Solution was the Nazi policy of exterminating all the Jews in Europe. It was agreed in 1941 and led to the building of gas chambers, first at Auschwitz concentration camp and then at five others. Jews were transported by train from all over Europe to these death camps, run by the SS. Altogether about six million Jews and five million others were killed in this way.

TUTORIAL

T1

a) *Kristallnacht was marked by utter lawlessness. The ordinary police did nothing as SS and other Nazis carried out these raids, often stealing from Jews' homes and doing exactly what they liked.*

b) *It was part of Hitler's beliefs that the people were there to serve the state, not the state to serve the people. Therefore, if people were not contributing to the state they were no use and could be put to death.*

c) *The Final Solution was industrialised death. Anti-Semitism had existed for a long time in Europe. Jews had been driven out of England from 1290 to 1655. There had been attacks on Jews in Russia in the late nineteenth and early twentieth centuries, encouraged by the Tsars, in which hundreds died. But only twentieth-century technology made the Final Solution possible.*

EXAM PRACTICE

Sample Student's Answers & Examiner's Comments

1 Write a sentence to explain the term 'November Criminals'   (2)

The 'November Criminals' was the name given to the Weimar politicians who made peace with the Allies in November 1918 when some people thought Germany should have gone on fighting.   **1/2**

EXAMINER'S COMMENTS

MARK SCHEME

Level 1	Explains one element in the term	**1 mark**
Level 2	Explains both elements in the term	**2 marks**

It is easy to drop a mark like this. The second part of the answer seems to suggest that you know why the term 'criminals' was used, but it is isn't clearly stated.

2 How did Stresemann revive the German economy?

(5)

Stresemann decided that if Germany was to recover, it had to get on better with other nations, even if this meant accepting the terms of the Treaty of Versailles which most Germans hated. In 1923 Germany was in a terrible state, with French troops in the Ruhr and an inflated currency. He therefore introduced a new currency, the rentenmark, and agreed to start paying reparations. This led the French to withdraw their troops. He then negotiated the Dawes Plan, 1924. This brought loans from the USA to revive the German economy. German industry could pick up, unemployment fell and some re-payment of reparations began. In 1929 the Young Plan reduced reparations to one-third of the original level.

5/5

EXAMINER'S COMMENTS

MARK SCHEME

Level 1	Vague and unsupported comments	**1 mark**
Level 2	Some relevant items listed	**2–3 marks**
Level 3	Account details problems and relates these to Stresemann's solutions	**4–5 marks**

This is a good answer: good enough for full marks to be awarded. There are other things which could have been said, but Examiners are not looking for perfection for full marks, just as good an answer as a sixteen year old could reasonably be expected to write.

The short opening sentence is worth having, as a general introduction before the answer gets down to specific facts. Don't waste too much time on generalities, though, or you will fall down to Level 1.

The student has realised that this is a question about *change* and questions about change require some sort of statement about what things were like before the change: imagine the answer starting at 'He therefore introduced...' and you can see what I mean.

Stresemann was hated by right-wing politicians like Hitler for apparently knuckling under to the Versailles Treaty terms. However, he was no different from other German politicians in his dislike of reparations. He worked to avoid paying them and in fact did get them reduced.

3 How successful were Hitler and the Nazis at bringing employment to the German people between 1933 and 1939? (15)

When Hitler became dictator of Germany in 1933, unemployment stood at nearly six million. By 1938 it was almost zero. He had won votes in the elections of 1932 and 1933 by promising to end unemployment and so it was a priority for him.

He expanded the National Labour Service, which had already been set up. This used government money to provide jobs in schemes such as building houses and schools, planting forests and, most popular of all with the Nazis, building motorways (autobahnen). At least 80,000 people were working on these motorways.

From 1935 all 18-25 year olds had to spend six months in the Labour Corps. They were not properly paid, receiving only pocket money, and treated like soldiers, wearing uniform and carrying out military drill. Hitler also expanded the armed services. This created lots of jobs and so took people off the unemployment lists. The army grew from the limit imposed by the Treaty of Versailles, 100,000, to 500,000 in 1935 and reached 1,400,000 by 1939. All these men had to be given uniforms, equipment, etc., so lots of jobs were created in several industries.

Hitler's readiness to break the restrictions of the Treaty of Versailles regarding weapons meant contracts for tanks, aircraft and battleships, all of which were forbidden by the treaty. This re-armament meant jobs in factories, building the weapons. Modern weapons require all kinds of supply industries apart from the iron and steel industries which build them: rubber for tyres, wood, glass, instruments, radios etc. They all have to be designed. All this meant jobs in many industries.

Hitler was thus highly successful at providing jobs for the German people from 1933 to 1939. It was one of the reasons for his popularity in the late 1930s and explains why the German people were willing to put up with other aspects of Nazism, such as the totalitarianism and dictatorship. 12/15

EXAMINER'S COMMENTS

MARK SCHEME

Level 1 Some accurate comments on one area of activity only or general, unspecific remarks **1–4 marks**

Level 2 Accurate account, giving broad coverage of issues, perhaps with some analytical comments. **5–10 marks**

Level 3 Accurate and balanced account covers all major areas with developed consideration of the issue of 'how successful...?' **11–15 marks**

The main merit of this answer is that it is a well-structured account. It is divided into paragraphs, which help to structure the argument. It starts with the problem as posed to Hitler in 1933 and ends with some evaluation of his success. The points made hang together in each paragraph. The student would be unlikely to achieve this without making some kind of written plan before starting to write. This might be only a few words, but a plan helps

- to ensure that you have covered all possible aspects of the question;
- to keep relevant points together: no wandering.

For this essay the plan might have looked like this:
1. Germany in 1933. 6m unemployed. H's promises
2. National Labour Service – describe. Autobahns
3. Labour corps – like army.
4. Conscription: figs.
5. Re-armament. Other industries
6. Success – no unemployment by 1938.

The only thing keeping this essay back from full marks is that the analysis of 'How successful...?' is a bit weak. It is arguable that quite a number of people had simply been removed from the figures without them actually having a job. Millions of women were forced to resign; many Jews had to quit their jobs; soldiers in the armed forces were not really in jobs.

Questions to Answer

The answers to Questions 4 and 5 can be found on p.269

4 Look at the chart. It shows unemployment and the number of votes received by the Nazis from 1928 to 1933.

How far do the unemployment figures on these graphs explain the voting figures? Explain your answer. (8)

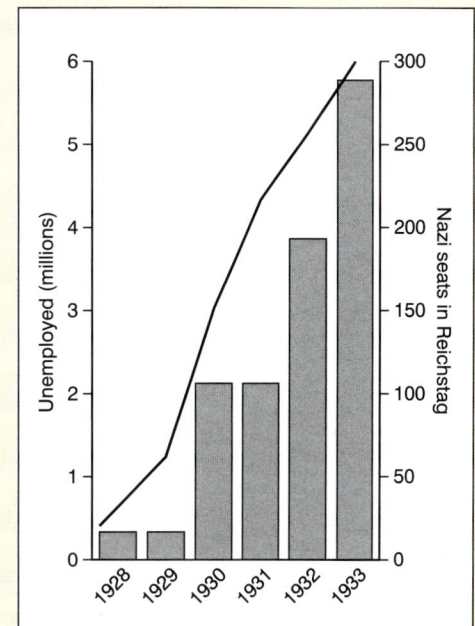

5 Look at the picture. It shows boys in the Hitler Youth.

a) Why are the boys doing this? (4)

b) 'Young people in Nazi Germany became nothing but servants of Nazism.'

Use this source and your own knowledge to comment on the accuracy of this statement. (10)

93

RUSSIA IN 1900

The central events in this chapter are the two revolutions which took place in Russia in 1917, but even in 1900 the government was finding difficulties in ruling the country.

WHY WAS RUSSIA IN 1900 SO DIFFICULT TO RULE?

- Russia was a vast country, 6,500 kilometres wide, a hundred times bigger than Britain. On the long Trans-Siberian Railway, completed in 1904 (see Fig. 5.1), it took a week to make the whole journey from Moscow to the far east.

- Travel was difficult. Roads were full of mud in summer, blocked by snow in winter. Great rivers ran north–south and were used a lot. Railways were beginning to help the situation, although total railway mileage in Russia was only the same as in Britain's.

- Only 40 per cent of the people were Russian-speaking. The country was an empire, of at least sixteen different nationalities, many of whom resented being forced to adopt the Russian language and customs.

- Divisions. Apart from these national divisions, Russia was deeply divided socially as well, with a huge gulf between the rich and the poor.

Figure 5.1
Map of Russia in 1900

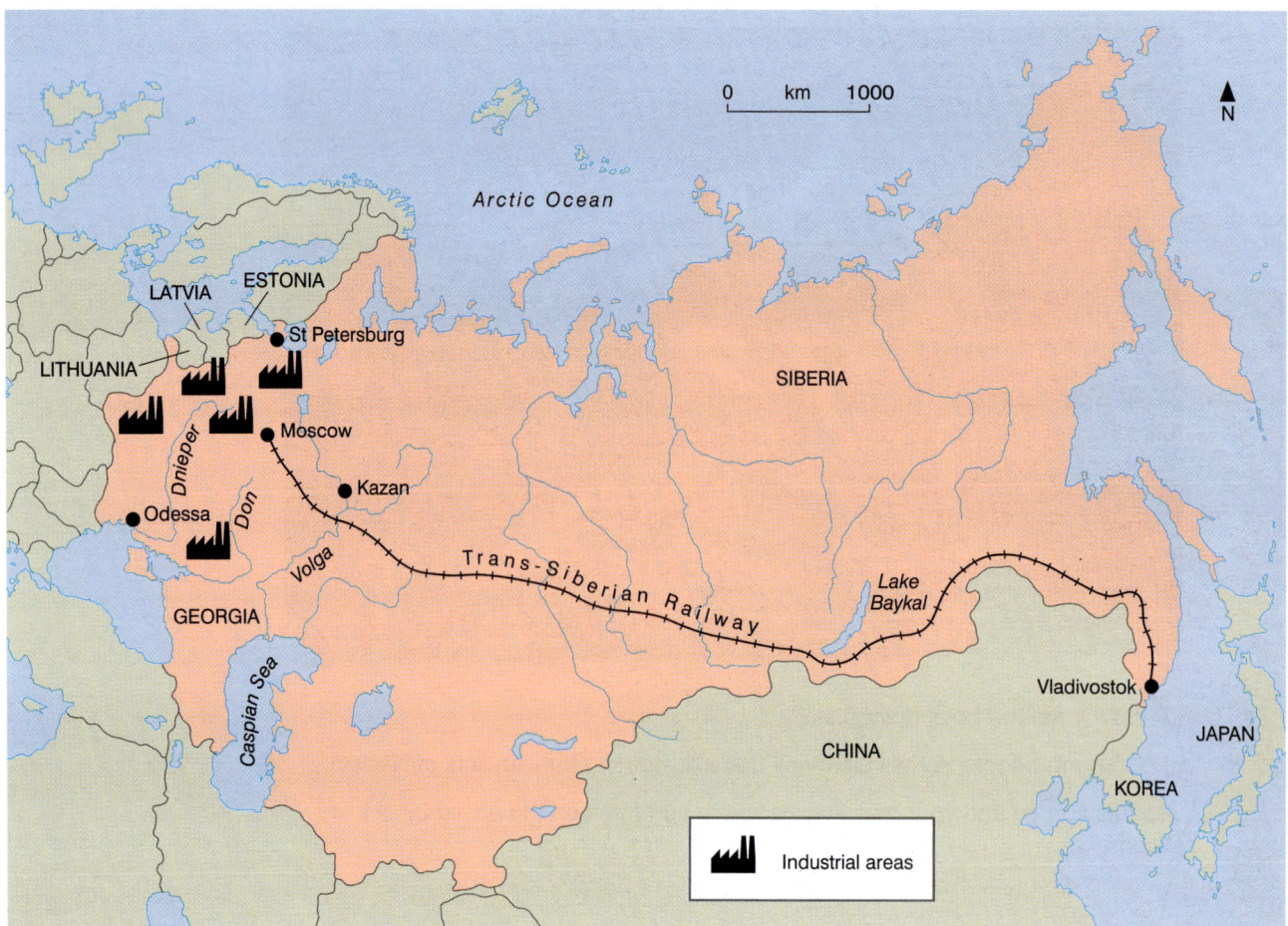

Peasants

Peasants made up 80 per cent of the people, living in villages, isolated by bad transport (see Fig. 5.2). Until 1861 they had belonged to their masters, like animals. They were freed in 1861 and given small amounts of land, for which they had to pay the government back. The result was that they were very poor, with heavy debts. This was made worse by the 50 per cent rise in population from 1860 to 1900. Peasants divided and sub-divided their land between their family, so their plots were very small. Most peasants could not read or write and still used old-fashioned farming methods, working their plots by hand. They were envious of the huge estates owned by the nobility (see below), but deeply suspicious of change. Disease was common and in years of bad harvest many died of starvation.

Figure 5.2
Peasants in a Russian village in about 1900

Nobility

The nobility made up only 1 per cent of the population but owned 25 per cent of the land. They were well-educated and rich (see Fig. 5.3) usually owning houses in Moscow or St Petersburg as well as on their country estates.

Figure 5.3
Guests at a countess' palace in St Petersburg

Industrialists

Russia had industrialised later than most European countries and was not so developed. However, by 1900 there were huge textile factories, ironworks and other industries (see Fig. 5.1). Many were partly owned by foreigners or the government, but industrialisation did bring a new and growing class of bankers and factory-owners. They were often resentful of the power and influence of the old nobles.

Industrial workers

Conditions for the workers in these new factories were as bad as, if not worse than, those in Britain in the early Industrial Revolution: low pay, long hours (15–16 hours a day), terrible living conditions (see Fig. 5.4). Many of the workers were peasants who only came to the cities to work for a few months. Housing was overcrowded and unhealthy.

Figure 5.4
Industrial workers' living conditions in Moscow

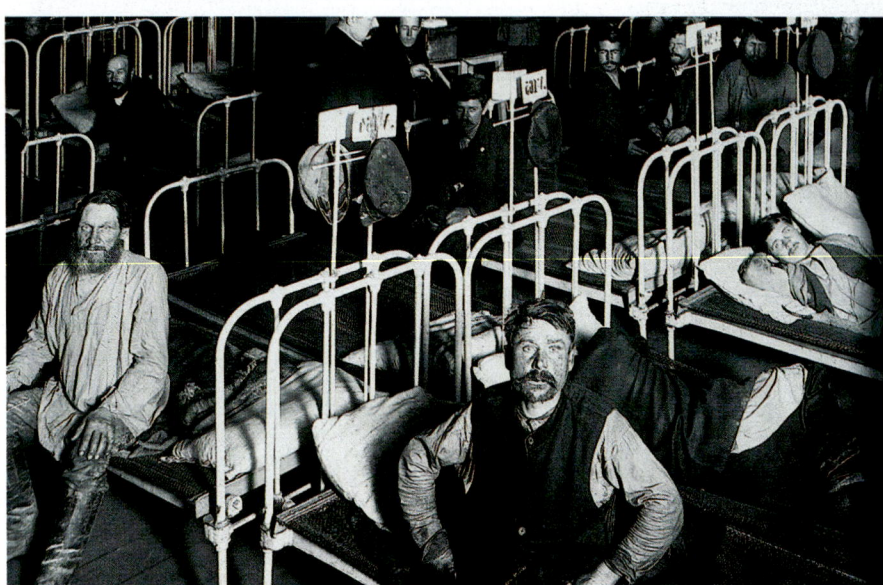

WHO RULED RUSSIA?

> **Autocracy means rule by one person.**

The ruler of Russia was called the Tsar. He had complete power over the country. He appointed ministers to advise him but he did not have to take their advice and took all decisions himself. There were no elections, no democracy at all. This system is called an **autocracy.**

The Church supported this autocracy by teaching the Russian people that God had chosen the Tsar to be their 'little Father on earth' to look after them.

Nicholas II (see Fig. 5.5) had become Tsar in 1896. In an autocracy obviously the personality of the autocrat is important.
Nicholas' good points:

- He was a kind and devoted family man.

- He believed he had been appointed by God to rule Russia well.

- He genuinely wanted the best for his people.

Nicholas' bad points:

- He had no idea how his people really lived and made no effort to find out.

- He could not rule alone, but employed large numbers of officials, many of whom were corrupt.

- He was weak: he usually agreed with the last person he had been talking to.

- He was cruel and obstinate. He clung to every bit of his power, hated opposition and used force to crush it.

- There was no free speech; there was censorship of newspapers and publishing; trade unions were banned; the secret police, the *Okhrana*, could arrest and imprison people without trial.

Figure 5.5
Tsar Nicholas II and his family

OPPOSITION

The key factors in Russia likely to cause change were the hardship of the peasants and the workers and a harsh, undemocratic govenment. All opposition groups were small, with little support among the masses of Russian people.

Cadets (from the first letters of the Russian words <u>C</u>onstitutional <u>D</u>emocrats)

They were admirers of the democracies of Britain, France and the USA and wanted Russia to have the same constitution. They were supported mainly by the small Russian middle class.

Social Revolutionaries

They wanted to seize the land of the rich and share it out among the peasants. They had some peasant support. Their tactics, in the absence of any democratic elections, were to try to cause a revolution by assassinating government ministers.

Social Democrats

They were a Marxist party.

> **Karl Marx** was a German writer who analysed society and political systems in Europe at the time (he died in 1883). He explained that:
> 1. The economic system called capitalism is unfair because the **capitalist** (investor) makes huge profits out of the labour of the **proletariat** (workers) who actually do the work.
> 2. All history shows struggles between different classes, e.g. the struggle between middle classes and landowners which, he said, had led to parliamentary democracy in Britain and elsewhere in the nineteenth century.
> 3. The next stage in the class struggle would be a violent revolution in which the proletariat would throw out the capitalists and take over the country themselves.

The Russian Social Democrats split in 1903 over tactics:

- The Mensheviks wanted to set up a mass party, including industrial workers and trade unions.
- The Bolsheviks wanted to build a party of dedicated professional revolutionaries. Their leader was Lenin. Because of the Tsar's police most of the Social Democrats lived in exile abroad. Lenin published his newspaper, *Iskra* (Spark) from London.

EXTRA POINTS ▶

1. Tsar Nicholas was supported in his views by his wife Alexandra. She encouraged him to spend his time with his family and discouraged him from giving way to anyone.

2. Tsar Nicholas also approved of, even encouraged, **pogroms** – attacks on Russia's Jews, as a way of distracting people from their problems and hardship.

3. Factories in Russia were very large. This meant that if there was a strike, or a shutdown, large numbers of workers were affected.

Check yourself

Q1 What problems were faced by (a) the peasants and (b) industrial workers in Russia in about 1900?

Q2 What were the main features of Tsarist autocracy under Nicholas II? How did he deal with opposition?

REMEMBER! Cover the answers if you want to.

ANSWERS

A1
a) The peasants were poor, with large debts to pay off for the land they had received in 1861. Each person's share of land was getting smaller as population was rising, and their farming methods were old-fashioned. Disease was common and bad harvests brought death from starvation.
b) Industrial workers were badly-paid, for long hours, with unsafe factories and overcrowded living conditions.

A2 The Tsar was an autocrat. This meant that his word was law. There were ministers and other advisers, but they were chosen by the Tsar, not according to democratic control. His government was carried out by a large number of officials who were often lazy and corrupt. Nicholas did not have strong views of his own, except an unwillingness to change anything. He was therefore very hostile to any form of opposition and fierce in his crushing of it, using his secret police, censorship and exile.

TUTORIALS

T1
a) A *better* way of putting this is to say that the peasants' real grievance was hunger for land: they could see that the Tsar, the Church and the nobles had lots of land, while they were struggling. They thought that if only they had more land their lives would improve.
b) These features were common enough in the early stages of industrialisation. What was special to Russia was the size of industrial enterprises – half of them had over a thousand workers. This was unlike Britain in the eighteenth and nineteenth centuries.

T2 The Church's view helps to explain Russian autocracy: he was chosen by God to rule Russia and so his word was law. You may remember from when you did seventeenth-century History, that English monarchs of that time held the same views. Nicholas did care for his people in a way, but from a distance: he was hopelessly out of touch with them. His attitude to opponents meant that many turned to violence, as all other doors were closed to them. His uncompromising attitude to reform brought about his own downfall in the end.

RUSSIA 1905–14

WHY WAS THERE A REVOLUTION IN 1905?

The key factors for change outlined in the previous section came together in the early years of the twentieth century to cause a revolution in 1905:

- Bad harvests brought hunger in the countryside.
- Depression in industry brought unemployment and wage cuts in the cities.
- The Tsar's government was seen to be incompetent and cruel.

THE RUSSO–JAPANESE WAR, 1904–5

Partly to distract the Russian people from their problems, the Tsar declared war on Japan in 1904. He expected to do well. Instead Russia suffered a series of humiliating defeats, culminating in the naval battle of Tsushima in May 1905, in which the Russian fleet was defeated in less than an hour.

THE 1905 REVOLUTION

Apart from what the war revealed about the Tsar's government, it brought further shortages and hardships for the people. Nicholas had decided that it would be better to allow some trade unions to be formed, under people he approved of, such as priests, as a way of avoiding more extreme protests. In January 1905 one of these leaders, Father Gapon, led a huge procession in St Petersburg to deliver a petition to him, asking for his help. They were met by troops who charged into the crowd and then fired at them. Many, perhaps thousands, were killed. It was called Bloody Sunday. This was followed by a year of protests by all kinds of different groups, with different grievances.

- There were demonstrations all over the country calling for democracy in Russia.
- Peasants seized land for themselves and burnt their landlords' houses.
- Non-Russians protested against Russian rule.
- In June, sailors on the battleship *Potemkin* mutinied.
- In September there was a General Strike (a strike of all workers).
- In October a *Soviet* (council) of workers was set up in St Petersburg.

There was no attempt by the different groups to work together, but Nicholas was put under pressure. He issued the **October Manifesto**. This promised:

- a *Duma* (Parliament)
- free speech and freedom of the press.
- freedom to set up and join political parties.

This achieved just what Nicholas hoped: his opponents split. Some, like the Cadets, called off their protests because this was just what they wanted; others did not trust Nicholas. Meanwhile he had made peace with Japan, brought his best troops home and paid them well. With his opponents divided, Nicholas used them to crush the revolution. Its leaders were put in prison or fled abroad and the revolution fizzled out.

Nicholas then passed the **Fundamental Law**, which said that the Duma would have little power, with its elections fixed to give more influence to the Tsar's supporters: there was to be one member per 2,000 nobles; there was only one member per 90,000 workers.

Even so, when the Duma met and began criticising him, Nicholas dismissed it. He did the same with the second Duma. Elections to the third Duma were even more weighted in the Tsar's favour and it sat, doing little, until 1912. His opponents reached these conclusions about the situation:

- The Tsar was not to be trusted.
- There would be no revolution in Russia as long as the soldiers were loyal to the Tsar.

1905–14: A NEW FUTURE FOR RUSSIA?

Nicholas then appointed an able minister: Stolypin. His policies had two angles:

Tough repression of all opposition

Contrary to the October Manifesto, censorship was re-introduced. The Okhrana increased its power. Twenty thousand opponents were exiled to Siberia. Over one thousand were hanged.

Land reform

Better off, more enterprising peasants (called *kulaks*) were allowed to buy up land from other peasants. Special banks were set up to help them. By this privatisation of land, Stolypin hoped to create a middle class of well-off farmers, supporters of Tsarism. He called it 'A wager on the strong and sober'.

Results

- About 15 per cent of peasants took up the offer and agricultural production went up rapidly.
- Industrial production doubled between 1900 and 1914. Russia became the fourth largest producer in the world of coal, pig iron and steel, and second largest producer of oil.
- Many peasants became poorer. Having sold their land they were reduced to landless labourers.
- Industrial workers were still doing long hours, for low pay, in bad conditions.
- Stolypin was assassinated in 1911. Nicholas did not appoint anyone as able as Stolypin to follow him.

◀ **EXTRA POINT**

Some think that Stolypin's ideas might have led Russia to a different future and so avoided revolution. They point out that Russia was now more prosperous, and did have the beginnings of deomcracy, the Duma. Others think that these reforms do not amount to much. Nicholas never really backed Stolypin and did not continue with his reforms after he was assassinated. The Duma was almost powerless, Nicholas would always resist change and Tsarism was doomed whatever happened.

Check yourself

QUESTIONS

Q1 Make a list of the long-term and short-term causes of the 1905 Revolution.

Q2 Why did the Tsar survive the 1905 Revolution?

Q3 Strikes in Russia, 1905–14:

1905	13,995
1906	6,114
1907	3,573
1908	892
1909	340
1910	222
1911	466
1912	2,032
1913	2,404
1914	3,534

Suggest reasons for the differences in the figures shown here.

REMEMBER! Cover the answers if you want to.

ANSWERS

A1 Long-term: poverty of the peasants; bad conditions, low wages suffered by city workers; weaknesses and corruption of the Tsar's government and lack of democracy. Short-term: Bad harvests 1903–5; depression in industry; defeat in Russo–Japanese War revealed incompetence of Tsarist rulers and officials; Tsar's troops fired on peaceful demonstration, Bloody Sunday.

A2 He survived by making concessions – the October Manifesto, offering relaxation of censorship and a Duma. This won over some of his opponents. He then used force to crush the rest.

A3 These figures show the massive number of strikes during the 1905 Revolution dying down afterwards. It shows things were quite peaceful from about 1908–11. It then shows growing dissatisfaction in the years just before the First World War broke out.

TUTORIALS

T1 A *few additional points:*
Long-term: Peasants wanted more land and were ready to seize it themselves if they were pushed to the limit. *Short-term:* Workers could be thrown out of work if trade slumped, with nothing to live on – there was no welfare system at all. The war brought food shortages and high prices, as in 1914–17. Conditions in the towns are important, as that is where revolution starts.

T2 He then broke his word over the October Manifesto: censorship was restored by 1906 and the Duma was not really democratically elected. In the long run, this probably sealed his death warrant. It shows, however, that if he could have made concessions earlier, and stuck to them, he might have survived longer. What do you think?

T3 This answer is good on describing, but does not really explain the decline from 1905 to 1910. It was partly that industry picked up, so there were fewer grievances, but also that Stolypin crushed strike organisers so effectively. The rise from 1911 is ominous for the Tsar. It shows that things were not looking too good even before war broke out.

THE REVOLUTIONS OF 1917

HOW DID THE FIRST WORLD WAR HELP TO CAUSE THE MARCH 1917 REVOLUTION?

When war broke out in August 1914 there was a wave of patriotic and pro-Tsarist emotion in Russia. Two and a half years later Nicholas was forced off the throne. How did this happen?

You know about the long-term causes of the Revolution; the short-term causes were:

Defeat

Before the end of 1914 the Russians had experienced two massive defeats at Tannenberg and the Masurian Lakes. One million men were dead, wounded or taken prisoner.

The war showed up huge faults in the Tsarist system. Soldiers were short of guns and boots. Many died from lack of medical supplies. Military leaders panicked and retreated. In September 1915 Nicholas decided to take over command of the army in person. Army morale improved, but it meant that he became associated personally with these faults.

Mutiny

Soldiers began to mutiny. Some formed soviets (councils). Some simply deserted and went home.

Alexandra and Rasputin

Nicholas and Alexandra's only son, Alexis, had haemophilia, a hereditary blood condition in which the blood does not clot properly and the subject can bleed to death. Alexandra found that a strange peasant 'Holy Man', Rasputin, had the power to stop Alexis' bleeding. She began to believe that Rasputin had been sent by God to help them. With Nicholas away at the war, Russia was run by Alexandra, who was under Rasputin's daily influence. In this situation even the upper classes lost support for Tsarism. Rasputin was murdered by a noble in 1916, but the damage had been done.

Shortages

With thirteen million men called up by 1916, the peasants were short of people to work the land. Less food was grown. Even worse, food was not getting through to the cities because the railways were in chaos. Food prices shot up in early 1917. There were also shortages of fuel.

> **Note on dates**
> At this time Russia still used the old calendar, which was thirteen days behind the rest of Europe. Thus the 'March' revolution took place at the end of February by the Russian calendar, and the 'November revolution' was called the October Revolution by Russians.

THE MARCH 1917 REVOLUTION

There were increasing strikes and protest demonstrations at the beginning of 1917. On 7 March there was a strike at the huge Putilov steelworks. It was joined by women protesting about bread shortages. On 12 March some soldiers refused to fire at the demonstrators and shot their own officers instead. At this point the ruling classes decided that something had to be done in order to prevent a total revolution in which they would be swept away. They therefore told Nicholas he had to abdicate (give up being Tsar). On 15 March he agreed.

HOW DID THE BOLSHEVIKS TAKE OVER RUSSIA IN NOVEMBER 1917?

The Tsar's abdication left two different authorities in Russia:

- The Duma became **the Provisional Government**; it was called 'provisional' (= for the time being) because they wanted to hold full democratic elections to a proper parliament.
- But the **Petrograd Soviet** also had a lot of influence, as the council of workers and soldiers representatives. (The name St Petersburg sounded too German so it had been changed to Petrograd at the begining of the war.) The Soviet agreed that, for the time being, the Provisional Government should be the government of Russia.

A key minister in the Provisional Government was **Kerensky**, who was also on the Soviet and so acted as a bridge between them.

THE FAILURE OF THE PROVISIONAL GOVERNMENT

The March Revolution was an abdication by the Tsar. The real revolution now follows: peasants seized land, workers took over control of factories, soldiers mutinied and deserted. For a little while, April and May 1917, the Provisional Government had a chance of seizing the initiative. The Bolsheviks were weak – Lenin was actually in Switzerland. They could have led the revolution to become the new popular, democratic government of Russia. They failed to do so. The Provisional Government was concerned to everything properly and legally. They therefore decided:

- Russia should have free speech, and free elections.
- To stand by Russia's alliances with France and Britain and so continue with the war.
- To leave all the other problems until the elections had been held.

These things were not what the people wanted to hear.

LENIN

At this point Lenin, the leader of the Bolsheviks, returned to Russia. The Germans had allowed him to travel by train through their country in the hope that he would stir up trouble in Russia and take it out of the war. They were not to be disappointed.

The April Theses

As soon as he arrived in Russia Lenin called on the Bolsheviks to seize power. His slogans were:

'All Power to the Soviets!' and 'Peace, Land and Bread!' His ideas were written up as the April Theses. Most Bolshevik leaders disagreed with him, but it was soon clear that his ideas were popular:

- the soldiers wanted peace,
- the peasants wanted land,
- the workers in the cities wanted bread, and they were all getting increasingly impatient.

The July days

In July Kerensky ordered a new advance against Austria but it brought only another defeat. Soldiers began to desert the army in thousands. They were mostly peasants. They had heard that the peasants at home were seizing land from landlords and they wanted to be there. There were huge anti-war demonstrations in Petrograd. The Bolsheviks tried to use them to seize power, but did not have enough support. Kerensky used soldiers to crush them and nearly arrested Lenin, who had to flee abroad again.

Kornilov

In September General Kornilov began to send his army towards Petrograd to remove the Provisional Government and restore the Tsar. In panic, Kerensky gave weapons to anyone who would use them to defend him. Many Bolsheviks formed Red Guard units (see Fig. 5.6). In fact, Kornilov's advance was stopped by Bolshevik railway workers who sabotaged his trains.

Figure 5.6
Armed Red Guard units

THE BOLSHEVIKS SEIZE POWER, NOVEMBER 1917

By October Russia was in chaos. The Provisional Government had failed to end the war, it had tried to stop peasants seizing land and had failed to deal with food shortages.

The Bolsheviks, on the other hand, had increased their support among soldiers, sailors and workers. They alone seemed to be willing to give people the changes they were looking for. They were armed. They had a leader, Lenin, who knew exactly what he wanted and an organiser, Trotsky, who could carry it out.

On the night of 6 November 1917, Red Guard units took control of key points in Petrograd: post office, stations, bridges over the rivers. They then took over the Winter Palace where the Provisional Government was, and arrested them. Kerensky fled abroad.

1. Clearly the behaviour of the troops on the streets of Petrograd in March was a crucial difference from 1905. They were actually raw recruits, peasants in uniform, and so likely to sympathise with the demonstrators. The Tsar dare not call up more disciplined, experienced troops for fear of weakening the battle front.

 **EXTRA POINTS**

EXTRA POINTS ▶

2. Many Bolshevik leaders disagreed with Lenin in April and in October. They expected the next stage of Russia's History, rule by democratic parliament, to last a long time. They thought Lenin was rushing things and this would lead them only to disaster. Lenin had to use all the force of his personality to persuade them to act.

3. The 'November Revolution' was not a revolution of the people on the streets like the March revolution. It was really a Bolshevik seizure of power, or 'coup'.

Check yourself

QUESTIONS

Q1 Look at the four factors listed as the short-term causes of the March Revolution. Write a sentence on each one, showing how it was linked to the war.

Q2 Why did the Provisional government only last eight months?

REMEMBER! Cover the answers if you want to.

ANSWERS

A1 The war went badly for Russia from the first. The soldiers could see that some of the reasons for their defeats were the fault of the Tsar's government, so they mutinied. Rasputin had more influence on Alexandra because Nicholas was away at the War Front from August 1915; he had also left her in charge of the government, so her influence was more serious. Shortages of food were brought about because of lack of peasants to till the fields and because much of the transport system was tied up with supplying the army.

A2 The Provisional Government failed to meet the hopes of the Russian people in 1917. They were popular at first, but the decision to carry on the war lost them support. They used force to stop peasants seizing land and they failed to halt the shortages of food in the cities: both these failures lost them support. They failed to call a general election. They were also faced with Lenin, determined to bring about a Bolshevik revolution against them.

TUTORIALS

T1 *At first the Russian peasants who made up most of the army went off to war willingly. Defeat and death demoralised them, but, as in France in 1916, see p.28, it was the stupidity of high command which tipped them into mutiny.*

To sum up, war imposed a stress on Tsarism which it was too weak to take.

T2 *The Provisional Government failed to realise that they were in the middle of both a war and a revolution. They had had no experience of running a government and tried to behave like the British or French parliamentary politicians they admired: sticking by Russia's treaties with France and Britain and so going on fighting; stopping the peasants from seizing land. They were ill-prepared for Kornilov's attempt at a counter-revolution. But most of all, they did not give the people what they wanted. After all, it was the people in the streets who had caused the abdication of the Tsar and so brought them to power.*

THE COMMUNISTS AND THE CIVIL WAR, 1917–21

Although they had seized power in Petrograd, the Bolsheviks were far from being in control of the whole of Russia. There were only 250,000 of them and they had very little support in the countryside. Even in Moscow they only took over after several days fighting.

HOW DID THE BOLSHEVIKS TAKE OVER RUSSIA?

The Bolshevik Government

They set up a government, called the Council of People's Commissars, or 'Sovnarkom' for short. Lenin was chairman, Trotsky was Commissar for War, there was one woman, Alexandra Kollontai and Stalin was Commissar for Nationalities. Several far-reaching decrees were passed quickly:

- All class distinctions were abolished. Instead of 'Your Grace', Your Excellency' etc., everyone now called each other *Tovarich* (comrade).
- All distinctions of rank in the armed forces were abolished.
- All land belonging to the Tsar, the Church and the nobility was taken over by the peasants.
- Workers should not work more than eight hours a day and forty-eight hours a week.
- All factories were taken over by the workers and all banks and foreign trade were taken over by the government acting in the name of the workers.
- Equal rights for women.

Figure 5.7 *Russian losses at the Treaties of Brest–Litovsk and Versailles*

--·--·-- Boundary of Russian Empire in 1914

---·--- Boundary of Russia after the Treaty in 1918

▮ Land taken away from Russia at Brest–Litovsk, but returned by the Treaty of Versailles in 1919

▮ Land *not* returned to Russia at the end of the war

0   km   500

All these decrees were simply telegraphed out to other parts of Russia in the hope that they would be obeyed.

The Cheka

Lenin also set up his own secret police. All non-Bolshevik newspapers were closed down. After three attempts to kill Lenin, the Cheka were given the power to arrest and execute opponents without trial. The 'Red Terror' began.

The Constituent Assembly, 1918

Lenin had to hold free elections to a Constituent Assembly which met in January 1918. The Bolsheviks only won 175 seats out of 707. The Social Revolutionaries (see p.97) won 370. Lenin surrounded the building with Red Guards and closed the Assembly after one day. So ended Russia's first freely-elected government, the last for another seventy-four years.

The Treaty of Brest–Litovsk, 1918

Lenin had to get Russia out of the war by making peace with Germany. He hoped that the revolution in Russia would spark off Communist revolutions elsewhere, but they did not happen. He was forced to sign harsh terms. As the map, Figure 5.7, shows, Germany seized lots of territory from Russia, some, but not all, of which was returned at the Treaty of Versailles. Russia lost 25 per cent of its people, 27 per cent of its best farmland, 26 per cent of its railway system and 70 per cent of its iron and coal industries.

THE CIVIL WAR, 1918–21

By 1918 there was civil war in Russia. On one side were the Communists (Reds), as the Bolsheviks were now called. On the other were all kinds of groups, called Whites, wanting to overthrow them. At one point there were thirty governments in different parts of Russia. The Whites were helped by other countries, angry at Russia pulling out of the war and determined to stop

Figure 5.8
Russia in the Civil War, 1918–21

the spread of Communism: Britain, France, USA. Japan and Poland invaded to see what they could get. There was also a legion of Czech prisoners-of-war who seized control of part of the Trans-Siberian Railway (see Fig. 5.8). It took over three years' fighting for the Communists to remove all their enemies from the country.

REASONS FOR THE COMMUNISTS' VICTORY IN THE CIVIL WAR

Unity

The Reds were united in wanting to hold on to power in order to build a Communist state. The Whites were not united. There were all kinds of groups: Tsarists, Cadets, Social Revolutionaries, who did not work together.

Geography

The Reds held the central heartlands of Russia. This meant they could use the core of the railway system to supply their armies. The Whites were huge distances apart (see Fig. 5.8), and had problems supplying their armies.

Leadership

The Reds had one dynamic leader, Trotsky. He travelled the country in an armed train, urging on his soldiers. He built up a Red Army from almost nothing, using Tsarist officers but controlling them by attaching a Communist Commissar to each one and sometimes by holding their families hostage. The three main White leaders: General Denikin, General Yudenich and Admiral Kolchak did not co-operate.

Patriotism

The Reds got more support from patriotic Russians as the Whites were helped by foreigners.

Peasants

The Communists had given the peasants the land they wanted. The peasants were not sure about the Communists, but they knew that if the Whites won the landlords would demand their land back.

Atrocities

The Reds used War Communism (see p.111) to get the supplies they needed. This included 'Red Terror' measures. Most famously, in 1918 the Tsar and all his family were murdered at Ekaterinburg. The Whites used 'White Terror' which was just as bad.

EXTRA POINTS

1. Lenin devised an idea called 'The Dictatorship of the Proletariat' to defend his own dictatorial rule. He claimed that, in the crisis Russia was going through, the Communists had to act dictatorially on behalf of the workers (proletariat) to ensure that the Bolshevik revolution was not crushed. This explained the Cheka and the rest of the 'Red Terror'. In time, he said, government would not be necessary, it would 'wither away'. See also War Communism, p.111.

2. Foreign help to the Whites was rather half-hearted. Allied soldiers were not keen to fight on behalf of Tsarism to crush a workers' government.

3. The situation in Russia was very confused in the Civil War. Some forces, often called 'Greens', supported neither the Reds nor the Whites but fought to be free of outside control. These were Anarchists and Nationalists.

Check yourself

QUESTIONS

Q1 Why did Lenin do the following things in 1917–18:

a) Give up so much land to Germany at the Treaty of Brest–Litovsk?
b) Put factories under the workers' control?
c) Take over all banks and foreign trade?
d) Set up the Cheka?

Q2 What part did Trotsky play in the Civil War?

Q3 Who supported the Reds in the Civil War?

REMEMBER! Cover the answers if you want to.

ANSWERS

A1
a) To get peace. The Germans had been victorious for four years and demanded their reward.
b) Because the Communists believed that the workers did the work and so should control the business. The capitalists, who owned the factories, simply exploited the workers.
c) Because the Communist State was acting on behalf of the workers.
d) Because the Bolsheviks were in a minority, with lots of enemies, and they were determined to succeed.

A2 He was organiser of the Red Army. He inspired the troops. He frightened them, if he thought they might change sides, or retreat. He made use of Tsarist officers, but kept political control of them.

A3 Communists supported the Reds wholeheartedly. Peasants supported them because they had given them land. Patriots supported them because the Whites had foreign support. Some supported them because their families were held hostage. Some were terrorised.

TUTORIALS

T1
a) Lenin had to buy peace. The terms make the German complaints about Versailles, in 1919, see p.52, seem silly.
b)&c) See the box on Marxism, p.98 for all the theory behind this. We would say Lenin 'nationalised' the banks and foreign trade by taking them into state ownership. Workers' control had rarely happened outside Communist countries – and did not last long in Russia, see p.111.
d) This is very controversial: What do you think? Was Lenin justified? Did the situation of 1917–21 justify the 'Red Terror'? He certainly gave Stalin plenty of examples to follow for his use of Secret Police in the 1930s.

T2 He showed brilliant skills as an organiser, as he had already shown in the November Revolution. He made brilliant use of the train, rushing through the countryside with guns, boots, uniform, alcohol, a printing press for pamphlets as well as his own living accommodation for weeks at a time.

T3 Although the motives were different, and some obviously not whole-hearted, the Communists did have considerably more support by 1921 than they had had at the time of the November 1917 Revolution.

LENIN'S RULE, 1917–24

WAR COMMUNISM

War Communism is the name given to the particularly harsh Communist measures Lenin introduced in the Civil War, while the Communists were fighting for their survival.

- All factories were taken over by the government. They were told what to make, at what price. Everyone, men and women, aged 16–60, had to work. There was strict discipline and strikes were illegal.

- Peasants were not allowed to trade the grain and other food they grew. The government simply took what they wanted. Detachments of soldiers, armed with machine-guns, went out into the country to seize grain.

- Food was rationed and only workers could have a ration card. Hoarding food was a crime for which you could be shot by the Cheka.

Results

- The peasants refused to co-operate and grew less grain.

- Coming on top of the First World War and Civil War, this led to a famine in 1921 in which perhaps seven million people died.

- In 1921 there was a serious mutiny of the sailors at the Kronstadt naval base near Petrograd. Sailors had previously been keen Bolsheviks and now demanded 'Soviets without Communists', free speech and free elections. The mutiny was crushed by Trotsky's soldiers, but it was a blow to Lenin and the Communist leadership.

NEW ECONOMIC POLICY (NEP)

Lenin introduced NEP in 1921. It was a dramatic change as it allowed several aspects of capitalism to return. He said it was only temporary, to revive the country until it was 'ready' for Communism.

- Small factories were given back to private ownership.

- Peasants were allowed to sell their grain and other food on the open market.

- The 'commanding heights' of the economy – heavy industry like iron, steel and coal, as well as railways, banking and foreign trade – were kept in the hands of the government. However, 'experts' were called in to manage them, and paid high salaries.

Results

- Some Communists were angry. They said it was a retreat for the Communist revolution.

- The Russian economy revived, quite rapidly and steadily. Food was on sale in the streets. Restaurants opened. Consumer goods reappeared in the shops.

- Some people got rich: 'Nepmen' were rich business people. Kulaks were better-off peasants.

UNION OF SOVIET SOCIALIST REPUBLICS (USSR)

In 1923 a new constitution was introduced. In *theory* it set up separate republics for each national group; *in practice* the whole country was run by the soviet Communist Party.

DID LENIN CHANGE THE LIVES OF THE SOVIET PEOPLE?

As we saw on p.107, the Communists were not widely supported in 1917. In the next few years they made a big effort to win people over.

- Propaganda in art. New ideas in art, particularly poetry, music and painting, especially posters, were encouraged. New techniques in film-making were developed by Eisenstein. Propaganda trains went out across the USSR with theatre groups and films.

- The Communists tried to bring about equality for women but met lots of resistance, especially in the countryside.

- The Church was attacked. Many Russians chose not to have a church wedding. Divorce was made easier.

- Education. A mass literacy campaign began. Peasants' children could go to university free.

- A large-scale electrification programme began, to bring electric power to every village in Russia. Lenin said 'Soviet Power plus electrification equals Communism'.

Most people remained unsure of Communism, but many were won over and became devoted party activists.

DEATH OF LENIN

Lenin had been shot in 1918 and the doctors had not been able to remove two bullets from his head. In 1922 he suffered a severe stroke and was unable to work. He died in 1924, aged only fifty-four. He was made a hero: his body was laid out in state and then embalmed.

EXTRA POINTS ▶

1. Note how governments had to pay attention to the demands of the peasants: Kerensky's failure to let them have the land they demanded led to his downfall. Lenin gained support by supporting their demands. He then had to deliver his promise, even though Communists did not support private ownership of land. After War Communism he had to give in and introduce NEP in order to halt the famine. Still 75 per cent of the population, their demands could not be ignored or over-ruled.

2. NEP was not so different from Stolypin's ideas for Russia's future, see p.101.

Check yourself

QUESTIONS

Q1 Why was the Kronstadt Mutiny so serious for Lenin?

Q2 What was new about NEP?

Q3 Look at this picture.

What did Lenin mean by 'Soviet Power plus electrification equals Communism'?

Figure 5.9
*Peasants watching the first
electric light in their village*

REMEMBER! Cover the answers if you want to.

ANSWERS

A1 The Kronstadt Mutiny was serious because the sailors had been important loyal Bolsheviks from the early days in mid-1917. They had played a big part in the November Revolution. Now they had turned against the Communist leadership.

A2 It was not that new: just a return to the situation of free enterprise which had existed under Tsarism only four years previously. However, several things were 'new' compared to the system the Communists had set up in 1917. All kinds of private trade were allowed: in food especially, but also in all consumer goods.

A3 By Soviet power, he meant the power of the new Soviet government to get things done. In 1921 electric power was only laid on in Russian cities. Electrification was supplying electricity to the hundreds of villages all over Russia. Communism was the ideal state which Lenin was trying to set up.

TUTORIALS

T1 The Communists had plenty of enemies and did not care what they did to them, but were concerned when their supporters turned against them. Note that the mutineers of 1921 were not the same sailors as had been involved in 1917: those men had gone off to fight in the Civil War.

T2 It was only partial privatisation. All major industries remained under government control. However the amount of private trade which arose annoyed many Communists. It abandoned (Lenin said temporarily) the state control and workers control of the early decrees of 1917 and restored capitalism.

T3 This electrification only began under Lenin and was put into effect under Stalin (see p.119), but it was Lenin's idea and it linked the new Communist government with the idea of modernity and progress. He hoped, as this slogan says, that people would be converted to Communism by the benefits it brought, such as electricity.

EXAM PRACTICE

Sample Student's Answers & Examiner's Comments

1 Look at this picture. It shows different Russian people reacting to the decrees of the Bolshevik government following the November 1917 Revolution. The painting was made by an official Soviet artist long after 1917.

Use your own knowledge to explain in what ways this is a propaganda interpretation of these events. (5)

The picture shows people reading a poster and talking about it among themselves. The attribution of the source explains that the poster is a list of the decrees passed by Lenin's new Bolshevik government. The picture was made long afterwards: it is not an eye-witness picture. It is propaganda because it shows everyone very happy – laughing and smiling. The artist wants us to think that the Bolshevik decrees were very popular.

4/5

EXAMINER'S COMMENTS

MARK SCHEME

Level 1	Describes picture or defines propaganda.	1–2 marks
Level 2	Explains that this is propaganda on basis of it not being an eye-witness description.	3 marks
Level 3	Explains propaganda on basis of other aspects of the picture	4–5 marks

This answer starts by simply describing what the picture shows. This is a good way of starting because it shows that you have looked hard at the source – an essential requirement. It also gets you started. The answer goes on to point to one key feature of the interpretation: the artist has made them all look happy. There is, however, one further aspect of what you can see which should have been spotted.

The artist has also put in one person from each of several types: a sailor, a soldier, a child, older people, a mother, a baby, a worker. These were all groups in Russia which the Bolsheviks were trying to appeal to. This picture is therefore propaganda in that the people are carefully selected according to the political aims of the Bolsheviks.

2 What were the aims of NEP? (8)

Russia in 1921, when the New Economic Policy was introduced, was in a poor state. There was a famine in some areas, agricultural production was low, industrial production was low. Lenin therefore had to make changes to revive the economy.

Peasants were allowed to trade in the food they produced, so they had an incentive to grow more. Private trade was also allowed in consumer goods, so that people could get hold of the things they wanted. Shops, small businesses and traders began to return to the streets, agricultural production recovered.

Heavy industry was kept under Communist control, but new managers were put in charge to help revive their businesses and make profits. Capitalist methods were therefore used and Marxist ideas rejected.

5/8

EXAMINER'S COMMENTS

MARK SCHEME

Level 1	Describes NEP only	**1–2 marks**
Level 2	Answer puts recovery as the aim and describes how this was to be achieved	**3–5 marks**
Level 3	Explains recovery as an aim but includes others, such as maintaining popularity and control.	**6–8 marks**

This question could have been answered in two lines, but this answer picks up the clue in the number of marks (8), that a longer, more detailed answer in required. In describing the situation in 1921, mention should have been made of the Kronstadt Mutiny.

The answer is only in Level 2 because it omits any mention of other aims for NEP. It is good as far as it goes, so it gets top marks for the level. Lenin knew that the Communists had not won anything like a majority in the Constituent Assembly of 1918. The Civil War had not increased their popularity and the hardship Russia was enduring would only make the Communists more unpopular.

NEP left what Lenin called 'the commanding heights' of the economy in the hands of the government. It was only a partial restoration of capitalism, therefore, and the direction of the economy was still clearly under his control.

Questions to Answer

The answers to Questions 3 and 4 can be found on p.270 and 271

3 Read this Source from the Tsarina's diary about events in Petrograd on 28 February 1917:

'This is a hooligan movement. Young people run and shout that there is no bread simply to create excitement. Workers prevent others from working. It will all pass and calm down if only the Duma would behave itself.'

(a) Write a sentence to explain the meaning of 'Duma'. (3)

(b) What can you learn about the situation in Petrograd in early 1917 from this Source? (6)

4 Why were the Bolsheviks unsuccessful in July, but successful in November, in taking over the government of Russia? (12)

STALIN BECOMES LEADER

Lenin died in 1924. He had no automatic successor: several of the leading Communists were able and popular. The least likely to succeed was Joseph Stalin, the General Secretary of the Communist Party. Yet by 1929 he had become undisputed ruler of Russia, a position he held until his death in 1953.

HOW DID STALIN BECOME LEADER?

Stalin's real name was Josef Djugashvili. He was born in 1879 in Georgia, of working-class parents. He began to train as a priest but soon became a Bolshevik revolutionary. The Tsarist secret police arrested him several times and he changed his name to Stalin (man of steel) in prison. He took part in the Revolution of 1917 and was made Commissar of Nationalities. One of the other Bolsheviks called him 'a grey blur'. He was not a great thinker, but was very hard-working and took on the boring but important job of General Secretary of the Communist Party in 1922. He used this position to build up support in the Communist Party: after a few years his supporters held key positions at all levels.

The one thing at which he showed tremendous skill was in out-manoeuvering his rivals, particularly Leon Trotsky.

Trotsky's real name was Bronstein. He was born in 1879, the son of Jewish farmers. He was leader of the Petrograd Soviet in the 1905 Revolution, but was a Menshevik and only joined the Bolsheviks in 1917. He played an important part in the November 1917 Revolution and a crucial role in creating the Red Army in the Civil War (see chapter 5). As a result the army supported him and he was made Commissar for War in 1922.

He was the most well-known Bolshevik after Lenin, a powerful speaker, thinker and organiser. However, he was arrogant and made no effort to build up support. Other Bolsheviks mistrusted him: they were suspicious that he was such a recent Bolshevik and feared he would use the army to become a dictator. He was also ill for much of the time following Lenin's death.

To outwit Trotsky and the others Stalin used:

- trickery
- rivalry between other Communist leaders
- his support in the Party
- policy differences

FIRST STAGE, 1924–5

Figure 6.1
Lenin with Stalin. Lenin and Stalin were not actually close friends and this picture may be a fake

Stalin told Trotsky that Lenin's funeral was a day earlier than the real date. Trotsky did not turn up; Stalin did, and made a great show of being Lenin's keenest follower. He made sure pictures like Figure 6.1 were published.

Trotsky put forward a policy of 'World Revolution'. He said Communism in the USSR would only survive if other countries became Communist too. This meant promoting revolutions elsewhere. Stalin put forward 'Socialism in one country': developing Communism in the USSR first. He managed to out-vote Trotsky with the support of:

- Other Communists, anxious to see Trotsky pulled down,
- His supporters in the Party.
- Ordinary Communist Party members, who feared that 'World Revolution' would involve them in more wars. They were fed up with war and keen only to get on with building Communism in the Soviet Union.

In 1925 Trotsky was removed from his post as Commissar for War.

SECOND STAGE, 1925–7

The USSR still faced the problem of how to develop industry and modernise peasant farming. The Communist Party was split over how to do this. Right-wing Communists wanted to keep on with NEP, slowly building up industry with peasant co-operation. Left-wing Communists wanted a crash programme of rapid industrialisation, forcing the peasants to join collective farms (for more on this, see p.124). For a while Stalin held the balance, then threw his weight in favour of the right-wingers. In 1927 Trotsky, leading left-wingers, and their supporters were expelled from the Communist Party.

THIRD STAGE, 1928–9

Stalin then turned on the right wing and began forcing collectivisation through. All right-wingers were removed from important positions. By 1929 all his opponents, to right and left, and their leaders, were out of power. Only Stalin's supporters remained.

Stalin was not a man to forgive and forget. Trotsky was sent to Siberia in 1928, expelled from the USSR in 1929 and murdered by one of Stalin's agents, in Mexico, in 1940. You can read what happened to his other former rivals on p.127.

◀ **EXTRA POINTS**

1. The leaders of the left-wing Communists were Zinoviev and Kamenev, both ex-Bolsheviks who had worked with Lenin for years. The leading right-winger was Bukharin, also a former Bolshevik and a popular leader and thinker.

2. Lenin, in his 'Testament' (a kind of will, read after his death) said Stalin was 'too rude', 'not cautious enough' and should be removed. Lenin also criticised Trotsky and other leading Communists and the Testament was not made public, much to Stalin's relief.

Check yourself

QUESTIONS

Q1 Make a list of points for and against Trotsky in the clash for the leadership of the USSR after Lenin's death.

Q2 Give an example of each of the four tactics used by Stalin to outwit his rivals between 1924 and 1929.

Q3 What have you learnt about Stalin's personality so far?

REMEMBER! Cover the answers if you want to.

ANSWERS

A1 **For:** skilled organiser; well-known; good speaker; clever thinker;

Against: arrogant; not prepared to get involved in building up groups of supporters among the Communists; late convert from Mensheviks to Bolsheviks

A2
a) Stalin tricked Trotsky over the date of Lenin's funeral.
b) Stalin used the rivalry other leading Comunists felt towards Trotsky in lining up massive opposition to him in 1924.
c) Stalin had lots of supporters in the Communist Party and used their votes against his enemies in all three stages of the leadership battle.
d) Over 'World Revolution' versus 'Socialism in One Country' Stalin's policy was more in touch with rank-and-file Communists. Over when and how to industrialise the USSR Stalin took up and put down policies as his tactics in the leadership contest demanded. Thus in 1927 he supported the right-wingers, who wanted to continue with NEP, against the Left, who wanted to force the pace. In 1928 he changed policies to force the fall of the Right.

A3 Stalin was tough, physically and emotionally. He was a hard worker and wanted power; this drove him on to overcome more talented men than him. Perhaps because he was an outsider (as a Georgian not a Russian) and perhaps because the others were rude about him because he was not such a good talker and thinker as they were, he carried personal rivalry to the limits, even having his former enemies killed.

TUTORIALS

T1 *Trotsky was probably shy and so found it difficult to make contact with what ordinary Communists felt. To be fair, the old Bolshevik Party had not been democratically-run: the leaders had made all decisions. He completely misjudged the new situation and his policy of 'World Revolution' was easily defeated by Stalin and his many supporters.*

T2
a) This enabled Stalin to manipulate a large-scale cult of Lenin, much to the scorn of Trotsky and Lenin's widow, but which promoted Stalin as the one true heir of Lenin.
b)&c) Stalin had used his position as General Secretary to keep in contact with Party members everywhere. Thus there were many people who owed debts of gratitude to him for little favours done over the years and would re-pay him with their votes. Members who supported his rivals found their careers in the Party did not go so well.

T3 *Stalin did have some positive qualities – he showed personal bravery in the Second World War – but, as you will see in the rest of this chapter, he was a ruthless monster, with little regard for human life or human feelings.*

STALIN AND INDUSTRY

When Stalin won the struggle to be leader in 1928, the USSR was not a heavily industrialised country. By 1941 it had the industry to support a massive and victorious war against Hitler's Germany, and after the war even to challenge the might of the USA in the Cold War.

WHY DID STALIN DECIDE TO INDUSRIALISE THE USSR SO FAST?

Industry in the USSR in 1928

- Some industry had been built up under the Tsars, but it was restricted to only a few areas (see Fig. 5.1, p.94).
- This early growth had been severely disrupted by the First World War, the Revolution (see p.103) and the Civil War (see p.108).
- Industry was not a big part of the USSR's economy. Only about 20 per cent of people worked in industry.

In 1928 Stalin decided to industrialise the USSR as rapidly as possible. His reasons were:

- Fear of other countries invading Russia. In fact, although many governments were hostile to Communism, no one had any plans to invade the USSR at the time. However, Stalin was naturally suspicious and (as we shall see) found threats everywhere. It is true that other countries were very hostile to the Communists and some had supported the Whites against the Communists in the Civil War. It is worth learning the italicised sentences from this famous speech of Stalin's from 1931, which explains his attitude: 'The history of old Russia consisted in being beaten again and again because she was backward. If you are backward you may be beaten and enslaved. If you are powerful, people must beware of you. *We are fifty or a hundred years behind the advanced countries. We must make up this gap in ten years. Either we do it or they crush us.*'
- He was fed up with the peasants charging high prices for food under NEP. Like several leading Communists, he suspected the peasants were cutting the supply of food to the cities in order to keep prices up. He was determined to smash their resistance. Rapid industrialisation would need rapid changes in agriculture and these would break their power.

HOW DID HE DO THIS?

He set up a **planned economy** with targets for each industry. The state planners, **Gosplan**, set:

- each industry a national target (see Table 6.1)

This was divided into targets for each region and further so that:

- each region set a target for each factory
- each factory set a target for each shift
- each shift set a target for each worker
- each worker had to produce a target.

Each industry had a Five-Year Plan to increase production:

- The first Five-Year Plan was 1928–32. It concentrated on heavy industry: coal, iron, oil, electricity.
- The second Five-Year Plan was 1933–37. It concentrated on heavy industry, but also on transport (new roads, railways, canals and the Moscow underground were built) and on mining, particularly in new areas.
- The third Five-Year Plan started in 1938 but was abandoned in the war. It concentrated on re-armament for the war.

Table 6.1 **The Five-Year Plans (output in millions of tonnes)**

	1928 output	1932 target	1932 actual production	1937 actual production
Coal	36	76	65	130
Iron	3	10	6	15
Oil	2	22	22	29

HOW WERE THE TARGETS TO BE ACHIEVED?

The increases in production in the targets were so great, as you can see in Table 6.1, that it was not going to be enough just to work a little bit harder.

Figure 6.2
The USSR under the Five-Year Plans

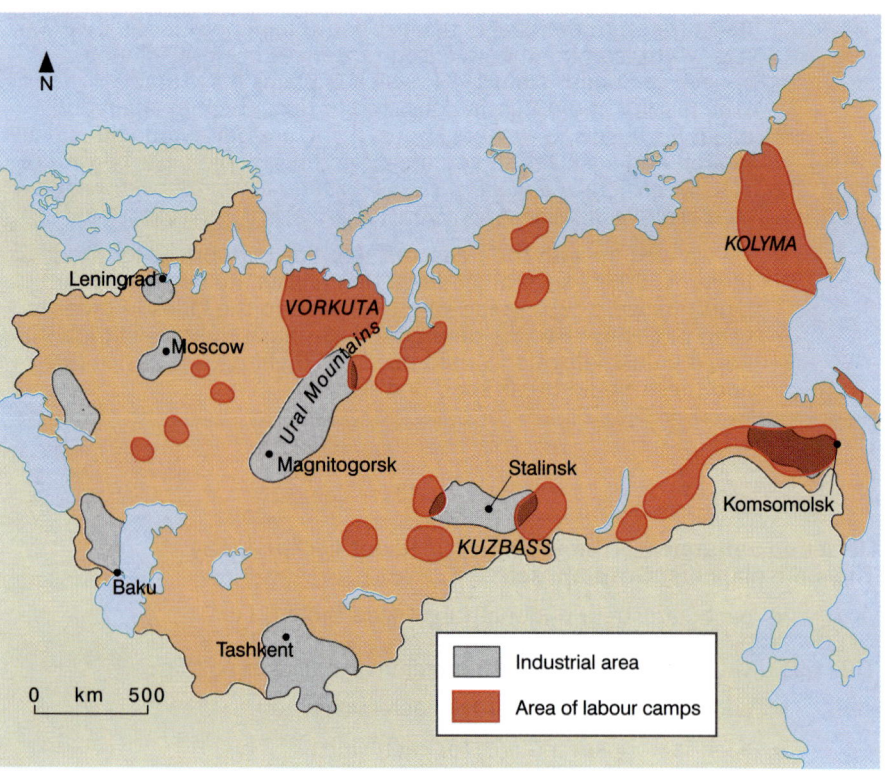

The whole Soviet Union was transformed:

- New areas of industry were opened up (see Fig. 6.2). There were new towns, with new factories and the houses for those who worked in them.
- Millions of new workers were needed.
  - Some were **foreigners**, skilled workers paid high wages to show the Russians what to do.
  - **Women** were recruited in large numbers; factories had nurseries so that women could soon return to work after their children were born. 80 per cent of new workers in the second Five-Year Plan were women. 40 per cent of industrial workers in 1937 were women, compared to 28 per cent in 1927.
  - **Peasants** were encouraged to leave the land to work in industry.
  - On many schemes Stalin used **forced labour** by convicts in the prison camps.
- These millions of workers had to be made to work hard to achieve their targets.
  - Hours were long.
  - Those who took time off were fined, or had their picture displayed in the factory. Those who made mistakes were accused of sabotage and sent to prison camps.
  - **Stakhanovism**. Certain workers, in favourable conditions, produced huge amounts. One of these was a coal-miner called Stakhanov, who dug 102 tonnes of coal in one shift – fourteen times the usual amount. Workers like Stakhanov were made heroes, with special housing, cars and honours. Other workers now had to work harder to produce the same as the Stakhanovites.
  - Government propaganda, in posters, slogans and on the radio bombarded the workers. They were told that that they were doing great things for their country and for Communism.
  - Safety was minimal and thousands of inexperienced workers died or were injured.
  - Stalin feared that the traditional way of life in Muslim areas of the USSR, where new industries were opening up, would stand in the way of industrialisation. Islam was therefore persecuted: mosques were closed and pilgrimages to Mecca were forbidden.

RESULTS

- The USSR became an industrial giant. The chart shows that the 1932 targets were rarely achieved, but that production by 1937 was way ahead of what it had been ten years earlier.
- Workers' standard of living fell. The concentration on heavy industry meant a shortage of **consumer goods** (the things people need, like shoes, clothes, household appliances). 'Real wages' (that is what you can actually buy for your money) fell. Conditions in the new towns were appalling. People lived in over-crowded flats, with expensive food and few amenities.
- On the other hand, there was no unemployment, there was free health care and education.

EXTRA POINTS ▶

1. The Tsars had tried to encourage the growth of Russian industry. Ever since they came to power, the Communists had been discussing how to industrialise. After all, they were the party of industrial workers. More industry would, they thought, mean more industrial workers, so more support among the people.

   The question for both the Tsars and the Communists was not really *whether* to make the USSR more of an industrial power, but *how*? Fast or slow? This was one of the main issues in the quarrels between Stalin and others after the death of Lenin, see p.117.

2. The system of central planning was very rigid. Local factories had no room to use their initiative: all they had to do was fulfil their targets. It might have been a good way to 'kick-start' industrial growth, but it made Soviet industry inefficient and slow to react to change. It was always unable to produce consumer goods in quantity and quality and was a major reason for the collapse of Communism in the late 1980s.

3. Compare the growth in Soviet industry in the 1930s with depression and unemployment throughout the capitalist world at this time.

Check yourself

QUESTIONS

Q1
(a) What were the Five-Year Plans?
(b) How did they work?

Q2 How did Stalin make his workers work harder?

Q3 What were the effects of industrialisation on the people of the USSR?
There is quite a lot you could write about here, but it needs to be planned if it is not to look haphazard. Various ways of splitting it up could be used: you could divide your answer into good and bad effects; or you could look at working and living conditions separately, as in this plan:
'At work, the Soviet people had to ...'

'Women's lives changed because ...'

'People's home life was changed because ...'

'There were some improvements to their out of work lives because ...'

REMEMBER! Cover the answers if you want to.

ANSWERS

A1
a) The Five-Year Plans were Stalin's method of industrialising the USSR completely and rapidly. The first started in 1928 and concentrated on heavy industry.
b) The Plans set targets for each industry. These were then turned into production targets which each region, factory, shift and even each worker had to meet.

TUTORIALS

T1
a) *Heavy industry – coal, iron, oil and power – had to be the starting-point, because all other industries needed them. The USSR continued with Five-Year Plans after the Second World War and other countries, such as India, also used them as a way of co-ordinating development.*
b) *The point of such centralised planning was that each industry was linked to each other. For example, new ironworks needed lots more coal: the Plans were there to ensure it was produced.*

A2 There were punishments for those who slacked or who did bad work. These included fines, being held up in front of everyone in the factory and, for serious cases, being sent to a labour camp. Specially good workers – called Stakhanovites – received rewards and were used to set standards for all the others.

All workers were subject to government propaganda telling them to work harder.

A3 At work, the Soviet people had to work very hard for long hours. They learned new skills and many millions left the land to become industrial workers. In comparison with other countries, where this was a period of high unemployment, Soviet workers had jobs and job security.

Women's lives changed because they were expected to join the workforce. Crèches and nurseries were provided and Soviet women were probably the most equally treated in the world at that time. However, few reached positions of responsibility, either at work or in government.

People's home life was changed because many moved to new industrial towns and cities. Many of these were inadequate at first as cities were built from scratch in the middle of nowhere. Flats were often very small and badly-built and there was a shortage of consumer goods, from clothes to household items.

There were some improvements: free health care was provided. Education was available for all, which it had never been before. In time, the new towns and cities had good, free leisure and cultural facilities.

T2 *Think of it as 'the stick and the carrot': the sticks were punishments, the carrots were incentives for fulfilling the targets.*

The workers in the new industries often came straight from peasant farms and were totally unused to the discipline of factory work. Some have argued that the strict controls were necessary to get these new workers to fit into the factory system.

Note also that Stalin emphasised the 'danger from abroad', even though there was no real threat to the USSR until well into the 1930s. This reflects Stalin's own paranoia (see p.127), but it built up an atmosphere of fear, in which superhuman efforts had to be made to save the country.

T3 *You could add a conclusion weighing all these things up.*

STALIN AND COLLECTIVISATION

WHY COLLECTIVISE?

Stalin could not turn the USSR into a modern industrialised state without changing agriculture. He needed:

- more food to feed the people in the new cities he was building.
- more workers for the new factories he was setting up.

- more food to sell abroad; this would give him the money to buy foreign industrial machines.
- more control over the countryside.

AGRICULTURE IN THE USSR IN 1928

Farming methods were old-fashioned, with few machines and lots of small farms. Many peasants had little or no land and so were very poor. Some peasants owned more land. These were called **kulaks** and were doing quite well under NEP. However, they grew what they liked and were only interested in making a profit for themselves.

COLLECTIVE FARMS

A collective farm was called a **kolkhoz**. It was intended to be **more efficient** because:

- All the land would be farmed together in much larger units.
- The government would provide tractors from MTS (Motor Tractor Stations) to work the land.
- All the tools and animals would be pooled.
- The peasants would work the land together (see Fig 6.3).

The government would tell the collective what to grow and buy a fixed amount. The peasants would be paid a share of the profits. In addition, they were allowed to keep small plots of land of their own to grow their own food.

Figure 6.3
A government propaganda poster which says 'Come and join our kolkhoz, comrade!'

OPPOSITION

At first, Stalin tried to persuade the peasants to join collectives voluntarily. Few did so. Then collectivisation was imposed by force. The peasants opposed collectivisation because it was the end of their whole way of life:

- They lost control over how they farmed: what they grew, when they planted, when they harvested, etc.
- They knew that the government would take their share of the crop in bad years and in good (Stalin called this 'The First Commandment'). This could leave them without food.
- They objected to control from the Communist Party. The chairman of every Collective was a Communist; every MTS had a secret policeman on the staff.

Kulaks

The peasants hated the idea of collectivisation. Many refused to hand over their farms and animals. In an attempt to win over poorer peasants, he attacked the kulaks. In fact anyone who resisted collectivisation was labelled a kulak and driven from their homes. They were put in forced labour camps or forced to settle on poor land. Most of the four million kulaks died. The rest of the peasants worked the land reluctantly.

RESULTS

- **Decline in output** Farming routines were disrupted. Animals had been slaughtered. Government experts made bad decisions. There was a serious decline in agricultural output:

Table **6.2 Agricultural output at the start of First Five-Year Plan (1928) and the second Five-Year Plan (1933)**

	1928	1933
Grain harvest	73.3 million tonnes	68.4 million tonnes
State grain demands	10.8 million tonnes	22.6 million tonnes
Numbers of cattle	70.5 million	38.4 million
Numbers of pigs	26.0 million	12.1 million

- **Famine** The government always took its share, as the figures above show, and this share increased. Armed convoys took food from starving villages. In 1932–33 at least five million died.
- **Control of agriculture** Stalin had what he wanted: agriculture was under his control.

EXTRA POINTS

1. The Communists had never been popular in the countryside. The Revolution of 1917 had been city-based (see p.103). The Communists also resented the fact that, under NEP, cities were often short of food as the kulaks restricted the supply to keep prices up. Changing agriculture would give Stalin more control over the peasants.

2. The long-term results of collectivisation for the USSR were bad:

   a) Peasants remained resentful; in the Second World War, in 1941, the German invading army was welcomed in the Soviet countryside.

   b) Agriculture under Communism remained inefficient in spite of efforts by other Communist leaders after Stalin to improve things. Although the USSR is a vast and fertile country there were always food shortages in the cities. [This failure was a major cause of the collapse of Communism in the late 1980s.]

Check yourself

QUESTIONS

Q1 Fill in the blanks at (a), (b), (c) and (d) on this chart.

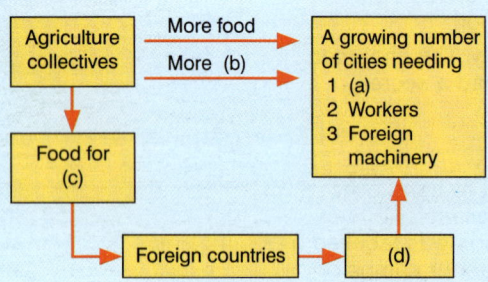

Agriculture collectives
→ More food
→ More (b)

A growing number of cities needing
1 (a)
2 Workers
3 Foreign machinery

Agriculture collectives → Food for (c) → Foreign countries → (d) → A growing number of cities needing

Q2 Give as many reasons as you can why the peasants opposed collectivisation.

Q3 What does the story of collectivisation of Soviet agriculture tell you about Stalin's methods?

REMEMBER! Cover the answers if you want to.

ANSWERS

A1
a) Food
b) Workers
c) Export
d) Machines

A2 They would not be making the decisions about how to farm, but would be told by someone else.

They feared that government targets for crop production would leave them starving.

They resented interference from the Communist Party.

A3 He was ruthless. He was prepared to overthrow centuries of traditional peasant farming in the USSR. He was prepared to send the kulaks to almost certain death. He was prepared to face famine by forcing collectivisation on the peasants. He did all these things to get his industrialisation carried out.

TUTORIALS

T1
a) *This is the obvious one. Stalin did not want to be dependent on the kulaks for getting enough food at a cheap enough price.*

b) *Stalin was short of workers. Remember that only 20 per cent of Soviet citizens were industrial workers. Stalin needed a much bigger labour force in industry so he had to draw on the peasants, and, at the same time put up agricultural production.*

c) *Don't forget this one. Food was all the USSR had to sell.*

d) *When your industry is as backward as the USSR's was, you need machines to make machines. The only way Stalin could get hold of them was by buying them from abroad.*

T2 *The main reason was that their whole way of life, which they and their forefathers had led for generations, looked like being utterly changed. The land they worked would not be theirs (apart from the little plots around their houses). The animals they tended would not be theirs. They would be expected to grow crops which the country needed, like flax, cotton or sugar-beet, but which were no use to them.*

In fact the government did seize the crops it wanted and the result was famine.

T3 *Compare these actions of Stalin's with others: his seizure of power in 1924-9, the industrialisation programme, the purges. Yet he did succeed in modernising the USSR: it survived the German invasion of 1941, it was victorious in the Second World War, and became one of the two super-powers afterwards.*

Are these achievements worth the cost?

STALIN'S DICTATORSHIP

In the years after 1929, Stalin built up a **totalitarian dictatorship** in the USSR. For what this means, and comparisons with Hitler's totalitarian dictatorship in Germany at much the same time, see p.74.

1. **Secret police**
   The Cheka, which Lenin had set up, changed its name over the years, to the OGPU, the NKVD and then, after the war, the KGB. Their job was to seek out and arrest anyone who was in any way critical of Stalin.

2. **Purges**
   Since 1918 (see p.108) the Communist Party had been the only party allowed, so Stalin's only critics were inside the Party. In 1934, Kirov, the popular party boss of Leningrad (as Petrograd was re-named in 1924) was murdered. Historians have accused Stalin of his murder, but he may not have been to blame. Nonetheless, Stalin took the opportunity to arrest many of his old rivals and their followers. '**Show-trials**' were held, in which lifelong Bolsheviks were accused of the most amazing things – spying for the West, or taking part in Trotskyite plots. They all 'confessed' and were executed. By 1938, every one of the Bolshevik leaders of 1917 had died or been executed, except Stalin. Ninety-eight of the 139 members of the Central Committee of the Communist Party of 1934 were shot. Half a million Party members were arrested.

   The other possible power-base for opposition was the Red Army, created by Trotsky in the Civil War. Stalin purged the army in 1937–38. One-fifth of all officers, including 90 per cent of all generals, were executed.

3. **Terror**
   Ordinary Soviet citizens suffered too. Two or three NKVD men would call in the small hours of the morning and take victims away. They used torture or simply interrogated people for days on end, without sleep, after which they would confess to anything.

   To be a kulak, or the son of a kulak, or to have supported one of Stalin's rivals in the leadership contest in the 1920s was enough. Trying to spread religious ideas or being a member of a church group could get you arrested. Teachers, doctors, scientists and poets all feared the knock on the door. The secret police encouraged informers to make accusations and arrested people as a result. Sometimes members of a family informed on each other. No one really knows exactly how many people were arrested, or what happened to them all. Some historians suggest ten million, some twenty million. Perhaps one million were shot.

4. **Labour camps**
   The rest were sent to labour camps. Here they toiled, unpaid, poorly fed, often in appalling conditions, building dams, canals, roads and other important projects (see Fig. 6.2). The Moscow Underground was built in this way (see Fig. 6.4). Millions died in the camps.

5. **Propaganda and censorship**
   The press, radio, cinema and publishing were all heavily controlled. The churches were not allowed to publish books. No critical word was ever heard. Only successes and achievements were described. Most Soviet citizens were not allowed to travel abroad to see what other countries were like for themselves.

6. **'Personality cult'**
   Stalin was the focus of the propaganda campaign. His picture was everywhere: in stations, offices, classrooms, factories. Huge statues of Stalin were set up. Several towns were named after him. Slogans gave him credit for everything: 'The country is being led from victory to victory by the steersman of the Party, the great Stalin.'

7. **The arts**
   In the first few years of Communism the arts had flourished under new freedom. Now censorship was imposed and every novel, painting, musical composition, film or play had to serve the state. Figure 6.5 is an example of Stalinist art.

Figure 6.4 *Moscow Underground*

Figure 6.5
Painting of Stalin talking with peasants and workers at a new dam

8. **Young people**

Special efforts were made to indoctrinate young people. In school, the curriculum was changed to explain the Communist Revolution and the heroic roles of Lenin and Stalin. Stalin himself wrote the history book all pupils used. Pictures of other Bolsheviks in old library books had pieces of paper glued over them. Instead of religious education, pupils had anti-religion lessons.

There were youth movements for young people: Octobrists from 8–10, Pioneers from 10-16 and Komsomol from 16–23.

HOW DID THE LIVES OF THE PEOPLE OF THE USSR CHANGE UNDER STALIN?

- Women and the family. In the early years of Communism divorce and abortion had been made much easier. Now restrictions were restored and the family was promoted, with the woman as wife and mother. At the same time, the industrialisation programme needed lots of women workers. The USSR therefore took the lead in providing crèches, nurseries and child-minding facilities at every workplace. Women continued to have equality in theory, probably more than in the West, but few reached top positions.

- Health services were provided, free. By 1939 the USSR had more doctors per head than Britain.

- Education also improved, although it was full of Communist propaganda (see above). A big effort was made to bring literacy to the mass of Soviet people.

- Living standards rose, although they remained considerably below Britain and the USA. Problems like food shortages, lack of consumer goods and lack of housing in cities (94 per cent of Russians lived in one room per family), were a continual annoyance. Party members and senior officials had extra privileges in food, shopping and housing.

- Leisure facilities improved. Every factory and new town had sports grounds, swimming pools, theatres, cinemas and social clubs.

1. The purges were a way of explaining things that went wrong in the Five-Year Plans. If there was a fault, or a train went off the lines by accident or bad work, for example, it was called sabotage and people were arrested, tried and executed. This happened in the Shakhty trial as early as 1928.

2. In the war, 1941–45, Stalin relaxed some of the censorship. He allowed the churches to open again as they encouraged Russian patriotism. After the war the terror and censorship returned. Returning prisoners of war were especially at risk as they had seen that the West was not as awful as Stalin's propaganda said. Stalin was planning new purges when he died in 1953.

Check yourself

QUESTIONS

Q1 Look at points 1 to 8. Which are examples of terror and which are examples of indoctrination?

Q2 Look at the picture of the Moscow Underground (Figure 6.4). Why do you think it was designed to look so grand?

Q3 Look at Figure 6.5. What message is it trying to give about Stalin?

Q4 Compare Stalin's dictatorship with Hitler's. What are the similarities and differences?

REMEMBER! Cover the answers if you want to.

ANSWERS

A1 1, 2, 3 and 4 are examples of terror under Stalin; 5, 6, 7 and 8 are examples of indoctrination.

A2 It was designed to look grand to impress visitors to the USSR.

A3 It is a piece of propaganda art about Stalin. Stalin looks gentle, friendly, fatherly, getting on well with a group of ordinary Russians. This fitted his propaganda image of the guide of his country and his people.

A4 There are striking similarities between Hitler's Germany and Stalin's USSR, even though they hated each other. Both used a mixture of terror, through secret police, prison camps, killing opponents and informers to force ordinary people into silence. They both used propaganda, the cult of the leader and censorship. Both only allowed approved art. Both put special efforts into indoctrinating the young, both inside and outside school.

TUTORIALS

T1 *There was some overlap, of course: the purges had a propaganda side, that the USSR was being attacked by enemies inside the country. Artists were terrorised into putting up with censorship.*

T2 *It was also designed so that each station looked like a palace – a palace for the people.*

T3 *It also shows the dam: a demonstration of the new and spectacular achievements of the Communist regime. Stalin, incidentally, never went out on trips around the USSR looking at the country and meeting people. He stayed in Moscow, speaking only to his dedicated followers and viewing his country through newsreel films.*

T4 *There are important differences too. Hitler was driven by racism and by far the greatest number of his victims were executed for racial reasons. Stalin had racist views too, but most of his victims were his own people. Hitler was also bent on war, which affected his economic planning; Stalin sought to avoid war.*

EXAM PRACTICE

Sample Student's Answers & Examiner's Comments

1 This poster was put up in the USSR in 1933. The booklet at the top is the Five-Year Plan of 1928. The capitalist – the man in the top hat – is saying 'Fantasy, Lies, Utopia'. The lower half of the poster shows the situation, and his reaction, in 1933.

(a) Use your own knowledge to explain the purpose of this poster.

(6)

> The lower half of the poster shows a great mass of industries forging ahead. So one purpose is to show that the industrialisation programme has been a success. It makes people feel better. The capitalist is shown in both scenes as a nasty man who mocks the Five-Year Plans as 'Fantasy' etc. Stalin believed that the USSR was in danger of being crushed by other nations. So another purpose of the poster is to remind people that the USSR has powerful enemies who want the Communist experiment to fail. (The USSR was the only Communist country in the world from 1917 to 1945). These enemies are being knocked aside by the success of the Five-Year Plans. Stalin used fear of outside interference to drive the workers on to make enormous efforts to fulfil the Five-Year Plan targets.

6/6

EXAMINER'S COMMENTS

MARK SCHEME

Level 1	Describes poster	**1–2 marks**
Level 2	Description adds some items of own recalled knowledge or explains purpose from within the source only	**3–4 marks**
Level 3	Uses own knowlege to explain purpose	**5–6 marks**

This is an example of the tricky question which asks you *both* to analyse the source *and* to add your own knowledge. It can be difficult to decide which aspect to concentrate on. The student here has used a useful but simple approach: start by working away at the Source – what does it tell us, what does it show etc. *Then* bring in outside knowledge to make more sense of it. The student only begins to do this in line 5: Stalin's paranoia about outsiders attacking the USSR explains why the poster shows this capitalist. It is almost as if the purpose of the Five-Year Plans was to bash the capitalists on the nose. What really makes this a quality answer is that the student has not allowed herself to get carried away with this aspect, but returns to the question (Explain the purpose...) in the last sentence.

b)   In what ways is this poster an example of propaganda?   (5)

> Propaganda is information that is given out for a purpose. It is often biased, either by saying things that are untrue, or by only telling part of the story. This poster fits this definition in several ways. It was carefully designed to influence the workers in the ways I have explained in the answer to Question (a). It is easy to see that it is biased: the first Five-Year Plan did not, in fact, fulfil most of its targets. The capitalist is a cartoon figure and anyway no nation was on the point of invading the USSR in 1933. However, there is some truth in the poster: production in the USSR did rise amazingly.

4/5

EXAMINER'S COMMENTS

MARK SCHEME

Level 1	Describes source again	**1 mark**
Level 2	Definition of propaganda, with only passing references to this poster	**2–3 marks**
Level 3	Uses this poster to demonstrate nature of propaganda.	**4–5 marks**

This question requires you start with a definition. Note that the excellent definition here includes not just bias but propaganda by selection.

The answer then goes on to point out three ways in which the real situation differed from the situation as depicted in the poster. Again, it would have been easy to stop there, but the student has remembered the idea of a balanced answer – so important in History – and found something about the poster which is actually correct. A more obvious point was that many people in the western world who had doubted whether Stalin's industrialisation programme could succeed were amazed.

2 (a) Why did Stalin modernise Soviet agriculture? (8)

The changes Stalin made to Soviet agriculture were because of the changes Stalin wanted to make to the whole USSR. He wanted to make the USSR a modern industrialised state.

New industries were being set up in new areas. They needed workers and 75 per cent of Soviet people were peasants. Agriculture had to be modernised to free workers to go to the factories.

Stalin also needed plenty of cheap food. He did not like being forced to pay what the kulaks, the better-off farmers, demanded for their grain. Agriculture was outside his control and he wanted to be able to ensure food supplies for his workers.

He also wanted surplus grain to sell abroad. This would give him the money to buy foreign machines which he needed to get Soviet industry started.

All these things could only be done by collectivising the farms. Collectivisation began in 1928 and by 1934 almost all farmland was in collectives.

5/8

EXAMINER'S COMMENTS

MARK SCHEME

Level 1	Describes one answer briefly or simply lists reasons	1–3 marks
Level 2	Describes a number of reasons, using own knowledge and relevant selected information.	4–6 marks
Level 3	Develops a number of reasons, using wider knowledge of historical context.	7–8 marks

This is a well-organised answer which starts by tying the collectivisation programme to the wider plan to modernise industry. The student gains credit for supplying several reasons, rather than just one. These are all accurately, if briefly, explained. The only possible motive for collectivisation which is not mentioned is the desire for political control of a large group, the peasants, over whom the Communists had always little influence or support.

What is missing, however, is any description of the state of agriculture in the USSR when Stalin became supreme leader in 1928. A change must describe situations 'before-and-after'. In this answer the candidate seems to have assumed a knowledge of the state of things which Stalin had to deal with. The only suggestion of this is the mention of the kulaks in line 5. The good explanations which the student offers are therefore weakened in their impact.

A more useful opening paragraph might have described the backwardness of Soviet agriculture in 1928: there were few machines, methods of farming were outdated, farms were small, there was little or none of the scientific approach that had revolutionised farming in Western Europe and the USA since the mid-nineteenth century. Most of all, attitudes were fixed, suspicious and hostile to change.

(b) How successful were the changes he made? (7)

The changes were not successful. Output fell because peasants killed their cattle and pigs rather then let them be taken over by the collective farm. They also destroyed tools and burnt crops. Many peasants were unhappy about working on the collective. Some of the new ideas brought in by the experts from Moscow did not work. The result was that farming production fell.

3/7

EXAMINER'S COMMENTS

MARK SCHEME

Level 1	General, personal comment on changes with some factual support.	**1–2 marks**
Level 2	Developed one-sided judgement or makes a number of unrelated points	**3–5 marks**
Level 3	Makes considered judgement, drawing on good factual support.	**6–7 marks**

This answer goes beyond a simple general statement, but only just. It is one-sided, having only critical comments to make. It would have been better to have mentioned some other reasons for failure – for example, the destruction of the kulaks removed all the most efficient farmers.

Most of all, it should have taken a wider view of the success or failure of the collectivisation programme, and that must mean some reference back to Stalin's aims. Certainly, in terms of food output, it was not successful. Nevertheless, Stalin did break the power of the kulaks, he did bring Soviet agriculture under state control and he did get his surpluses for export and the industrial areas. These should have been included.

Question to Answer
The answer to Question 3 can be found on p.272

3 'Stalin brought nothing but hardship to the lives of the Soviet people.'
How accurate do you think this description of Stalin's rule in the USSR is? (12)

ISOLATIONISM

The First World War ended with over a million US soldiers fighting on the Western Front. The US President, Woodrow Wilson, was adoringly welcomed when he arrived in Europe to take part in the peace negotiations, the first US President to visit Europe during his term of office. He had Fourteen Points for a new, better, peaceful world after the war, including a League of Nations, and played a big part in drawing up the Treaty of Versailles. (For more on all these issues, see chapter 3.) Yet when Wilson returned to the USA, he found that the mood of the country had changed. Many American people seemed to want to return to **isolationism**. This meant that they did not want the USA to join any foreign alliances or take much part in world affairs.

WHY DID THE USA TURN TO ISOLATIONISM IN 1919?

- **Tradition**
  Isolation was the traditional US policy towards the rest of the world. Woodrow Wilson had in fact been re-elected President in 1916 on a promise to keep the USA out of the First World War. In a world before air travel the USA was much more cut off from the rest of the world than it is today. Apart from other countries in the Americas, everywhere else was at least six days sea journey away.

- **Dislike of the 'Old World'**
  The USA is a country of immigrants. In 1919 the majority of US citizens had been born in Europe and their experiences and memories of Europe were not happy ones. For them, Europe spelt poverty, lack of freedom, exploitation, oppressive governments. Not surprisingly, they wanted to forget Europe and get on with building new lives for themselves.

- **Dangerous ideas**
  The Europe of 1919 was full of revolutionary ideas – Socialism, Communism, Anarchism. There had been the Communist Revolution in Russia in 1917 (see chapter 5) and attempted Communist revolutions in Germany, Hungary and elsewhere. Many people in the USA hated and feared these ideas. Any further contact with Europe was therefore to be avoided.

- **100,000 US soldiers had died in the First World War**
  Many Americans regretted this and wanted to pull out of any more entanglements which could lead to further wars.

ISOLATIONISM IN PRACTICE

- **Rejection of the Peace Treaties**
  Under the US constitution, peace treaties have to be agreed by the Senate – one of the elected houses of the US Congress. The Senate was isolationist and would not agree to the Treaty of Versailles because it involved joining the League of Nations. The Treaty, into which Wilson had put so much energy and hope was rejected. The USA never joined the League of Nations.

- **Restrictions on immigration**
  Thirteen million immigrants had come into the USA between 1900 and 1919. Many of these were 'new' immigrants from southern and eastern Europe: Italy, Greece, Poland and Russia (see Fig. 7.1). They were often Catholics and some were socialists.

Figure 7.1
*Immigrants from Italy
arrive in the USA*

Immigrants who had arrived in the eighteenth and nineteenth centuries were mainly from countries in northern and western Europe like Britain, Germany, Scandinavia and the Netherlands. They were nicknamed 'WASPs', (White Anglo–Saxon Protestants). Wasps were worried about these new immigrants and restrictions were placed on immigration in 1921:

- The total number of immigrants let in was limited.

- In 1917 a literacy test was imposed on all immigrants.

- A 'quota' system was introduced: numbers were only let in according to the proportion of people from that country already in the USA. For example, this meant a large quota from Britain, which was hardly ever filled, while the countries of 'new' immigrants only had small quotas.

The 'open door' which the USA had always offered to anyone who wanted to come had closed.

● **Tariffs**
The Fordney–McCumber tariff put high duties on 28 products coming into the USA from other countries. This made them expensive for US customers.

EXTRA POINTS ▶

1. Wilson was very keen on his League of Nations. On his return from Europe he made an exhausting speaking tour of the country by train, trying to whip up support. He suffered a stroke and the important negotiations with the Senate were conducted from his sick-bed. He could have got the Senate to agree to sign the treaty if he had compromised, but he refused to budge at all and lost the vote.

2. Quite often the Congress, including the Senate, is controlled by a different party from the one the president belongs to. Wilson was a Democrat, but the 1918 elections gave the Republicans a majority in the Senate. The Republicans were more isolationist than Wilson.

Check yourself

QUESTIONS

Q1 What are: (a) isolationism; (b) WASPs; (c) tariffs?

Q2 Why didn't the USA join the League of Nations?

REMEMBER! Cover the answers if you want to.

ANSWERS

A1
a) Isolationism is an American feeling of wanting to keep isolated from the rest of the world. It meant not joining any alliances, not getting involved in commitments to other countries, cutting off trade and immigration.
b) WASPs are White Anglo–Saxon Protestants.
c) Tariffs are duties which foreign-made goods had to pay on entering the USA.

A2 The USA did not join the League of Nations because the US Senate refused to ratify (agree) the Treaty of Versailles. The Senate was dominated by isolationist views and they feared that membership of the League would lead the USA into all kinds of foreign wars and obligations.

TUTORIALS

T1
a) *It is right to describe isolationism as a mood, rather than a policy. It was a feeling, an attitude, which led to all kinds of policies: refusal to join alliances, economic policy (tariffs), immigration policy. It also had a racist and intolerant side, which you will find out more about later in this chapter.*
b) *WASPs, as early arrivals in the USA, were more powerful than other national groups.*
c) *High tariffs were intended to help US industry by removing foreign competition.*

T2 *This US isolation is an important moment in twentieth-century history. You will see that it was one of the factors in the weakness and failure of the League (see chapter 8). You will also see how the USA tried to reverse the isolationism of 1919 by adopting the opposite policy after the Second World War (see chapter 10).*

PROSPERITY IN THE USA IN THE 1920S

The US economy was booming in the 1920s. Look at these figures of sales of goods:

	1919	1929
Cars	9 million	26 million
Telephones	10 million	20 million
Radios	60,000	10 million

The figures give you two main features of this boom:

- There was a huge increase in production in the 1920s. It has been called a second Industrial Revolution.
- It was a boom in **consumer goods** that is goods which people bought and used themselves. This compares with the first Industrial Revolution, which took place in the USA in the last part of the nineteenth century and was a boom in heavy industry: coal, iron, steel etc.

WHY DID THE US ECONOMY BOOM IN THE 1920S?

Raw materials

The USA is rich in the raw materials industry needs, like coal, iron and oil.

The results of the First World War

The USA had stayed out of the First World War for three years, until 1917. This meant:

- US industry did well selling weapons, ammunition and food to the warring countries of Europe.
- While the European countries were busy fighting, the USA took over many of their colonial markets.
- The great German chemical industry, which led the world before 1914, was held back by the war. The US chemical industry developed in its place, making fertilisers, dyes, plastics and explosives.
- US investors and bankers did well out of the war, so they had money to invest in new industries in the USA.

Tariffs

Tariffs on imports protected US industry from foreign competition (see p.136).

Laissez-faire

President Woodrow Wilson had put restrictions on US industry to protect the public. His successors as president in the 1920s (Harding 1920–23, Coolidge 1923–28, Hoover 1928–33) believed in leaving industry and business alone and kept taxes low. This policy is called *laissez-faire*.

New technology

Many of the successful industries of the 1920s were based on new technology: telephones, radio, artificial fibres, fridges and other electric goods. There was a huge electrification programme so that most US citizens, at least in the cities, could use electric home appliances.

The film industry boomed

California, with its months of clear sunshine, was ideal for filming and a suburb of Los Angeles called Hollywood grew up as the home of the industry. By 1930 eighty million cinema tickets were being sold a week in the USA alone, and Hollywood films were entertaining the world.

But the greatest success story was the car industry.

Henry Ford and the car industry

The first cars were all individually hand-made. Henry Ford revolutionised car production by setting up an **assembly-line** at his factory in Detroit in 1913. Each worker only had to do some small task as the car moved past. By 1927 one of Ford's famous Model T cars was coming off the assembly-line every ten seconds. Fifteen million were made in all.

The car industry led to the growth of the other industries which supplied it: plate glass, leather, rubber and steel. Increased car ownership led to more economic growth: road-building, the oil industry, petrol stations and repairs.

Not many of the goods sold so widely in the 1920s were new. But the effect of new technology was to make them cheap. Cars, radios, vacuum cleaners and so on had existed before 1920, but they were expensive luxuries. Now lots of people could afford them. The average price of a car in 1908, for example, was $850; in 1925 it was $250.

Advertising and sales

Selling millions of goods to a mass market needed new techniques of advertising. Posters and magazines all told the US public, in glowing terms, about the new goods on offer. Radio commercials brought the desire for new goods into every home. Teams of commercial travellers took samples to persuade local stores to order them. Shopping habits changed as chain stores, like Woolworths, expanded: there were 29,000 chain stores in 1918, 160,000 by 1929. Many more people began to buy on hire purchase: six out of ten cars were bought this way.

DID EVERYONE SHARE IN THIS PROSPERITY?

Foreign visitors were flabbergasted by what they saw of the USA in the 1920s, with its booming, bustling cities, full of cars. But that was not the whole picture, by any means.

Farmers

US agriculture was not prospering in the 1920s.

- Farmers had increased production during the First World War to sell food to Europe, but by the 1920s Europe was growing its own food again.

- High US tariffs protected US industry, but meant that foreigners did not have any dollars to buy US farm produce. Many countries put up their own tariffs in retaliation.

- US farmers suffered competition from Canadian farmers.

- US farmers were really the victims of their own success: they had cultivated new land, taken on new machines, so that they were **overproducing** food: more farm produce than they could sell. The result was lower and lower prices for their produce: wheat which sold for $1.83 a bushel in 1920 only fetched 38 cents a bushel in 1929.

The average annual income per head in the USA in 1929 was $681; the average farmer's income was $273. Nor were these just a small group: half of all US citizens lived in rural areas. Those people in rural areas who were not actually farmers worked in businesses dependent on agriculture, and shared the hard times. Not for them the new fridge and vacuum cleaner: even if they could afford it, very few rural areas had electricity. Rural Americans felt left out and isolated; six million left the land for the cities in the 1920s. Many of these were black farm labourers and small farmers from the southern USA.

The poor

Historians estimate that 42 per cent of US citizens were living below the poverty line. That is, they did not have enough money to feed, clothe and house themselves. These people were:

- The unemployed. New technology in industry often replaced jobs with machines. There were around two million unemployed throughout the 1920s.

- Workers in old industries – coal, textiles. They were facing stiff competition for their goods. Wages were low. At a time when $48 a week was considered a minimum, male coal miners were earning $18 and women $9 a week.

- Those in unskilled or casual jobs did not share in the boom, their wages were low and jobs uncertain. Only three in a hundred semi-skilled workers owned a car. Many of these poor workers were recent immigrants: Italians, Poles, Mexicans and black Americans recently arrived in the cities of the north from the southern states.

EXTRA POINTS

1. It was a very optimistic time: people believed that the USA was 'the land of opportunity'. Being optimistic about the future actually helped business grow: if things were going to get better then it was worth expanding your factory, or buying something more on hire purchase. And for the years 1920 to 1929, things *did* get better.

2. Low food prices were bad for farmers, but good for business, because it meant that workers did not have to be paid high wages.

3. The system of production which Henry Ford and other industrialists used, in which making something was broken down into lots of small tasks, was called Taylorism.

Check yourself

QUESTIONS

Q1　Look at this picture:

(a)　Use this picture to explain what an assembly-line is.
(b)　How did assembly-line methods change industry?

Figure 7.2
Henry Ford's assembly-line. The bodywork is just about to be slid on to the chassis

Q2　How widespread was prosperity in the USA in the 1920s?

Q3　Which groups did *not* take part in the boom?

ANSWERS

A1   a)   An assembly-line is a way of making complicated industrial goods by splitting up the whole process into lots of little tasks. One worker can then just do one task, over and over again, as the car (or whatever) goes past on a conveyor-belt.

       b)   Assembly-line methods changed industry by enabling goods to be made in huge quantities, more cheaply.

A2   The boom was really confined to well-off, city-dwelling Americans. This meant that over half the American people did not share it.

A3   The groups which did not take part in the boom were rural Americans, unemployed, those on low wages.

TUTORIALS

T1   a)   *The answer could refer more closely to the picture: it is not just a stimulus to get you started. So, you could point out that this is one of the big moments in the assembly-line, where the body is put on the chassis. the bodywork is lowered on to the chassis under its own weight.*

       b)   *You could also say that assembly-lines are expensive to set up: lots more capital is needed than for building a car in a workshop. It also means that workers do not have to be skilled, and so do not have to be paid high wages.*

T2   *It is hard to be exact of course – see answer to Question 3.*

T3   *A disproprtionate number of these were black or recent immigrants into the USA.*

THE ROARING TWENTIES

WHAT WAS IT LIKE TO LIVE IN THE USA IN THE 1920s?

The cities

It was in the huge, bustling cities of the USA that the Twenties seemed to roar the most. Just before 1920 the number of US citizens living in towns and cities exceeded the number living in rural areas for the first time in the history of the USA.

Cities were:

- Bigger, as people moved out to new suburbs and travelled in to work in their cars or by train.

- Higher, as skyscrapers were built (see Fig. 7.3).

In the streets of the cities there were:

- Lots of cars and lorries.

- Shops, especially large chainstores and department stores, where all the new consumer goods were on display.

- Cinemas, where Hollywood films were shown.

- Bars, where you could get a drink (illegally) (see p.142)

Figure 7.3
Skyscrapers in New York in the 1920s

- Clubs, where people danced new and lively dances, like the Charleston, to Jazz music, often played by black musicians (the other name for this period is 'The Jazz Age').

Rural Americans looked at this situation with dismay. The USA seemed to be passing them by. They disapproved of what they saw as a new immorality: more freedom for women (see below), easy sexual relations in films, divorce, buying things on hire purchase rather than paying for them outright.

Women

- **Before 1920**
  As in Britain, women in the USA in the early twentieth century were not equal with men and were subject to many restrictions. Girls were not allowed to mix freely with boys. They were expected to get married and stay at home looking after their children. For working-class women this was not possible as their families needed money, but most jobs were closed to them and any others were low-paid. They did not have the vote in most states. In New York it was illegal for women to smoke in public. Fashion reflected their restricted lives, with long dresses, tight waists and elaborate hairstyles.

- **The First World War and the Roaring Twenties**
  Women took on new jobs in the First World War while the men were away. In 1920 all women were given the vote. By 1929 ten million more women were working than in 1920, a 25 per cent increase. Divorce was made easier and the number of divorces doubled. '**Flappers**' was the name given to young, liberated women of the 1920s. They wore short hair, short skirts, smoked in public, drove cars, danced wildly, had their own sex lives.

- **Judgement**
  As with other aspects of the 1920s, the evidence can be misleading. Women did not enter a new age of equality. In spite of having the vote, hardly any women made careers in politics. They may have had jobs, but they were paid less than men for the same work and unable to get promotion. The flappers were a few, well-off, city girls. Most girls, especially in rural America, still had less personal freedom than boys, got married and stayed at home.

Prohibition

One cause which women, particularly rural and small-town women, took up passionately was the banning of alcoholic drink, known as Prohibition. Prohibition was introduced because organisations like the Anti-Saloon League (a saloon is an American word for a bar) and the Women's Christian Temperance Union believed that alcohol damaged family life: men spent money on alcohol which should have gone to buy the family food and clothes, it ruined their health, it caused them to lose their jobs, and so on. Many religious organisations and politicians supported Prohibition.

In 1919 the Eighteenth Amendment to the US constitution made the sale, manufacture or transport of alcohol illegal. At the same time the Volstead Act made the buying of alcohol illegal.

The Prohibitionists may have been right about the dangers of alcohol, but millions of US citizens were used to having a drink. They were not going to change their habits because of a change in the law. So ways were found, especially in the cities, of getting round it:

- Speakeasies: illegal bars.

- Moonshine: illegally-made alcohol.

- Bootlegging: smuggling alcohol into the USA.

A whole new police force had to be set up to enforce the law. In 1929 they poured over fifty million litres of illegal alcohol down the drains, although this was only a tiny fraction of the amount actually made.

The problem with Prohibition was that it made ordinary citizens into criminals. Ordinary police were reluctant to enforce the law and took bribes to 'turn a blind eye'. **Gangsters** took the place of ordinary drink manufacturers. Prohibition was an enormous opportunity for them. They controlled speakeasies and illegal alcohol supplies. The Chicago boss, Al Capone, made $100,000 a year from illegal businesses and openly murdered four hundred of his rivals. He claimed: 'All I do is supply a public demand' and in the circumstances of Prohibition, he was right. (In 1933 the government judged Prohibition to have failed and, by the Twenty-First Amendment, it was abolished.)

Intolerance

- **'Red Scare'**
  Some powerful Americans were scared of left-wing, or 'red', ideas. Known Socialists or Anarchists were harrassed by police. Some immigrants with these beliefs were deported back to Europe. Trade unions were attacked and some industrialists, like Henry Ford, refused to allow their employees to join a trade union. Trade union membership fell from five million to three million over the 1920s.

- **Racism**
  The Ku Klux Klan increased in membership in the 1920s. The roots of the Klan were among poor whites in the south, but it also had members in northern cities. Their leader was called the 'Imperial Wizard'. They wore white sheets with pointed hoods, and marched with burning crosses. They attacked mainly black Americans, but also Roman Catholics, Jews and foreigners. Victims were bullied, beaten up, even lynched. The Klan had five million members by 1925.

Black Americans

There were twelve million black Americans in the USA in 1920, the descendants of African slaves. Three-quarters of them lived in the south, where they suffered not only from the Ku Klux Klan, but from poverty and discrimination. They had been freed from slavery in 1865, but southern whites still kept them down. Black farmers were kept in debt. 'Jim Crow' laws ensured that they did not have the right to vote. They had separate and poorer schools and were barred from the using the same restaurants, transport, cinemas, toilets, beaches, parks, even the same drinking fountains as whites.

Over the 1920s 1.5 million black Americans left the south for the cities of the north.

In many ways their lives improved:

- They had a chance of getting a job.
- Some blacks did well and formed a new black middle class.
- They could get educated at black universities and colleges.
- There were black newspapers, magazines, literature.
- Popular black heroes appeared – sportsmen and jazz musicians. Jazz itself, created by black musicians, swept first the USA and then became the popular music of the western world.
- There was less obvious discrimination – no segregated buses or restaurants, for example.

In other ways they still faced difficulties.

- There was discrimination in jobs. Blacks were the last to be taken on, the first to be fired.
- There was discrimination in housing. Blacks were forced into ghettoes, like Harlem, New York and South Side, Chicago. Even recent immigrants, discriminated against by most whites, were hostile to blacks.

EXTRA POINTS ▶

1. Among the scandalous examples of intolerance in the 1920s were:

   a) The trial of two Italians, Sacco and Vanzetti. They were accused of robbery and murder, but the evidence against them was slim. However, the judge was biased against them because they were Anarchists. They were executed in 1927.

   b) In some states it was made illegal to teach Darwin's theory of evolution because it conflicted with a literal interpretation of the Bible.

2. The Ku Klux Klan declined rapidly after 1925 when one its leaders was convicted of a sex scandal.

3. The roots of Jazz lie in the country music of southern blacks – the blues – and the marching bands of New Orleans. These were adapted by black musicians in northern cities to fit new instruments and the tastes of mixed black and white club audiences.

Check yourself

QUESTIONS

Q1 What were: (a) skyscrapers, (b) flappers, (c) speakeasies, (d) Jazz?

Q2 Prohibition was called 'A great social experiment?' What does this mean and why did Prohibition fail?

Think about the word 'experiment'. What do you think it means? Think about the reasons *why it failed* – this is not a description of what happened. Make a list. Which do you think is the most important reason? Now use the writing plan below.

Start paragraph 1 by writing: 'Prohibition was an experiment because ... '

Start the next paragraph by writing: 'The main reason it failed was ... '

Put any other reasons you can think of into a paragraph starting: 'Other reasons for the failure of Prohibition are ... '

Q3 What problems are there in deciding whether the 1920s brought improvements to the lives of (a) American women, and (b) black Americans?

ANSWERS

A1
a) Skyscrapers were very tall buildings put up in US cities in the 1920s.
b) Flappers was the name given to young women of the 1920s who broke the rules about how women were supposed to behave by, for example, smoking in public, going out alone with men.
c) Speakeasies were bars, made illegal by Prohibition.
d) Jazz is a kind of popular music invented by black Americans.

A2
Prohibition was an experiment because it was an attempt to change people's habits, to make them more 'moral', by law. It was something no other country had tried – hence an experiment, something new.

The main reason it failed was because people were not willing to change their habits. The result was that ordinary people doing ordinary things were now breaking the law. Even after ten years, they were not willing to change. Millions of people, including the police, found ways of getting round the law, which brought it into widespread disrespect.

Other reasons for the failure of Prohibition were that it opened the way for gangsters to move into the drink business. In this way it did more harm than good. It also cost the country lots of money in trying to enforce the law.

A3
The main problem is that we are dealing with a large number of people. It is hard to generalise: *some* women may have gained more freedom, but many didn't. *Some* black Americans benefitted by moving north, but still 10.5 million stayed in poverty and segregation in the south.

TUTORIALS

T1
a) *Skyscrapers began in New York, where there was a shortage of space for offices on Manhatten Island, so they built upwards. Other cities were so impressed that they copied the style. New techniques of steel construction were needed.*

c) *Speakeasies usually had to pay the local police to leave them alone; if you didn't pay enough the police would 'raid' them.*

T2
See how the writing plan makes a nice, organised case out of a few basic ideas taken from this chapter.
What other ways can you think of in which governments have tried to make people better by law? Did it work?

T3
This answer has got the main point, which is that the focus of the question is on problems of finding out, not on describing what happened. Apart from the problem of making generalisations about the lives of millions of people, there is a problem of definition: what is improvement? Was a black American in an overcrowded apartment in a ghetto in a northern city, on low, casual wages, but able to walk down the street and go into any café or cinema, better or worse off than a relative who stayed back in the south?

There is also the problem of the sources: we may need to use more diaries and personal reminiscences to see how people really felt, rather than relying on secondary sources.

THE WALL STREET CRASH AND THE GREAT DEPRESSION

THE OVER-PRODUCTION CRISIS

As the 1920s drew towards the end, the US economy faced a crisis, although few people recognised it at first. It was a crisis of **over-production**. That is, US industry was producing more than it could sell. The boom had been based on selling consumer goods; this meant finding more and more people to buy fridges, telephones, vacuum cleaners etc. By the late 1920s the market was running out of customers. We have seen most of the reasons for this:

- Many Americans, probably more than half, were too poor. Farmers, unemployed and low wage earners had no money to spare for consumer goods after they had fed, clothed and housed themselves.

- Even the well-off could not go on buying and buying. There are limits to how many fridges you need.

- US industry could not sell abroad because other countries had put up tariffs on US imports in response to the US Fordney–McCumber Tariff (see p.136).

The most spectacular sign that all was not well was the Wall Street Crash.

THE BOOM IN SHARES

Suppose you want to start a company. You need money (capital). You may not have enough yourself, so you sell shares in your new company to get the money to set it up. For their shares, investors get two benefits if your company does well: first, you will pay the shareholders interest, a dividend, from your profits; second, because your company is doing well, other people might want to buy the shares at a higher price. Shareholders could sell their shares for more than paid you for them.

In the USA, shares are bought and sold in Wall Street, in New York. In the 1920s, dividends went up and share prices went up, year after year. It seemed an easy way to make money: you bought some shares, perhaps on borrowed money, and sold them again six months later at a profit. Lots of people were eager to join in: in 1920 four million Americans owned shares; by 1929 it was twenty million.

Then, in autumn 1929, some people began to get rid of their shares. Suddenly, there was a panic: everyone rushed to sell and prices fell fast. On 24 October 1929, thirteen million shares were sold. Prices plummeted. A share in one cigar company, for example, fell from $113 to $4 in a day. This was the Wall Street Crash.

WHAT CAUSED THE WALL STREET CRASH?

- Loss of confidence. Shares are only worth a lot of money if people believe things are going to go on getting better. As soon as there is any doubt, everyone loses confidence, no one will buy and prices drop. Some investors could see that the over-production crisis was looming and began to sell, sparking off the crash.

- Some people had bought shares 'on the margin'; that is, they had only paid 10 per cent of their value, expecting to pay off the rest when they sold them at a profit. When prices began to fall these **speculators** were in trouble and rushed to sell in order to cut their losses.

- Some banks had lent money to speculators to buy shares. They needed to cover their loans and rushed to sell.

WHAT WERE THE RESULTS OF THE WALL STREET CRASH?

- People who had invested heavily in shares were ruined. Speculators who had bought shares on the margin, at higher prices than they could sell them for, were bankrupted.

- Banks began to fail. There were lots of small banks in the USA. Some had lent out more money than they had on deposit. When the loans could not be paid back, the bank went broke. This meant that people who had put money in the bank, believing it to be safe, lost it all. Five thousand banks went broke between 1929 and 1933.

- There was a tremendous loss of confidence and fall in demand, which helped to cause the Great Depression.

THE GREAT DEPRESSION

By 1933, the worst year of the Depression:
- industrial production had fallen by 40 per cent
- wages had fallen by 60 per cent
- share prices had fallen by 80 per cent
- 14 million Americans were unemployed.

The diagram below shows how the US economy became locked into a downward spiral. You can see that the main cause was over-production, but that the Wall Street Crash made it all worse.

Figure 7.4
Causes of the Great Depression

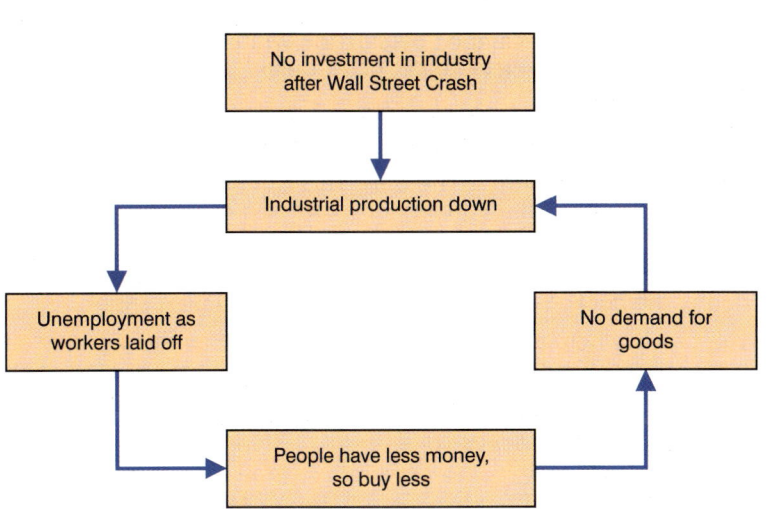

HOW DID THE GREAT DEPRESSION AFFECT THE AMERICAN PEOPLE?

Farmers

Farmers were already in an over-production crisis in the early 1920s. In the Depression things only got worse. It was not worth some farmers taking crops to market, because the price they would get was less than the freight charges. Many could not meet their mortgage repayments and had to sell up the farm they had worked on all their lives. In some cases farmers ganged up and forced banks at gunpoint not to put the farm up for sale.

In parts of the Mid-West soil erosion led to a 'dust bowl', in which the over-cropped soil on the farms simply blew away. Some farmers, forced off their land, loaded up their family and belongings and headed for California, hoping to find work picking fruit. These 'Okies' (from Oklahoma) or 'Arkies' (from Arkansas) found lots of others had the same idea.

In the cities

Americans believed in 'rugged individualism'; that is, each person should look after his or her own future. There was therefore no system of unemployment benefit ('dole') at all. Americans had grown up believing that in their 'land of opportunity' anyone could succeed. Now that things had gone wrong, they thought it was their fault and felt ashamed.

The busy streets were now quieter, with people who had lost their jobs begging or selling small items. Many had to resort to picking over the city rubbish dumps in search of food or something to sell. Those who could not pay their rent were forced out and slept in the parks, on benches or in shacks made of cardboard packing-cases. They queued for charity soup kitchens or bread hand-outs. Some left home and travelled around, looking for work. These 'hoboes' often rode illegally in railway goods wagons.

The government

President Hoover had been elected just before the boom ended. He believed it would go on for ever and claimed that the USA was going to be the first country in the world to put an end to poverty. When the Depression came, he stuck to his belief that it was not the job of government to interfere in business and things would get better in time. He also insisted it was not the job of government, but of charities, to help those in poverty.

He was deeply unpopular as a result. People in cardboard shacks called them 'Hoovervilles'. In 1932 20,000 ex-soldiers went to Washington to ask for their 'bonus', their war pension, to be paid early, as they were in financial trouble. Some of this Bonus Army camped outside the White House. Hoover sent troops, with guns and tear-gas, to get rid of them.

EXTRA POINTS ▶

1. Clearly one of the reasons for the over-production crisis was the **distribution of wealth** in the USA. This can be put statistically: the richest 5 per cent of the population earned 32 per cent of earnings, while the poorest 42 per cent earned only 10 per cent of earnings.

2. The boom in shares was spectacular: share prices rose 60 per cent during the decade, while wages only rose by 10 per cent.

3. The Crash, when it came, was also made worse by the fact that some companies did not really make anything at all: they just made money by buying and selling shares. When confidence in these companies collapsed, it brought down proper companies too.

Check yourself

QUESTIONS

Q1 Describe in one sentence each:

(a) The Wall Street Crash.
(b) The Great Depression

Q2 Look at the main central spiral in Figure 7.4 (p.147) and explain it in your own words.

Q3 Explain President Hoover's attitude to the Depression crisis.

REMEMBER! Cover the answers if you want to.

ANSWERS

A1
a) The Wall Street Crash was a rapid fall in the value of shares in October 1929.
b) The Great Depression was the mass unemployment and hardship in the USA which began in 1929.

A2 Industry was over-producing, so production was cut. If you were producing less you did not need so many workers, so some were sacked, some worked part-time on lower wages. People who were unemployed or on lower pay had less money to spend. This meant less demand for goods. So industry made less and needed less workers, and so on.

A3 Hoover believed what nearly everyone believed in the USA in the 1920s: that if you leave the capitalist economy alone, if you let business look after itself and keep government interference to a minimum, everything will go well. And up to 1929 it did. Like everyone else in the 1920s, too, he believed in 'rugged individualism': people should not be coddled, supported by government welfare because that made people weak and dependent. The trouble was that these views were no longer appropriate for the Depression years.

TUTORIALS

T1 *It is useful sometimes to get your thoughts together into one sentence: sometimes this is harder than writing several descriptive sentences! In (a) it is worth saying what Wall Street is: the New York Stock Exchange. In (b) the unemployment was the result of a decline in economic activity, both in industry and agriculture: this was the real Depression.*

T2 *The Wall Street Crash made this situation worse by cutting investment in industry and undermining people's confidence. It was very hard for the USA to break out of this cycle, once it was locked into it. Trying to sell abroad was no answer as most of the world was in depression at this time. This is why the Depression lasted so long.*

T3 *Hoover was not a nasty man, but too rigid in his ideas. Individuals were unable to deal with the Depression because the forces at work were beyond their control. It may be that the economy would right itself again: but what was the starving family going to eat tonight?*

As you will see on the next page, a new President was coming along with very different answers and a more understanding outlook.

ROOSEVELT AND THE NEW DEAL

Hoover's opponent in the 1932 Presidential election was Franklin D Roosevelt.

Franklin Delano Roosevelt (FDR), was born in 1882 into a rich family and led an easy life as a young man. Then, in 1921, he caught polio. For three years he struggled to regain the use of his limbs, to sit and then to stand. His own suffering seemed to give him more understanding of other people's. He was elected Governor of New York in 1928 and made the state government do what it could to relieve the hardship of the Depression.

FDR ran an inspiring campaign. He did not have any detailed worked-out plans, but he seemed ready to try something new to improve the situation. Unlike Hoover, he was not stuck in 1920s' ideas about keeping government out of things. He was even prepared to spend government money to start the economy going again, something Hoover regarded with horror. Above all, he seemed optimistic. His most striking promise was 'I pledge you, I pledge myself, to a new deal for the American people'. He won the election easily and immediately began his New Deal. His aims were:

- Relief for those in hardship.
- Recovery of the economy so that people could get jobs.
- Protection of people's homes and savings.
- Improvement of the USA.

As you look at the New Deal measures described below, try to see which one of these four aims he was trying to meet with each one.

THE FIRST HUNDRED DAYS OF THE NEW DEAL, 1933

In his first hundred days in office FDR began a whirlwind of activity. New government agencies were set up, often known by their initial letters.

Emergency Banking Act

On the second day of his presidency, he ordered all the banks to be closed. Government officials looked at their records and those that were financially sound were allowed to re-open. Public confidence in the banks was restored.

FERA (Federal Emergency Relief Agency)

$500 million was made available to help those in dire need. It was spent on soup kitchens, blankets, free nursery schools for children of the unemployed, etc.

CCC (Civilian Conservation Corps)

Young people were given a job for six months at a time so that they could get used to the idea of work. They did environmental work: planting trees in National Parks, digging drainage ditches, flood prevention schemes. The government paid them a wage of $30 a month, of which they had to send $25 home to their families. Two million people (of whom only 8,000 were women), worked on CCC schemes.

AAA (Agricultural Adjustment Administration)

Prices of farm produce were raised by setting fixed quotas for most products, so that they did not grow too much. The cotton crop was ploughed into the ground, and pigs slaughtered in order to keep up the price. Farmers were paid not to cultivate some land. Farm incomes rose by 50 per cent by 1936.

NIRA (National Industrial Recovery Act)

This had two parts.

- **Part 1 set up the PWA (Public Works Administration).**
  This spent $3.3 billion on building schools, roads, bridges, airports, etc. and giving jobs to millions of people.
- **Part 2 The 'Blue Eagle'.**
  The government worked with employers in setting decent wages and working conditions. Goods made under this agreement displayed a 'Blue Eagle' badge.

TVA (Tennessee Valley Authority)

The land of the Tennessee River valley was badly eroded, there were frequent floods, farmers were poor, hardly any had electricty. Seven states were involved, so no one was able to deal with it.

The TVA was set up to cover the whole area. Dams were built on the rivers (see Fig. 7.5).

Figure 7.5
Dam in the Tennessee Valley

These controlled floods, created lakes which made a new inland waterway and generated electicity. Building them also created jobs. Industries which needed lots of water and electricity, like aluminium smelting and paper making were established and provided more jobs. The number of farms with electricity rose from 3 per cent to 80 per cent by 1943. Farmers were taught new farming techniques to prevent soil erosion and 'model farms' were encouraged to try out new ideas.

● **Government spending**
FDR believed in spending government money – even more than he could raise through taxes – to get the economy going again. This diagram shows the idea:

Figure 7.6
New Deal spending

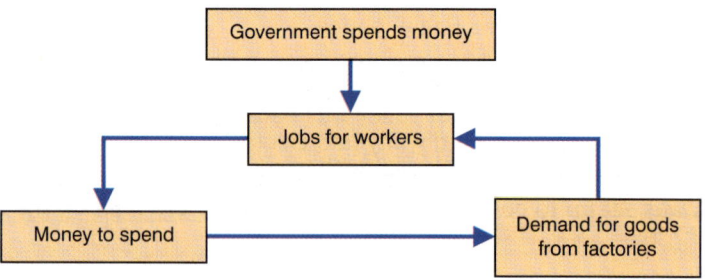

The British economist J.M.Keynes approved of this way of 'spending your way out of trouble'. Many conservative Americans and business people did not. They argued that FDR should not spend what he did not have.

● **The Supreme Court**
Under the US constitution, laws passed by the government can be reviewed by the Supreme Court to see if they are in line with the constitution of the USA drawn up in 1787. It takes time, but in 1935 the Supreme Court declared the NIRA illegal and did the same in 1936 to the AAA.

Despite these problems FDR won the 1936 election easily: 'Everyone is against the New Deal except the voters,' he joked. With this support, FDR thought of adding enough new judges who agreed with him to the Supreme Court in order to out-vote the others, but his supporters warned him that he should not meddle with the constitution. In fact the NIRA and the AAA had done most of what they were set up to do and new laws were passed in a Second New Deal. Gradually the Supreme Court changed its view anyway.

THE SECOND NEW DEAL

● The Wagner Act, 1935 gave US workers the right to join a trade union.

● Social Security Act, 1935 began a basic system of welfare – old age pensions, unemployment benefit and sick pay. It did not cover health care, and was set at a lower level than welfare in Europe, but it was better than nothing.

● WPA (Works Progress Administration) involved more public spending to provide jobs. 8.5 million people worked on WPA schemes, for parks, hospitals and schools. Writers, artists and photographers were also employed.

CRITICISMS OF THE NEW DEAL

● It was inconsistent. For example, measures intended to help farmers actually made life harder for the poor by making food more expensive.

● Right-wing Americans complained that the New Deal was spending money FDR did not have and just turning millions of Americans into government employees. In 1937 he decided to try to meet these criticisms by cutting government spending. Unemployment immediately rose again.

- Left-wingers criticised the New Deal for not doing enough to change the USA.
  - The New Deal did little for the very poor.
  - Black Americans continued to be disadvantaged and made no progress towards civil rights in these years. FDR was dependent on support from white southern Democrats, who would have blocked any attempt to help black people. New Deal laws allowed blacks to be paid lower than whites. The AAA quota system led to millions of poor black farmers being pushed off their land.
  - Women made little progress towards equality. For example, they were still paid less than men for the same work. FDR did appoint one woman to a senior position in his government – Frances Perkins, Secretary of Labor.
  - Revolutionary ideas like the TVA were not copied elsewhere.
- Recovery was only partial: spending in 1937 was only 75 per cent of what it was in 1929. Unemployment was still 9.5 million when the Second World War broke out in 1939. Contracts for war industries began to bring down the figures.

In spite of these criticisms the New Deal did:

- Restore the confidence of the American people in their country and in their capacity to deal with their problems.
- Retain democracy and most of the basics of US economy and way of life intact.

Roosevelt was immensely popular. He was able to communicate with ordinary Americans, especially through his 'fireside chats' – radio broadcasts. He is the only US President to have been elected four times: 1932, 1936, 1940 and 1944.

 **EXTRA POINTS**

1. Two further New Deal agencies protected people's property by giving money loans. These were the FCA (Farm Credit Administration) and the HOLC (Home Owners Loan Corporation).

2. The New Deal used **federal** powers (that is, the government of the whole USA, based in Washington) to deal with the crisis of the Depression. During the twelve years of Republican rule, 1920–32, federal power had been little used. FDR gave the Federal government a new role: dealing with a crisis which was too big for individual states to deal with.

Check yourself

QUESTIONS

Q1 List the New Deal measures which:
(a) restored confidence (b) provided jobs
and (c) improved the USA.

Q2 Compare the diagrams of Figure 7.4 (p.147)
and Figure 7.6 (p.152). How did the New
Deal change the downward spiral in Figure
7.4 to the upward spiral of Figure 7.6?

Q3 Do the criticisms listed here mean that the
New Deal was a failure?

REMEMBER! Cover the answers if you want to.

ANSWERS

A1
a) Emergency Banking Act.
b) CCC, PWA, TVA, WPA.
c) CCC, TVA, WPA.

A2 When unemployed people got jobs, they got
money in their pockets. This meant they
could buy goods, so there was some revival
of demand. Factories felt it was worthwhile
taking on workers, or putting their staff on
full pay again, because someone wanted
their goods. This meant more money to
spend, and so on.

A3 The New Deal was clearly only a partial
success. With unemployment still high even
when the USA entered the Second World
War in 1941, and demand still not up to
1929 levels, it did not achieve total
recovery.

The criticisms of the right may by true, but
the New Deal never set out to abide by
right-wing economic ideas. The left-wing
criticisms are fair points, but the New Deal
was not a radical government; it did not try
to reform US society, or change it. It set out
to preserve it and restore it.

The New Deal should only be judged by its
own aims. In these it was quite successful:
probably as successful as possible in a
worldwide depression. FDR's underlying
intention was to give people back their
optimism, their hope in the future, and in
this he largely succeeded.

TUTORIALS

T1 *This list is worth doing to get you thinking about the
New Deal, but really several of the agencies had
overlapping aims. Job-creation, through the PWA, for
example, helped to restore confidence that the USA was
on the road to recovery. The TVA certainly achieved all
three aims.*

T2 *The key difference, which reversed the spiral, was
government intervention: spending money to create jobs.
FDR was prepared to do this, to spend money, even money
the government did not have, to achieve this reversal.*

T3 *The New Deal was not like Stalin's Five-Year Plans (see
chapter 6) or like Hitler's Germany (see chapter 4).*

*That is, it was not calculated by the government to a
blueprint. It was a bunch of ideas, some of which
worked and some of which did not: FDR expected some
not to. It is not surprising that it was inconsistent.*

*Even more, it was democratic. FDR had to stand for
election four times. People were not put in labour camps
if they disagreed with it or did not fit in with it. It did
preserve a lot of things in US society which were wrong:
racial discrimination, low pay, sex discrimination, for
example. But it also preserved a healthy democracy.*

EXAM PRACTICE

Sample Student's Answers & Examiner's Comments

---

1 Why did the 1920s boom in the USA end? (15)

The boom in the USA in the 1920s was based on selling consumer goods. By 1929 it was clear that US industry was producing more than it could sell. Income was unequally distributed in the USA, with some very rich and lots of people very poor. This meant that many people were too poor to buy consumer goods which were still luxuries to them, while the very rich could not go on buying for ever.

Some people realised this by 1929. They began to sell their shares. This led to a financial collapse, the Wall Street Crash. Millions of shares were sold, at lower and lower prices. Many people were ruined and some banks collapsed. The bankruptcy of many people, and the bank failures, shattered people's confidence in the future. The boom ended and the USA entered the Great Depression.

8/15

EXAMINER'S COMMENTS

MARK SCHEME

Level 1	Describes boom and crash	1–3 marks
Level 2	Describes and blames Wall Street Crash	4–7 marks
Level 3	Explains one reason for end of boom	8–11 marks
Level 4	Developed account includes several reasons, well-explained and supported.	12–15 marks

The candidate here has realised that the boom ended for reasons deeper than just the Wall Street Crash, so goes into Level 3. However, it is very thin on detailed factual support, so stays at the bottom of that level: only 8 marks.

The kinds of information which, if included, would have got the answer up to 11 (still in Level 3) are, for example:

● What kinds of things are consumer goods? (cars, radios, telephones, electrical appliances like fridges etc.)

● Some of the people who missed out on the boom (unemployed, farmers, people on low wages).

● Distribution of income (see figures on p.139).

To reach Level 4, the answer should have dealt with other causes of instability: export trade was weak because of high US tariffs; speculation on Wall Street; lack of government intervention.

> 2   Read this source and answer the questions which follow:
>
> 'He drove his old car into a town. Where can we sleep the night? Well, there's a Hooverville on the edge of the river.
>
> He never asked again, for there was a Hooverville on the edge of every town.
>
> The rag-town lay close to water. The houses were tents, weed-thatched enclosures, paper houses, a great junk-pile.
>
> He scoured the countryside for work and the little money he had went for petrol to look for work.'
>
>   from *The Grapes of Wrath*, by John Steinbeck, published in 1939
>
> (a)   How did Hoovervilles get their name?   (2)
>
>   They were named after President Hoover   *1/2*

EXAMINER'S COMMENTS

MARK SCHEME

Level 1	Names President Hoover	**1 mark**
Level 2	Notes sarcasm in using his name	**2 marks**

The mark scheme tells you what you need to know. The two marks should have been a clue that just mentioning Hoover was not quite enough. Hoover had claimed that the USA was about to abolish poverty, so poor people took his name for their shacks.

> (b)   Why were so many people living in Hoovervilles at that time?   (5)
>
>   There was a Hooverville in every town, as the source says, because of the Great
>   Depression. This had made many people homeless and so they had to go there.   *3/5*

EXAMINER'S COMMENTS

MARK SCHEME

Level 1	Explains in terms of Depression being widespread and severe	**1–2 marks**
Level 2	Explains in terms of homelessness and people moving around seeking work	**3–4 marks**
Level 3	Includes understanding of lack of any welfare as contributing to problem	**5 marks**

The lack of any form of welfare system in the USA during the Great Depression meant that people had to get out of their homes or farms if they could pay the rent and had to look for work or starve. Hence the scale of the Hoovervilles, a feature not seen in Britain or Germany even at the height of the Depression.

Questions to Answer

The answers to Questions 3 and 4 can be found on pp.272 and 273

3   Look at this picture of a migrant family's shack.

Which of the two sources, the extract from the novel *The Grapes of Wrath* or
the photograph, do you consider most useful for finding out about the effects
of the Depression on the USA? Explain your answer.   (7)

4   Why didn't the USA join the League of Nations?   (10)

HOW WAS THE LEAGUE OF NATIONS SET UP?

After the mud, death and destruction of the First World War, many ordinary people felt a strong desire to find a peaceful way of solving disputes between nations. US President Woodrow Wilson expressed this in a proposal for a League of Nations, the last of his Fourteen Points (see chapters 2 and 3). It was one reason why he was so enthusiastically welcomed when he visited Europe in 1919.

But how should it work? Who should be members? What powers should it have?

Wilson was told to come up with the details. Through all the tough bargaining of the Treaty negotiations he clung hard to his idea of a League of Nations. It was written into each Treaty.

The plans were based on what they thought had gone wrong in 1914. One historian has pointed out that the League was really set up to prevent the First World War happening again! Events from 1919 to 1939 proved rather different from 1914, however, which caused problems, as we shall see.

WHAT WAS THE LEAGUE SUPPOSED TO DO?

- Bring together all nations in a parliament to discuss and settle disputes peacefully.
- Improve people's living and working conditions; help people to become better off by improving international trade. They believed that injustice and poverty were important causes of war.
- Make war impossible by persuading all nations to disarm.
- If one country was aggressive to another, the League would force the aggressor to back down by:
  - Pressure of world opinion
  - World trade ban
  - Force if necessary.

HOW WOULD IT WORK?

The Assembly was a parliament of all nations. It met once a year. One nation, one vote. Decisions had to be unanimous.

The Council met more often. It could meet quickly in an emergency. Its permanent members were Britain, France, Japan and Italy plus between four and eleven other countries. The four permanent members had a veto. It could recommend action to stop an aggressor.

Secretariat The officials of the League.

Court of International Justice at The Hague was intended to settle disputes by international law.

International Labour Organisation (ILO) worked to improve conditions for workers all over the world.

Commissions These special agencies dealt with mandates (former colonies of Germany and her allies, see chapter 3); refugees; slavery; health.

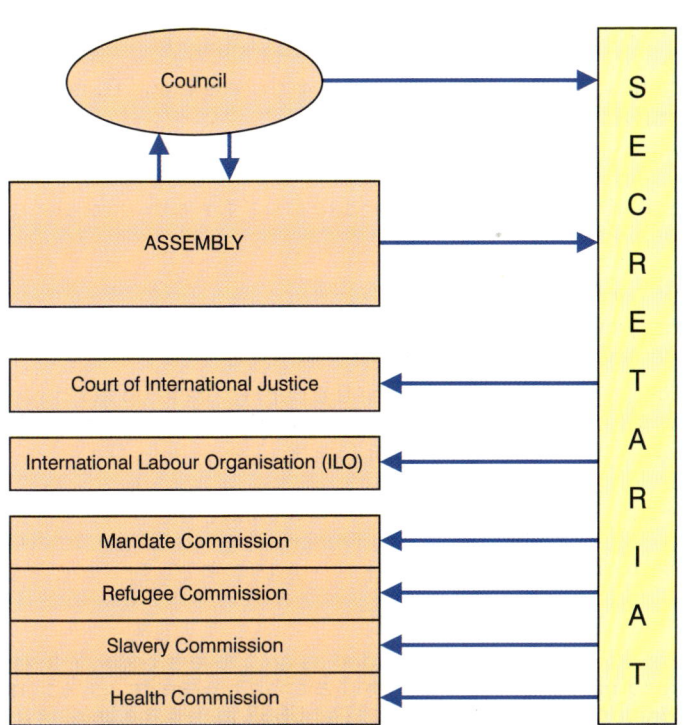

Figure 8.1
*The structure of the
League of Nations. It met
at Geneva in neutral Switzerland*

Figure 8.2
*The Assembly of the
League of Nations in session*

PROBLEMS OF MEMBERSHIP

There were forty-two members at the beginning. This rose to a peak of sixty in the 1930s.

The USA never joined

When President Wilson returned to the USA he found that public opinion had turned against him. This change is explained more fully in chapter 7, p.134, but in summary, many US citizens:

- feared membership of the League would drag the USA into more wars.

159

- disagreed with the terms of the Treaty of Versailles, and membership of the League involved signing the Treaty.
- were not keen on joining closely with Britain and France, two imperialist countries.
- did not agree with trade bans as a weapon.

So the country with the greatest power and moral force to make the League work was not a member.

Britain and France

This threw the weight of making the League work on to Britain and France. But they each had their own priorities:

- Britain wanted to hold on to the Empire, build up her trade again and stay clear of European conflicts.
- France wanted to keep Germany down.

Which would Britain and France put first in a conflict: their own aims or the aims of the League? Would Britain and France act on their own, or always work through the League?

The USSR

This other powerful country was regarded as an outsider because it was Communist and because Lenin's government had broken its agreements with its allies in order to get out of the war. (The USSR joined the League in 1934.)

The victors of 1918

The League was dominated by those who had won the war and dedicated to enforcing the terms of the Treaties. Germany and other defeated nations were not members at first. They bitterly resented the terms of the Treaties of 1919 (see p.52) and wanted to change them. They also therefore resented the League.

White Imperialists

White European nations dominated the League. Britain refused to build an anti-racist statement into becoming a member of the League.

EXTRA POINT ▶

The commitment of Britain and France to the League was always a matter of doubt. They had set up a Conference of Ambassadors in 1919 to ensure that the Treaty was kept to. When the League was set up this group was no longer needed, but they found it convenient to keep it going, often by-passing the League.

Check yourself

QUESTIONS

Q1 Where did the League of Nations meet, and why?

Q2 Which nations were on the Council of the League, and why?

ANSWERS

A1 The League met in Geneva. This is because Geneva is in Switzerland, a country which was always neutral.

A2 Britain, France, Japan, Italy plus other nations in rotation. The League had to combine the idealism of making all nations equal in the Assembly, with the realistic fact that some nations were much stronger than others. Putting these four nations on the Council recognised that the League could not do much without them anyway.

TUTORIALS

T1 *It is important to realise that the League was set up with great popular idealism. Many ordinary people hoped it would succeed. Neutrality, not belonging to one side or the other, and acting on behalf of the League, not yourself, were an important part of this idealism.*

T2 *The inclusion of these four nations on the Council also kept in being some of the criticisms of the League: they were the victors of 1918; three were white European imperial nations; when Germany and the USSR joined, should these powerful countries become permanent members of the Council?*

WAS THE LEAGUE SUCCESSFUL IN THE 1920S?

SUCCESSES

The agencies of the League showed the need for an international organisation to solve international problems:

- Millions of refugees from the First World War were helped to return to their homes;
- The Health Committee began work to reduce leprosy, yellow fever and malaria worldwide;
- An international highway code and shipping signals were agreed;
- Slave labour and the use of dangerous chemicals were stopped.

Border disputes settled included:

- **Upper Silesia, 1921**
  This area was disputed between Poland and Germany. The League held a plebiscite (vote) and used the results to split the area according to what its people wanted.

- **Åalund Islands, 1921**
  These islands in the Baltic were disputed by Finland and Sweden. After an enquiry, the League awarded them to Finland, which Sweden accepted.

- **Greek invasion of Bulgaria, 1925**
  The League condemned Greece, which withdrew its troops.

FAILURES

- **Vilna, 1920**
  This was the largest city in Lithuania, and was made the capital of the new country. However, the majority of its population were Poles and a Polish army seized the city. France wanted to keep on the right side of Poland and Britain was not prepared to act alone, so the League did nothing.

- **Greece and Turkey, 1920–22**
  Turkey refused to accept the terms of the Treaty of Sèvres (see p.50). They attacked the Greeks and drove them out of Smyrna. The League failed to stop this war, even though one of its main purposes was to enforce the 1919 peace settlement.

- **The Ruhr, 1923**
  When Germany stopped reparations payments, France and Belgium did not refer their grievance to the League, but acted on their own. They sent troops into the Ruhr to seize German industries (for more on this, see p.54).

- **Corfu, 1923**
  An Italian general was murdered in Greece. Mussolini, dictator of Italy, was furious. He sent Italian forces to shell and then occupy the Greek island of Corfu. Greece appealed to the League. This looked like a serious dispute and the League acted fast: Italian troops had to withdraw and Greece would have to pay compensation when the general's murderers were found. Mussolini then went behind the back of the League to Britain and France who made Greece pay up at once. Mussolini boasted of his triumph: he had got what he wanted by using aggression – a bad sign for the future.

DISARMAMENT AND PEACE

Several attempts were made in the 1920s to ensure peace in the world. These were often made outside the League. Did this matter?

- **1922, Washington Treaty**
  An agreement was signed by the USA, Britain, France, Japan and Italy to limit the size of their navies and not to build any more battleships for ten years. This seemed a positive step, and the fact that the USA was not in the League did not seem to matter.

- **1923, Proposals for a Disarmament Treaty**
  These were rejected by Britain. Plans for a Disarmament Conference were drawn up in 1926, but not fully agreed until 1931 (see p.166).

- **1925, Locarno Pact**
  At a conference held at Locarno, Switzerland, Germany's Foreign Minister, Stresemann, agreed:
  - To accept the boundaries with France and Belgium laid down at Versailles.
  - To accept that the Rhineland was a de-militarised zone.

■ To refer any disputes to the League.

Germany had apparently accepted the terms of the Treaty of Versailles at last.

● Under the Dawes Plan of 1924, the German economy was reviving and reparations were being paid. The British and French economies were also doing better. In this general atmosphere of co-operation – called the Locarno Honeymoon (see p.64) – Germany joined the League in 1926.

● 1928, Kellogg–Briand Pact. Kellogg (representing the USA) and Briand (France) got fifteen major nations, including the USSR, and over thirty smaller ones to sign an agreement never to go to war.

CONCLUSION

By 1928 the prospects for peace looked quite good. Business was doing well; world leaders had made agreements outlawing war; Germany seemed to have put aside her bitterness; the League had had some success in solving disputes.

But underlying resentments were unchanged:

● Many Germans were still bitter about the Treaty of Versailles. The Locarno Treaty secured Germany's western boundaries, but made no mention of those on the east: that seemed to suggest that they could be altered.

● If so, where did that leave countries like Poland and Czechoslovakia?

● France was still terrified of Germany. They viewed German economic recovery with alarm and made military alliances in eastern Europe. How did these square with France's support for the League?

 **EXTRA POINTS**

1. 1922, Rapallo Treaty: USSR and Germany re-establish diplomatic relations.

2. Stresemann believed that he could get more for Germany by negotiation than by defiance, but his aims were still to alter the terms made at Versailles. The Young Plan, 1929, further reduced the reparations Germany had to pay.

Check yourself

QUESTIONS

Q1 How much disarmament had been achieved by the end of the 1920s?

Q2 'Making the League work meant sinking your own interests and putting the League first. Nations were usually reluctant to do this.' How accurate is this statement? Use examples from the 1920s to illustate your answer.

163

ANSWERS

A1 Very little. The Washington naval agreement stopped any new ships being built, but that is about all. It seemed impossible even to get a disarmament conference started. The Kellogg–Briand Pact, 1928, did nothing to reduce arms, although nations promised not to use them.

A2 This statement is mostly true. There are examples, from the early 1920s, when the post-war determination to seek peaceful settlements was strong, of nations agreeing to accept the League's decisions even if they went against what they most wanted: Silesia, 1921 and the Åalund Islands, 1921.

There are more important examples on the other hand: Mussolini was prepared to bully and threaten over the Corfu Incident, 1923, to get his own way. France and Belgium chose to invade the German Ruhr in 1923. Even more seriously, France made military alliances with Poland and Czechoslovakia.

Most of the serious diplomacy of these years went on outside the League: the Dawes Plan 1924, the Locarno Pact, 1925, the Kellogg–Briand Pact, 1928. Clearly, most countries still preferred to do things the old way.

TUTORIALS

T1 *The nations which had been disarmed by the Treaties, Germany, Austria and Hungary, were very bitter about the failure of disarmament plans. They felt they had been forced to disarm and that the other nations were hypocrites. It increased their suspicion of the League.*

T2 *This is a well-organised and well-balanced answer. It makes good use of factual information to support the points you want to make: it does not just tell us the whole story of the 1920s from one end to the other. It has a point of view.*

None of the criticisms you make of countries in the 1920s mattered much at the time: there were no serious crises, economies were improving and all seemed well. With hindsight, however, we can see that attitudes had not in fact changed: France still feared Germany; Germany still wanted revenge; Italy wanted glory; Britain wanted to keep clear; eastern European nations wanted security, and so on. Nearly all of these national aims were being met outside the League.

When things got serious in the 1930s the League had not established itself as the 'normal' way of doing things.

WAS THE LEAGUE SUCCESSFUL IN THE 1930s?

We have seen that the League did not always work very well in the 1920s; how would it work in the period of the great worldwide depression?

HOW DID THE GREAT DEPRESSION AFFECT THE LEAGUE OF NATIONS?

- Depressed economies, unemployment and falling trade meant that countries found it hard not put themselves first. Banning trade with a country which had been aggressive, for example, could hit the trade of those imposing the ban as much as the one they were trying to punish.

- Some countries turned to dictatorship and dictators turned to foreign wars as a way of distracting their people from hardships at home. Japan, Italy and Germany all did this.

- Countries became more selfish, clearly putting their own interests first. France, for example, began work on the Maginot Line, a huge set of fortifications along the German border.

In three crises, in Manchuria in 1931, over disarmament in 1933, and in Abyssinia in 1935, the League was seen to fail. They are like case-studies of the problems which in the end stopped the League from being an effective peacekeeping organisation.

Manchuria

Japan had become a successful industrialised nation, but the Depression forced them to find new markets. Many leading Japanese, especially in the powerful and important army, looked with envy at European empires in the East and wanted to build up an empire of their own. They already possessed Korea and had their eyes on the huge and badly-governed provinces of China.

Figure 8.3
China, Japan and Manchuria

In 1931 the army invaded Manchuria, in northern China (see Fig. 8.3). All efforts by the Japanese government to stop the army action failed. By 1932 they had taken over Manchuria, and began to move into the rest of China. Although Japan was on the Council of the League it seemed a classic case of right and wrong: what would the League do?

- It took nearly a year to investigate the situation, while Japan completed her conquest.

- The report said Japan was wrong. Japan simply left the League.

- Sanctions were imposed on Japan, but the two nations which did most trade with Japan – the USA and the USSR – were not in the League and so not bound to take part in the trade ban. The nations in the League could not even agree to ban sales of weapons to Japan.

Conclusion:

- The League seemed powerless to stop the aggressive actions of a powerful nation.

Disarmament

The nations of the League had failed to agree about disarmament in the 1920s but a Disarmament Conference finally got under way in 1932. The problem was: should all nations reduce their armaments to Germany's level, or should Germany be allowed to rearm up to everyone else's? Both options were very unpopular.

In 1933 Hitler became Chancellor of Germany and immediately began to rearm. He rejected disarmament plans from League members as hypocrisy and took Germany out of the League in 1933.

Conclusions:

- The failure of the League to disarm in the 1920s left it in a weak position to argue against Hitler.

- France and Britain were split over how to treat Germany: France wanted to keep Germany weak; Britain felt Germany had a point. In fact, in 1935 Britain made her own naval agreement with Germany, allowing German naval rearmament up to 35 per cent of British strength.

- In a depression, rearmament was one way several countries took of helping industry. Several countries began to rearm from 1933 onwards.

- The Disarmament Conference failed totally: another war seemed to loom ahead.

Abyssinia

This country, now called Ethiopia, was one of the few countries left in Africa which was not a colony. Back in 1896 the Abyssinians had defeated an Italian invasion. The Italian dictator Mussolini wanted a glorious victory to win popularity at home. In 1935 he threatened to invade (see Fig. 8.4). Haile Selassie, the Emperor of Abyssinia, appealed to the League. Again it seemed a clear-cut case of right and wrong, and much nearer home than Manchuria. What would the League do?

The problem this time was that Britain and France did not want to make an enemy of Mussolini; they saw him as an important ally against Hitler. They feared that tough policies against him would push him into friendship with Hitler. For most of 1935 they did nothing. They even made an alliance with Italy, the Stresa Front, at which Abyssinia was not discussed.

Thinking he could get away with it, Mussolini invaded Abyssinia, using all the weapons of modern warfare such as gas and flame-throwers. The League called for sanctions against him. There were delays for two months while they discussed whether to include oil and fuel. Britain and France could have stopped all supplies getting to the Italian troops as they controlled the Suez Canal (see Fig. 8.4), but kept it open for Italian shipping. Some idea of the

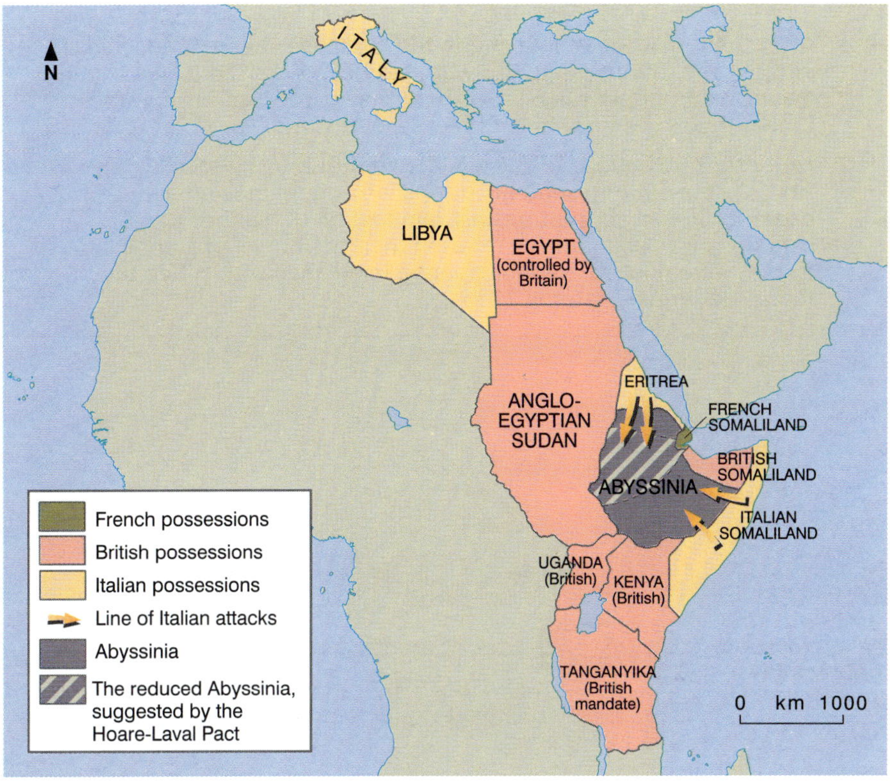

Figure 8.4
Map of Abyssinia

dilemma which sanctions produced was the information the British government received that a ban on coal exports to Italy would cost 30,000 coalminers their jobs: was this too high a price to pay for acting as League police?

The reluctance of Britain and France to work through the League was shown by the Hoare–Laval Plan. This was a secret plan worked out by the foreign ministers of Britain and France on their own to let Mussolini have most of Abyssinia. There were howls of protest when it was revealed.

Conclusion:

- The League was seen to have totally failed. War now seemed likely sooner or later.

SUMMARY OF THE PROBLEMS OF THE LEAGUE

- Membership. The absence of the USA in particular, but also the USSR, severely weakened the League.
- It was too closely linked to the Treaties of 1919. This meant it was regarded with suspicion by those who had lost badly by those treaties.
- Members of the League, especially Britain and France, who, in the absence of the USA had to take the lead, were always torn between self-interest and the needs of the League. Usually self-interest won.
- Sanctions were hard to put into action.
- It had no armed force to keep the peace or intervenen in a war.
- It worked too slowly.
- By the 1930s dictators, like Mussolini and Hitler, or army leaders, as in Japan, were quite prepared to defy the League.

167

EXTRA POINTS ▶

1. After their invasion of Manchuria the Japanese called it Manchukuo, and put the Chinese Emperor who had been deposed in 1911 on the throne as a puppet ruler. From there they carried on further into China. It was the beginning of the Second World War in the East.

2. Hitler took advantage of the world's attention being focused on Abyssinia in 1936 to send his troops into the Rhineland. France was eager for Italian support against him and all thought of tough sanctions was abandoned. Yet even then the hopes of France and Britain were dashed: Mussolini joned in alliance with Hitler, the Rome–Berlin Axis, later in 1936.

Check yourself

QUESTIONS

Q1
(a) Which country was the aggressor in (i) Manchuria and (ii) Abyssinia?
(b) Why did they get away with it, in each case?

Q2 What lessons do you think Hitler learned from the two crises?

Q3 Look at the cartoon.

How does the cartoonist make clear his view of the League in the Manchurian crisis?

THE DOORMAT.

Figure 8.5 *British cartoon of 1931 called* The Doormat. *The document the Japanese soldier has trodden on is named 'Honour of the League'; the elderly man is using a 'face-saving outfit' on the face of the woman who represents the League.*

ANSWERS

A1

a)   (i) Japan (ii) Italy

b)   (i) Japan got away with it because the League took so long to report on the invasion that it was all over before they decided what action to take. Also sanctions could not work because Japan's main trading partners were USA and USSR, neither of whom were in the League.

(ii)   Italy got away with it because Britain and France were more worried about Hitler and did not want to drive the Italian dictator into an alliance with Hitler by imposing tough sanctions on Italy. Sanctions were imposed too little, too late.

A2   Hitler would have learnt that if you were going to break the rules of international behaviour, the League would not stop you if you went ahead and took no notice. This was particularly the case if you were a strong nation.

A3   The cartoonist is critical of the League – he calls it a doormat. He shows the Japanese walking over the League's body into its building in Geneva. The diplomats try to save some of the reputation of the League with cosmetics.

TUTORIALS

T1

(i)   *It was hard for the League to react to the Manchurian Crisis. China was in chaos; the civilian Japanese government had no control over what its army was doing in China. Further, Japan was a fellow Council member and Britain and France did not want to alienate her.*

(ii)   *Britain and France may have felt some guilt that they were imperialist powers trying to stop Italy building up her own Empire. In the end they got the worst of all worlds: Abyssinia was seized; the world's smaller nations despised them; and Italy and Germany made an alliance.*

T2   *He could see that Britain and France, the only two countries with the economic and military power to give the League some 'teeth', usually did what they wanted, in a crisis, not what the League wanted.*

T3   *Japan should really be shown walking out of the building because she merely left the League when it criticised her. The cartoonist has shown the Japanese treading on the 'Honour of the League'.*

HITLER AND THE CAUSES OF THE SECOND WORLD WAR

DID HITLER PLAN FOR THE SECOND WORLD WAR?

Historians have argued long over this: it depends what you mean by 'plan'. If you mean did he have a blueprint of events, which would lead, stage by stage, to war when he wanted it, then the answer is probably no. If you mean, did he expect to have to go to war sometime, then the answer is probably yes.

HITLER'S IDEAS

The problem starts with what he said in *Mein Kampf*. This was his long, rambling autobiography, written in 1924 when he had time on his hands, serving his prison sentence after the Beer-Hall Putsch (see chapter 4, p.68). He made several points:

- The German people are a superior race. All Germans should be in the same country. He criticised the Treaty of Versailles for leaving German-speaking people in Austria, Czechoslovakia and Poland.

- Once all Germans are united, they will need more land. This will be taken from the land to the East: Poland, Russia. These are lived in by Slavs, whom Hitler believed to be inferior people; Hitler also hated the USSR because it was Communist.

- This will mean war. Germany should ignore the Treaty of Versailles and rearm so as to be ready.

Are these just vague ideas? Or a statement of intentions? Let's see what happened when he got into power, nine years after he had written *Mein Kampf*.

HITLER'S GERMANY

(This section is just a reminder; for more, see chapter 4).

- Rearmament. Hitler set about building weapons and increasing the size of the German armed forces (see below). Partly this was to solve the unemployment problem, but it also made Germany strong again.

- The German economy was put on a war footing. By 1939 more than half the German economy was devoted to war preparations.

- The Hitler Youth movement was designed to prepare young male Germans for war.

But this still doesn't mean that he had a plan. Look at the events of 1933 to 1938, below. Notice how cleverly Hitler uses events to get what he wants, choosing his time perfectly. Notice also how ruthless he was, prepared to use force, murder, threats, or whatever suited him.

1933

Germany leaves the League over rearmament. Hitler is indignant that other countries have not disarmed while Germany was forced to do so in 1919. Britain, among others, thinks he has a point. Secret rearmament of Germany begins.

1934

Austrian Nazis, on Hitler's orders, assassinate Austrian Chancellor Dollfuss. Hitler prepares to take over Austria but Mussolini moves Italian troops up to the border to stop him. Hitler, lacking strong armed forces, backs down.

1935

January   Plebiscite in Saar, as arranged at the Treaty of Versailles, votes to join Germany: a minor victory for Hitler.

March   Germany openly rearms, particularly building up the air force, the *Luftwaffe*, from 36 planes in 1932 to 8,250 by 1939 and the army, from the limit of 100,000 imposed at Versailles to nearly 1,000,000 by 1939.

June   Anglo–German naval agreement allows Germany to build a fleet up to 35 per cent of the size of the British navy.

1936

March   While the rest of the world is watching Abyssinia, Hitler orders his troops to occupy the Rhineland. This is German territory but was declared demilitarised at the Treaty of Versailles. Hitler and his generals are nervous. If French troops are sent against him, he will have to back down as he does not yet have a strong enough army. France, in the middle of an election campaign and unsure of British support, does not act. Hitler gets away with it.

November   Mussolini, fed up with the attitude of France and Britain over his Abyssinian invasion, makes Rome–Berlin Axis agreement with Hitler. This was extended in 1937 when Germany, Italy and Japan signed the Anti-Comintern Pact, so lining up one of the alliances in the Second World War. (Comintern was the international Communist organisation.)

1937

The Spanish Civil War started in 1936. Hitler (and Mussolini) decided to support the anti-Communist leader, General Franco. Hitler used the war as practice for his new *Luftwaffe*. Guernica was destroyed by the German Condor Legion in a bombing raid (see Fig 8.6).

Figure 8.6
Guernica, in northern Spain, destroyed by German bombers in April 1937

Figure 8.7
Map of Europe, 1936–38

1938

March Hitler threatens to take over Austria. He bullies Austrian Chancellor Schuschnigg, pointing out that Italy would not rescue Austria as it had in 1934, France would not act and neither would Britain, Schuschnigg prepares to defy Hitler by holding a plebiscite on the issue, but Hitler forestalls him by taking over Austria. This is called the **Anschluss**.

April Sudetenland. Hitler then began to threaten to take over the Sudetenland, the border areas of Czechslovakia where three million Germans lived.

As Hitler begins to move towards new lands Britain becomes heavily involved through Chamberlain's efforts to keep peace by appeasement (see next page).

EXTRA POINTS ▶

1. Another excuse Hitler could use to defend his rearmament programme was the alliances France had built up with several eastern European countries: Poland, Hungary, Czechoslovakia, Hungary, Romania. They had looked for France's protection against any attempt by Germany to alter the eastern boundaries laid down at Versailles. Hitler said he was being surrounded and had to defend himself.

2. Historians argue about the Hossbach Memorandum. This document came out of a meeting held in 1937 in which Hitler told his generals to be ready for war within five years. It gives strength to the idea that Hitler planned for war, but did not necessarily plan when it would happen.

Check yourself

QUESTIONS

Q1 Look at Figure 8.7.

a) Describe what action Hitler took over areas *a* and *b* on the map.

b) What was he trying to do in each case?

c) Was he: lucky? clever?

Q2 Was Hitler solely to blame for the drift to war up to 1938?

REMEMBER! Cover the answers if you want to.

ANSWERS

A1

a) At *a*, the Rhineland, he sent in soldiers in 1936. This was supposed to be a demilitarised zone.
At *b* he took over Austria in 1938, the Anschluss, by a mixture of threats and force.

b) Over the Rhineland he was just showing that he was master in his own country. Over Austria, he was determined to unite the two German-speaking countries.

TUTORIALS

T1

a) *Both these actions were against the terms of the Treaty of Versailles. Hitler had long condemned the Treaty and many Germans agreed with him.*

b) *In both cases he was serving notice that he was not going to observe the terms of the Treaty of Versailles. We might assume the joining of Austria and Germany in one state meant a lot to Hitler. He was, after all, born an Austrian. 1938 was his second attempt, following his threats in 1934 when he was forced to back down by Mussolini.*

It is worth noting just how weak Hitler felt in 1934 and 1936, before he had built up his armies. By 1939 he was prepared to take on the French army and regarded the Italian Army with contempt.

ANSWERS

c) Over the Rhineland, he was clever in seizing the opportunity of other European countries being absorbed in the Abyssinia affair, and France being paralysed by being in the middle of a general election campaign.

Over Austria, he was much more calculated. After 1934 he knew he had to get Mussolini on his side. His armed forces were also stronger by four years' growth and he could now steamroller Schuschnigg when Schuschnigg tried to defy him.

A2 Hitler was moving towards a war in Europe from the moment he came to power in 1933. But he was not solely to blame: there are other factors.

The League of Nations was supposed to keep the peace, and it was seriously undermined before Hitler even became Chancellor. Several nations, including the USA, share the blame for this.

Nor was Hitler to blame for the terms of the Treaty of Versailles, which led so many Germans to want revenge, a feeling Hitler was able to use.

TUTORIALS

c) *The reoccupation of the Rhineland was a huge risk – he would have looked very silly if anyone had kicked up a fuss. It was a calculated risk: he was clever in choosing his moment, but slightly lucky in getting away with it.*

Over Austria we can see the results of clever planning: the Rome–Berlin Axis, the added strength of Germany's forces.

T2 *Britain and France failed to act to stop Hitler. They were torn between their duty to work within the League and their wish to follow their own interests. Their failure to work together to find a way of halting Hitler means they both have a share in causing the war. There is also the matter of appeasement (see below), which may have led Hitler into thinking that he could get away with aggressive actions without their leading to war.*

APPEASEMENT

Appeasement

By the mid-1930s British and French leaders adopted a policy of **appeasement** towards Hitler (and also Mussolini). They felt that the Treaty of Versailles had been too harsh and that some of the dictators' demands were fair. They hoped that if Hitler and Mussolini got most of what they wanted, they would be satisfied and start behaving reasonably – they would be 'appeased'.

THE SUDETENLAND CRISIS, 1938

In 1938 some German Nazis in the Sudetenland, part of Czechoslovakia, complained that they were being badly treated by the Czech government. Hitler threatened to invade Czechoslovakia to protect them. War seemed quite likely: Czechoslovakia had a modern and well-equipped army and was ready to fight. It also had an agreement with France that they would protect each other if either was attacked. The war could spread.

In this situation the British Prime Minister, Chamberlain flew to meet Hitler in Germany in September. He thought he had persuaded Hitler to calm down and allow a plebiscite to be held in the Sudetenland, but at the next meeting Hitler stepped up his demands and threatened war. Chamberlain called a conference at Munich, attended by Germany, France, Italy and Britain. They agreed that the Sudetenland should be handed over to Germany.

RESULTS

- The Czechs were furious – they had not been consulted and had lost the Sudetenland and their defences against Germany.

- Hitler was jubilant – he had got what he wanted without a shot being fired. He promised Chamberlain: 'I have no more territorial demands in Europe.'

- Chamberlain was welcomed by the British public as a hero, a peace-maker. 'I believe it is peace in our time,' he said.

- Winston Churchill, out of favour with the government, warned: 'We have suffered a total defeat. You will find that in time Czechoslovakia will be engulfed in the Nazi regime.'

In March 1939 Hitler's troops invaded Czechoslovakia (see Fig. 8.8).

Figure 8.8
A Czech woman watches German forces march into Prague, the Czech capital, 1939

WHY DID THE BRITISH ADOPT A POLICY OF APPEASEMENT?

- A majority of the British people hated the idea of another war. Almost all that generation of British leaders had fought in the First World War and never wanted to fight again. 'I am a man of peace to the depths of my soul. Armed conflict between nations is a nightmare to me,' said Chamberlain.

- Government experts had told Chamberlain, based on the wars going on in China and Spain, that another war would be devastating. They estimated 1,800,000 British civilians would be killed in bombing raids in the first sixty days of a war.

- Britain was not ready for war. The armed forces were run down. British military planners had believed German propaganda about rearmament and thought Germany was more prepared for war than she really was.

- Many British were not prepared to go to war over a European crisis. Chamberlain called Czechoslovakia 'a far-off country of whose people we know nothing'. To many British the overseas Empire was far more important. They preferred to buy peace at the price of the Sudetenland.

- Many British feared Communism far more than Nazism. Some even admired Hitler for the stand he was taking and felt a strong Nazi Germany was a good defence against the USSR.

THE DRIFT TO WAR

Hitler and Chamberlain misunderstood one another.

- Chamberlain thought Hitler could be trusted and meant what he said. He had never dealt with anyone who was prepared to lie, bully and break his word as Hitler did. As soon as Hitler invaded Czechoslovakia in March 1939 it was obvious that Poland would be his next target. Chamberlain therefore made an alliance with Poland to support her if she was invaded. France already had such an alliance.

- Hitler thought Chamberlain was so set on peace at all costs that Britain would never go to war. He thought he could go on seizing land to the east while Britain and France did nothing.

The Nazi–Soviet Pact, 1939

The only country which could interfere in Hitler's planned seizure of Poland was the USSR. To the astonishment of the world the two arch-enemies, Germany and the USSR, signed an agreement in August 1939 not to attack each other. This was the Nazi–Soviet Pact and contained secret clauses to divide up Poland between them.

It was a dishonest deal on both sides: Hitler knew he would attack the USSR sooner or later (it happened less than two years later). Stalin hoped it would buy him time while Hitler made war in western Europe first. In September 1939 German forces invaded Poland. Britain and France stood by their alliance with Poland and declared war on Germany. The Second World War had begun.

 **EXTRA POINTS**

1. Other examples of appeasement in action are: the Hoare–Laval plan to carve up Abyssinia in 1935 (see p.167); the agreement between Britain and Germany allowing Germany to rebuild her navy (see p.170); the failure to take any action over Hitler's reoccupation of the Rhineland in 1936, and the Anschluss in 1938.

2. Appeasement, far from preserving peace as it was intended to do and as the great mass of the British public hoped it would, may have made war more likely. This is because appeasement may have encouraged Hitler to think he could get away with all kinds of aggression.

Check yourself

QUESTIONS

Q1 Describe what Hitler was up to at each of these four moments.

(i) Sudetenland; (ii) Invasion of Czechoslovakia; (iii) Nazi–Soviet Pact; (iv) War with Poland.

Q2 Why did Chamberlain adopt a policy of appeasement?

Look at the five reasons given. They are different types of reasons: some public statements, some private attitudes, some secret information. Sort the reasons into different types; explain your decisions, using these paragraph headings:

'The reasons Chamberlain gave for appeasement were … '

'He also had information which could not be made public. This was … '

'Some people in Britain also thought … '

REMEMBER! Cover the answers if you want to.

ANSWERS

A1

(i) Hitler was trying to create an excuse for invading Czechoslovakia by stirring up trouble in the Sudetenland. Then Chamberlain asked for a meeting. Hitler was co-operative at first but then thought he might be able to force Chamberlain to let him have the Sudetenland without a war. Chamberlain agreed to this at Munich, provided Hitler signed a piece of paper promising not to go to war. Hitler signed, with no intention of keeping his promise.

(ii) Czechoslovakia was now severely weakened. It was easy to capture the country.

(iii) Poland was next and Hitler needed breathing space to capture Poland. Britain and France would not lift a finger for Poland – after all they'd done nothing over the reoccupation of the Rhineland, Mussolini's invasion of Abyssinia, the Anschluss. But it was necessary to square things with the USSR. They could agree to carve up Poland between them, hence the Nazi–Soviet Pact.

(iv) Poland was invaded, but, to Hitler's surprise, Britain and France declared war.

TUTORIALS

T1

(i) *Remember that Hitler had no idea why Chamberlain wanted to meet him. Chamberlain was quite an old man; air travel was unusual: What did he want?*

At Munich, Hitler was able to put on a show of anger, having to go to war to defend Germany's pride, etc. He played on Chamberlain's fear of war and guilt over the terms of the Versailles Treaty brilliantly.

(ii) *This was a deep shock to Chamberlain: all he had worked for was in vain.*

(iii) *The Nazi–Soviet Pact was the end of all the idealism of the inter-war years: here were two real enemies sinking their differences to carve up a weaker neighbour. They were just as bad as the pre-1914 nations.*

(iv) *This is the moment Hitler makes a miscalculation: he was going to have to fight in the west before invading Russia. But, thanks to the Nazi–Soviet Pact, he wasn't going to have to fight a two-front war, like the Kaiser's generals did in 1914.*

ANSWER

A2

The reason Chamberlain gave for appeasement was that he wanted peace. Most British people felt the same and this is why Chamberlain was given a hero's welcome when he returned from Munich.

He also had information which could not be made public. The first was that war would bring huge casualties to the civilian population. Chamberlain was thus even less ready to consider war. The second was that Britain was simply not ready to fight a war.

Some people in Britain also thought that the real menace to Europe was Stalin and Communism. Some even approved of Hitler as a bulwark against Stalin. There was also an unwillingness to go to war for a distant country.

TUTORIAL

T2

The secret reasons are not unreasonable considerations and Chamberlain did start to make hurried preparations for war. You could argue he gained Britain twelve months. In fact, the experts were wrong and casualties were not that serious but Chamberlain could not know that in 1938, of course.

Any judgement which puts Stalin or Hitler one above the other is at fault. There were plenty of people in Britain who apologised for Hitler, although Chamberlain himself was not one of them.

EXAM PRACTICE

Sample Student's Answers & Examiner's Comments

---

1 Why did German soldiers marching into the Rhineland in 1936 cause a crisis? (6)

The German occupation of the Rhineland in 1936 was a crisis because the Rhineland had been declared a demilitarised zone at the Treaty of Versailles in 1919. This meant that it was against the terms of the Treaty for any soldiers to be in the area. Hitler's decision to send his troops in caused a crisis because it was a breach of the Treaty. **4/6**

EXAMINER'S COMMENTS

MARK SCHEME

Level 1	Describes incident	**1–2 marks**
Level 2	Explains illegality of invasion	**3–4 marks**
Level 3	Explains crisis it caused	**5–6 marks**

This answer is fine as far as it goes, but doesn't really explain 'crisis'. Hitler had broken the terms of the Treaty, but how were the countries enforcing the Treaty – Britain and France – to react? Should they take tough action? Invade? If so, who should do it? Both countries were busy trying to deal with the illegal Italian invasion of Abyssinia. France, which was most keen on keeping up the terms of the Versailles Treaty, was in the middle of an election campaign and no politician wanted to commit France to military action which could lead to war. Many people in Britain thought there was nothing wrong with Hitler moving troops around inside his own country. The 'crisis' was in the response – or lack of it – as much as the action.

---

2 Look at the cartoon. It is a Soviet cartoon from 1939. The policemen are Britain (Chamberlain, *right*) and France (Daladier, *left*). The people in the car are German Nazis (Hitler, Goering and Goebbels). The signpost reads: 'Western Europe' on the left arm and 'USSR' on the right.

(a) What is the Soviet cartoonist's view of what is happening in Europe? (4)

The cartoonist feels that Britain and France are sending Germany to attack the USSR in order to divert them from attacking western Europe. **3/4**

EXAMINER'S COMMENTS

MARK SCHEME

Level 1   Explains points from the cartoon   **1–2 marks**

Level 2   Explains main theme of cartoon   **3–4 marks**

Cartoons are often packed full of symbols and this is no exception. Being from the USSR it gives us a good insight into their attitudes at this important time. The only other major points to make are the portrayal of the Nazis with guns and an axe: the cartoonist sees Germany as hell-bent on war. Also France and Britain as timid policemen.

· ·

(b) Use this cartoon and your own knowledge to explain the Soviet agreement to the Nazi–Soviet Pact of August 1939.   (7)

> The cartoon does help to explain the Nazi–Soviet Pact. It shows the USSR's fear that Germany was going to attack them. It shows the Soviet fear that France and Britain were actually enouraging Germany to do this as an alternative to attacking them.
>
> Germany seized the Sudetenland in September 1938 following the Munich crisis and then took over the rest of Czechoslovakia. Poland would obviously be the next target and after Poland then the USSR. The Nazi–Soviet Pact of August 1939 was an agreement between the USSR and Germany not to attack each other. It also had secret clauses on how they would divide up Poland between them.

6/7

EXAMINER'S COMMENTS

MARK SCHEME

Level 1   Describes Nazi–Soviet Pact   **1–2 marks**

Level 2   Explains Soviet motives with
            little or no reference to cartoon **3–4 marks**

Level 3   Uses cartoon to explain motives   **5–7 marks**

The answer gets into Level 3 because it combines some knowledge with an understanding of the cartoon, however, it stays with the events of 1938–39. The motives for the Nazi–Soviet Pact go back further: they were always afraid of attack, from the western intervention in the Civil War in 1919–20. They knew that most European countries were totally hostile to them. They knew that Hitler was fanatically hostile to Communism and to the Russian people, who he regarded as inferior.

They had tried to get other nations to unite against Germany but had usually been given the brush-off. They were not invited to the Munich Conference and regarded appeasement with dismay. They felt that the western Europeans would happily see Hitler invade the USSR, as the cartoon suggests.

3 Choose *two* of the items in the table and explain how they weakened the League of Nations. (10)

Decisions were slow	USA not a member
Linked to the Treaties of 1919	Sanctions ineffective
Self-interest of leading members	1930s Depression

The League was linked to the Treaties of 1919. It was set up as part of each of the Treaties. It was supposed to support and enforce the terms of the treaties. This meant that the defeated countries who disliked the treaties, disliked and mistrusted the League.

Sanctions did not work and so the League was weakened. In the case of the Japanese invasion of Manchuria, 1931, economic sanctions could have been imposed, but the main country involved in trading with Japan was the USA which was not a member of the League and unwilling to harm its own trade by applying sanctions.

In the case of the Italian invasion of Abyssinia, 1935, sanctions could have hurt Italy but Britain and France could see that tough economic sanctions would hit their own economies at a time of depression. They were therefore unwilling to include items, such as oil and coal, which would really bite on the Italian economy.

3/5 + 5/5

EXAMINER'S COMMENTS

MARK SCHEME

In this style of question each answer is marked out of 5, to a simple mark-scheme:

Level 1	Describes item chosen	**1–2 marks**
Level 2	Explains how item links to weaknesses	**3–5 marks**

Note the difference between 'describes' and 'explains'.

The answer about the treaties is only a description of the situation, with a remark about the defeated countries resenting the League. There is more to it than that: it meant the League was frozen in time to 1919. To several countries, notably Britain, 1919 was not a perfect settlement. But if changes were made to one part of the treaties, then perhaps other changes could be made. The League in the later years was thus weakened.

The answer for the second item is much better. Note that the United Nations (see chapter 11) took on this matter of sanctions and tried much harder to make them work. Even then they take a long time to have an effect.

Question to Answer

The answer to Question 4 can be found on p.273

4 How much did the failure of the League of Nations contribute to the outbreak of the Second World War? (12)

THE ROOTS OF APARTHEID

Race – a person's racial group – has always been regarded as important in South Africa. In 1946 the census classified the 11.4 million people living in South Africa as: 69 per cent African; 21 per cent white; 8 per cent coloured; 2 per cent Asian.

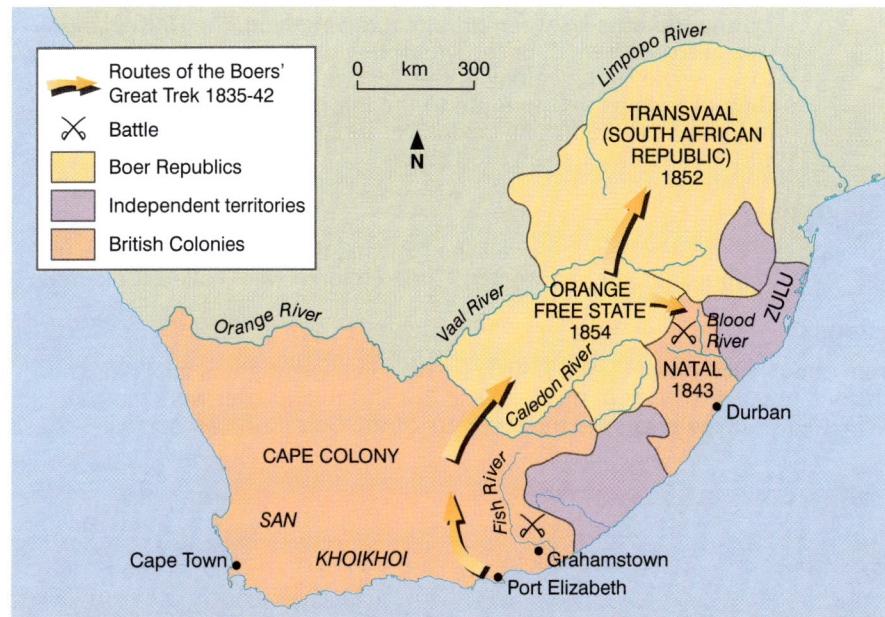

Figure 9.1
Map of South Africa

WHAT ARE THE ROOTS OF THESE DIFFERENT RACIAL GROUPS?

Africans

- The African people living in the Cape area had been there for at least 2,000 years. They were light-brown skinned, small people and belonged to two tribes, the Khoikhoi and the San (see Fig. 9.1). These are the people the whites called 'Hottentots'.

- To the east and north lived larger numbers of black Africans who arrived about 400 AD. They spoke Bantu languages and belonged to several tribes of whom the most numerous were the Xhosa and the Zulu (see Fig. 9.1). They were well-organised and, particularly the Zulus, great warriors.

All of these Africans were mainly herdspeople, who moved over wide areas with their animals. They did not 'own' land as settled farmers do, but they regarded the lands their tribes had grazed for centuries as their own.

Whites

- **The Dutch**
  In 1652 the Dutch set up a base at Cape Town to supply ships of the Dutch East India Company on their way to and from the East. Soon they moved inland and eastwards, taking land from the Khoikhoi and San to farm and graze cattle. The Africans were killed, or died of European diseases for which they had no immunity, or were made slaves. The Dutch settlers gradually lost contact with Europe and developed their own way of life:

- They were farmers – Boers in Dutch.
- They were Protestants, mainly of the Dutch Reformed Church, with a strong sense that God had marked them out as special people, superior to other races.
- They spoke their own language, Afrikaans. This was mainly Dutch, but with some words from African languages and the languages of other Europeans who had settled in the Cape.

- **The British**
  During the wars between Britain and Napoleon, the Netherlands was allied with the French. The British used this as an opportunity to seize the Dutch colony in the Cape in 1795 as a useful base for their own ships on the route to the important British possessions in India. It was officially taken over by Britain in 1805 and British settlers increased from the 1820s.

Coloureds

Although the Dutch settlers regarded the Africans they met as inferior, many had sex with Khoikhoi and San women. Their children were called 'Coloureds'.

Asians

From about 1860 onwards the British set up sugar plantations in Natal. The Africans refused to work in them, so the British brought over workers from India. Many stayed and were the founders of the South African Asians.

WHY WAS THERE HOSTILITY BETWEEN THE BOERS AND THE BRITISH?

The Great Trek

The Boers disliked being ruled by the British. They objected to British criticism of the way they treated the Africans. The last straw was the abolition of slavery in British colonies in 1833. From 1835, over the next ten years, 14,000 Boers left the Cape and travelled inland, northwards and eastwards (see Fig.9.1) in wagons drawn by oxen. By 1854 the Boers had set up two new independent republics, the Transvaal and the Orange Free State.

Meanwhile the British had developed two colonies in the Cape and Natal.

The 'Great Trek' in history

The story of the journey out of the Cape in 1835, the 'Great Trek', is tremendously important to the Boers. The Boer leader, Piet Retief, drove off some Africans but was killed by Zulus in 1836. This was avenged at the battle of Blood River in 1838, when 500 Boers faced 10,000 Zulus. The Boers put their wagons in a circle, a laager as they called it. From the laager they defeated the Zulus, killing 3,000 of them. No Boers lost their lives. They took this as a sign of God's approval of their desire to be left alone.

Later the story was built up by Afrikaner Nationalist politicians as a key moment in their history and a justification for apartheid (see Fig 9.2).

Figure 9.2
Huge crowd of white South Africans at the opening of the Trekker monument in 1949

Diamonds and gold

The Boers were not to be left alone for long. In 1867 diamonds were discovered at Kimberley in the Orange Free State and in 1871 gold was found at Johannesburg in the Transvaal. Boer farmers were not interested in developing these resources, but British businessmen were. Soon the diamond industry was controlled by an Englishman from the Cape, Cecil Rhodes. The gold deposits were deep, requiring lots of money and workers to get it out. Big companies were involved. Only twenty-five years after gold was discovered, Johannesburg had grown from nothing to 250,000 people and was the largest city in southern Africa.

Most of the 100,000 black workers in the mines were migrants. That is, they came to work from their villages for a fixed period. They did not bring their families with them and were housed in large compounds. They had to carry a 'pass' to show who they were and where they came from. Because they housed and fed them, the mining companies paid them very low wages. The system may have suited unmarried young men, but was hard for families, especially for the women left at home far away, to till the ground and bring up the children. It also ensured that few blacks were classified as city residents.

British imperialism

In the late nineteenth century the British were keen to expand their Empire. They took part in a 'scramble for Africa' with several European countries. One of the keenest imperialists of all was Cecil Rhodes. He saw British possessions stretching 'from the Cape to Cairo'. Both the Zulus and the Boers were in the way.

- The Zulus defeated the British at Isandhlwana in 1879, but were then overcome by the sheer numbers of British.

- The Boer War, 1899–1902. At first the Boers used their knowledge of the land and their skill as guerrilla fighters to inflict defeats on the British. In time, however, greater British numbers and resources forced the Boers to surrender. The two British provinces and the two Boer republics were joined in the Union of South Africa, part of the British Empire.

Results of the Boer War

- **Concentration camps**   In order to win the war, the British had to control the countryside. They adopted the tactic of burning down Boer farms and putting women and children in concentration camps. Bad food, poor hygiene and overcrowding in the camps led to 27,000 deaths of women and children – compared to 4,000 Boers actually killed fighting.

- **Language**   Having forced the Boers into the British Empire, they were now forced to speak English. Afrikaans was banned in schools and English was the official language.

Both these issues left a huge legacy of bitterness towards the British.

THE GROWTH OF SEGREGATION, 1902–48

Although the British had promised non-whites political rights if the Boers were defeated, this promise was broken. The new government of the Union of South Africa began to pass the segregationist laws which the Afrikaners wanted. The British probably did this for two reasons:

- guilt over the treatment of Boer families in the camps;
- wish to get on well with the Afrikaners (as the Boers were now more often called) in order to ensure British control of the gold and diamond mines.

1911 Mines and Works Act

This excluded non-whites from many jobs. It also made it legal to pay blacks less than whites for the same work.

1913 Land Act

Black people could not own land, except in the 7 per cent of the country reserved for them. (This was increased to 13.5 per cent in 1936.) They could be evicted from white-owned land which they rented. Many were, causing great hardship.

1920s and 1930s

Unemployment among whites rose in these years. The government response was to create jobs for whites by sacking black people. 13,000 poor whites took over black people's jobs on the railways. More jobs in the mines were reserved for whites.

It seemed as if the Afrikaners had lost the war but won the peace. The kind of segregated, white-controlled state they had always wanted was being set up within the British Empire.

EXTRA POINTS ▶

1. During the 1820s and 1830s there had been great upheavals and movements of people in a huge area of south-east Africa. This is called the *Difaqane* and was caused when other tribes in the area were attacked by the Zulus led by their great chief, Shaka. Many died and tribes were weakened. The land was temporarily almost empty when the Boers arrived as they trekked north-east from the Cape in the 1830s.

2. In 1890 Cecil Rhodes sent settlers into the area north of the Boer republics. He tricked the chief into handing over land and set up a colony. This was called Rhodesia and is now the independent state of Zimbabwe.

Check yourself

QUESTIONS

Q1 Who are the Boers, or Afrikaners?

Q3 Why was the Boer War fought?

Q2 Why is the memory of the Great Trek so important to them?

REMEMBER! Cover the answers if you want to.

ANSWERS

A1 The Boers were the Dutch who settled in the Cape from 1652. Boer means farmer. They developed their own language, Afrikaans, and their own way of life, based on farming, the Dutch Reformed Church and black slave labourers.

A2 The Great Trek was the movement of the Boers out of the British-governed Cape in 1835 and after. A great deal of interest was taken in this event after their defeat by the British in the Boer War, especially during the revival of Afrikaner Nationalism in the 1930s. The Great Trek symbolised their wish to turn their backs on the British and live their lives in their own way.

A3 The Boer War was fought because the British wanted to control the two Boer republics, the Orange Free State and the Transvaal. They wanted the land, to build up a British-held ribbon of territory from the Cape to Cairo and they wanted the mineral wealth of gold and diamonds in the republics.

TUTORIALS

T1 *Through the twentieth century the word Boer dropped out of use. For one thing, it was obviously wrong to call all whites of Dutch origin 'Boers' when lots of them were no longer farmers – three-quarters of all whites lived in cities by 1951. Also, after their defeat in the Boer War, 1899–1902, the former Boers wanted to resist British takeover. They began to emphasise their own history and call themselves 'Afrikaners'.*

T2 *The success of the Great Trek, especially the victory at Blood River in 1838, was taken by many Afrikaners as a sign from God that he was on their side and approved of them. The symbol of the laager, the tight circle of wagons fending off a numerous and hostile enemy also became important as world criticism of apartheid increased.*

This whole incident is a good example of history being used at a later time for different purposes.

T3 *The British of course offered better reasons for the Boer War than those given in the answer. Many of the miners living in the Boer republics were British and the Boers gave them no political rights at all. The British also offered political rights to the black people living under the Boers. There is some truth in both these claims.*

APARTHEID BEGINS

Although they had lost the Boer War and were now part of the British Empire, the Afrikaners were determined to keep their separate identity. Some refused to fight for Britain in the two World Wars, although many did. In 1924 the Afrikaner leader, General Herzog, became Prime Minister and restored the use of the Afrikaans language in schools. We have seen that tough segregationist laws were passed.

In the 1930s an Afrikaner politician, Dr Malan, started the Purified National Party. He wanted Afrikaner control of South Africa. In 1948 his Nationalist Party won the General Election and Malan became Prime Minister. The Nationalist Party were to rule South Africa for the next forty-six years.

WHY DID MALAN WIN THE 1948 ELECTION?

- Only whites (and some Coloureds in the Cape) had the right to vote. He had the support of most Afrikaners, a majority of the white population (although only 12 per cent of the total population of South Africa).

- He had the support of the pro-Afrikaner Dutch Reformed Church, of which he had once been a minister.

- He had the support of the **Broederbond**. This was an influential, secret, all-male, Afrikaner, anti-British organisation.

- He played on white fears of blacks by talking of the 'black peril'. During the Second World War industry had boomed. Many blacks had moved into the cities. Segregation in jobs and housing had been relaxed. Poor and unemployed whites were worried about losing their privileged position.

- He offered **apartheid** – apartness – a stricter separation of blacks and whites, with whites, of course, in control.

WHAT WAS APARTHEID AND HOW WAS IT PUT INTO PRACTICE?

Malan appointed an all-Afrikaner government and Afrikaans became the language of government. Apartheid was built up by a series of laws – see below.

The theory

- Racial groups were to be strictly defined.

- The races were to be kept apart as far as possible.

- Black Africans were regarded as rural people and land was to be set aside for them.

- This would mean that they were only visitors in the cities. They could not live or work there permanently.

- Whites were a superior race and should rule alone.

- Anyone who opposed this or argued for racial equality was a Communist and a menace to the state.

- Within twenty years everyone in South Africa and the world would accept that apartheid benefitted everybody.

Apartheid laws

- **Prohibition of Mixed Marriages Act, 1949**

- **Population Registration Act, 1950**
  Every South African was classified as either Black, White, Asian or Coloured. Coloureds felt the craziness of this law most because, as they were the result of mixed marriages in the past, different members of their families ended up being classified White and Black.

- **Group Areas Act, 1950**
  Certain areas were declared white only. It was illegal for other racial groups to live in these areas. They included the cities and the best farmland. Over the next thirty-five years four million black people were removed from their homes in 'white' areas. In some

cases the homes where they had lived for generations were bull-dozed. Thirteen per cent of the land was set aside as 'black homelands', for the 70 per cent of the population who were black.

- **Suppression of Communism Act, 1950**
  This banned the Communist Party and any organisation which opposed apartheid.

- **Abolition of Passes Act, 1952**
  Despite its name, this act enforced the system of passes which already existed. Having declared urban areas to be 'whites only', black people were treated as temporary migrant workers. Any black person living in a white area had to carry a 'passbook', which was like a passport. Police used the pass laws to harrass black people.

- **Separate Amenties Act, 1953**
  All public facilities – buses, trains, shops, cinemas, hospitals, post offices, parks, libraries, beaches – were segregated. Signs were put up like those in Figure 9.3.

Figure 9.3
Signs in South Africa during apartheid

- **Bantu Education Act, 1953**
  All schools were brought under government control. There were separate schools for whites and blacks. The latter were much less well-funded, with bigger classes and worse buildings. There were separate national curriculums. Black Africans were not taught any black history and only prepared for life in the homelands. Government inspectors enforced the curriculums.

- **Separate Representation of Voters Act, 1956**
  Cape Coloureds lost the right to vote.

VERWOERD AND THE SECOND PHASE OF APARTHEID

Verwoerd was a staunch supporter of apartheid and Prime Minister from 1958 to 1966, when he was assassinated by a government official.

The logical next step for apartheid was make the black homelands self-governing. On the other hand, Verwoerd believed that blacks were 'uncivilised' and incapable of ruling themselves. The result was the **Bantu Self-Government Act, 1959**. ('Bantu' was the Nationalists' term for black Africans.)

The plan was for eight of the homelands to become independent tribal 'states'. This, of course, meant that any person from these homelands could be treated as a 'foreigner' in South Africa. The first of these 'Bantustans' to be declared independent was the Transkei in 1976. No other country recognised these so-called states.

- They were little scattered patches of land.
- The South African government looked after their defence and foreign policy.
- Their rulers were not elected and had no popular support.
- They were only kept going by huge amounts of money from South Africa.

A POLICE STATE

The enforcement of racial segregation and white supremacy did not, of course, go unchallenged. Gradually the South African government built up a police state to suppress opposition.

- **Banning orders**   Organisations like the African National Congress and the Pan-African Congress (see pp.190 and 191) were banned. The Minister of Justice could ban meetings. He could put a ban on individuals. This meant the person could not write, meet others, broadcast or travel.
- **Detention without trial**   The Minister of Justice could have people detained by the police without trial: from 1963 this could be for ninety days at a stretch.
- **Press censorship**   Newspapers could not criticise the government; editors were arrested.
- **Police violence**   The atmosphere of terror was increased by the violence used by the police, who seemed to be above the law. Many people were tortured or beaten, sometimes to death, while they were in police hands.
- **BOSS (Bureau of State Security)**   The Minister of Justice under Verwoerd was Vorster. He became Prime Minister from 1966 to 1978. In 1966 he set up the Bureau of State Security, a secret police.

EXTRA POINT ▶

As Minister of Education under Malan, Verwoerd had told black pupils that they could not expect equality and that those who believed in equality were not suitable people to be teachers. As late as 1983, 2,088 rand per year was spent by the government on every white child and 211 rand per year on every black child.

Check yourself

QUESTIONS

Q1 What were the *black homelands* and why are they important to apartheid?

Q2 In what ways was apartheid new?

Tackle this question by making two lists: things were new; things that were not new.

Use these sentences to open your first two paragraphs:

'Apartheid was not new because ... '

'What was new about apartheid was ... '

Add a third paragraph starting:

'In my opinion, the new/old aspects of apartheid were more important than the old/new, because ... '

REMEMBER! Cover the answers if you want to.

ANSWERS

A1 The black homelands were the areas which the Nationalist government allocated to black Africans. They were all rural areas, some of them remote, and made up 13 per cent of the land area of the country – black Africans made up 70 per cent of the population.

They were important to apartheid because if black people belonged to those areas they were visitors, migrant workers, in the rest of the country. They could then be made to live in certain areas, separate from the white population and made to carry passes at all times.

A2 Apartheid was not new because South Africa had had segregationist laws for some time, for example the 1911 Mines and Works Act and the 1913 Land Act. Already black people were treated as inferior, with low wages, no political rights, and racial discrimination in jobs and housing. The hated passbooks already existed.

What was new about apartheid was Malan's and Verwoerd's determination to set up a white racist state. The laws passed between 1949 and 1953 created a complete system and rules to back it up.

In my opinion the old aspects of apartheid were more important than the new because South Africa was already a racist state. The attitudes of the Afrikaners go back a long way.

TUTORIALS

T1 *Part of the racism on which apartheid was based was the belief that black people were all farmers and so should be forced to live in rural areas. In fact, many of the rural areas classified as homelands were on very poor agricultural land. Verwoerd's plan to turn the black homelands into independent states was the logical next step of the 'homelands' policy. The intention was that, in time, the cities would become all white.*

T2 *You could argue the last paragraph the other way, too. What apartheid and its leaders did was to give racial discrimination a theory, a whole belief about race and God's support for the Afrikaner people. On the basis of these crazy ideas, the builders of apartheid tried to create a white-run state which would last for ever: Verwoerd said black people would only be ready for self-government in two thousand years' time.*

RESISTANCE TO APARTHEID

In the early years of the Boer and British conquest of South Africa the African population had fought the seizure of their lands. Although many tribes had put up fierce resistance, notably the Zulus, the whites' superior guns and numbers always overcame them in the end.

The growth of segregation in the early twentieth century was opposed by the few better off and educated black Africans. In 1912 they formed the South African Native National Congress, which changed its name in 1923 to the African National Congress (ANC). They campaigned against the 1913 Land Act, even travelling to London to see King George V. Their efforts were all in vain. They also failed to block any of the growing racial discrimination laws of the 1920s and 1930s.

Strikes in the mines did bring some improvement in wages. There was some trade union growth. Many Africans left the white churches for their own. On the whole, however, the lives and rights of black people grew worse up to the Second World War, with little effective resistance.

WHY WAS BLACK RESISTANCE SO INEFFECTIVE UP TO THE 1940s?

- Black Africans were not used to acting together: their first loyalty was to their tribe.
- Few Africans had the education to take on the white government successfully
- The ANC was a middle-class organisation. They were wary of mass protest and especially of the South African Communist Party, founded in 1921 and the main white anti-racist group.
- The ANC was committed to non-violence, but its protests were timid and ineffective.
- The government and the police dealt with opposition harshly, arresting leaders and giving long prison sentences. Most whites wanted to 'keep the blacks in their place', as they put it.
- The British government was unwilling to interfere in South African politics to help black people. Anyway, most British were casually racist: black people had few rights anywhere in the British Empire.

The rise of the ANC

In the war years South Africa changed more rapidly. More black Africans flocked to jobs in the towns. Young, able black leaders appeared. From 1944 the ANC formed a Youth League. Among its outstanding members was Nelson Mandela, a chief's son, tall and striking, training to be a lawyer.

In 1949 many of these young men became leaders of the ANC. In 1952 Chief Luthuli, an impressive leader with a deep commitment to non-violence, took over as President. At the same time, the Nationalist Party was erecting the apartheid system.

OPPOSITION CAMPAIGNS

1952, Defiance Campaign

Hundreds of demonstrators deliberately defied the law and walked into 'white only' parks, offices, streets and other areas. Thousands were arrested but ANC support rose from 7,000 to 100,000.

1955, Freedom Charter

ANC President Luthuli proposed a congress of all anti-apartheid groups, including Asians, coloureds and white Communists, to draw up a statement of the kind of South Africa they wanted – an alternative to apartheid. This was agreed at a mass meeting of 3,000 people in 1955:

- Everyone, whatever their race, should have the right to vote
- Everyone, whatever their race, should have equal rights
- State ownership of industries and mines in the name of the people
- No racial restriction on ownership of farmland
- No police state
- Human rights: freedom of speech, no pass laws
- Equality in jobs and wages
- Free and equal education
- Better housing and health care for everyone

1956 Treason Trial

In retaliation, the government arrested 156 people and put them on trial for treason and communism. It is true that Communists had taken part in drawing up the Freedom Charter, but that is because the ANC was prepared to work with anyone who opposed apartheid. All of the 156 accused were eventually found not guilty and the trial gave an opportunity for ANC members like Nelson Mandela to make powerful speeches in their own defence. However, it took five years, during which the opposition was without many of its leaders.

Women protest

The apartheid system hit women hard. They were left in the homelands to bring up their children without their husbands, who were away working in areas where wives could not follow. Women had to farm the land as well. In 1955 the pass laws were extended to women. They organised their own mass protests:

- Demonstrations against the pass laws.
- Protests in rural areas against unfair land ownership.
- **Bus boycotts**   Many black people, particularly women, were dependent on long bus journeys to get to work, but the buses were expensive. When the bus companies put up fares the women organised bus boycotts. Despite police support for the bus companies, the boycotts were successful.

SHARPEVILLE, 1960, AND THE END OF NON-VIOLENCE

In 1959 some ANC members had split off to form a more militant organisation, the Pan-African Congress (PAC), led by Robert Sobukwe. In 1960 they held a demonstration at Sharpeville. The police opened fire on them; sixty-nine people were killed and at least 180 wounded. In another demonstration at Langa two people were killed and forty-nine wounded. There was a worldwide storm of protest. Thousands of people were arrested. The ANC, PAC and Communist Party were banned.

Ironically, Albert Luthuli received the Nobel Peace Prize in 1961. In his acceptance speech he said that:

'Thirty years of my life have been spent knocking in vain, patiently, moderately and modestly at a closed and barred door. What have been the fruits of moderation? The past thirty years have seen the greatest number of laws restricting our rights, until today we have reached a stage where we have almost no rights at all.'

Mandela and some other ANC members, after long discussions, decided that non-violence was not working in the face of a harsh and oppressive government. He formed 'Umkhonto we Sizwe' ('The Spear of the People') to carry out acts of sabotage, destroying property but trying to avoid loss of life. In their first actions, in 1961, Umkhonto we Sizwe blew up power lines.

Nelson Mandela was now banned and on the run. The police eventually caught him and he was put on trial, with eight others, at Rivonia in 1964. He made a passionate four-hour speech in his defence and was sentenced to life imprisonment. As prisoner 466/64 he began his sentence on Robben Island, a prison island off Cape Town. Other ANC leaders went into exile, some to win support across the world, some to organise and train guerilla soldiers.

STEVE BIKO

In 1969 a twenty-two-year old medical student, Steve Biko, formed an all-black students organisation, the South African Students Organisation. He argued that black people had to raise themselves up by their own efforts, not through multi-racial groups in which whites usually took the lead. He campaigned for 'Black Consciousness', increasing self-awareness and confidence among black people in South Africa, which they preferred to call by an African name: Azania. He was a powerful writer and speaker. Naturally this brought him to the attention of the government. He was expelled from university and banned. In 1977 he was arrested, tortured and beaten to death, aged thirty. The police and the government denied all guilt.

SOWETO RIOTS, 1976

Figure 9.4
Police in armoured cars disperse demonstrators in Soweto, 1976

Soweto simply stands for SOuth WEst TOwnships, a huge collection of black housing areas outside Johannesburg. In 1976 the schoolchildren of Soweto erupted into riots (see Fig. 9.4).

Reasons for the Soweto riots:

- The spark which set off the riots was an order from the government that half their lessons were to be in Afrikaans. The schoolchildren saw Afrikaans as the language of their oppressors and a useless language in the wider world, spoken only by some white South Africans. It seemed to be preparing them only for life as servants or ill-paid workers in Afrikaner-ruled South Africa.

- They were also protesting at inadequate funding for black education, in comparison to white schools. This meant black schools were overcrowded, with classes of sixty or seventy, no textbooks and poorly-trained teachers.

- They could see the wider problems their parents suffered: rising unemployment, housing shortage, rising rents.

- Black Consciousness had influenced many young people.

The police used force to disperse the demonstrators. Two died on the first day, but more demonstrations followed all over South Africa. By the end of the year nearly 600 people had been killed, hundreds of buildings, especially schools, had been burnt, thousands of pupils had gone to join the ANC guerillas. Unlike after Sharpeville in 1960, the police did not easily re-establish control. It was a turning-point.

◀ **EXTRA POINTS**

1. More names from the opposition to apartheid:
   ANC colleagues of Nelson Mandela who joined with him and helped to change the ANC in the 1940s:
   Walter Sisulu, a trade unionist, later Mandela's closest friend in prison;
   Oliver Tambo, teacher and organiser;
   Anton Lembede, young schoolteacher who died in 1947 aged only 33.

   Key women:
   Albertina Sisulu; Winnie Mandela, wives of ANC leaders who became leaders in their own right.
   Helen Suzman, for a long time the only MP to speak out against apartheid.

2. Parallels with the civil rights movement in the USA are worth making. Both were heavily influenced by non-violence (Martin Luther King in the USA, Albert Luthuli in South Africa). Both found bus boycotts an issue which caught popular imagination and support (1955 in Montgomery, USA and in South Africa). Steve Biko's 'Black Consciousness' echoes the views of Marcus Garvey, a Jamaican who founded the Universal Negro Improvement Association in 1914, and the Black Power movement in the USA from the late 1960s.

3. The Soweto rioters also targeted beer-halls in black townships. They saw alcoholism as weakening black resistance and demeaning black pride.

Check yourself

QUESTIONS

Q1 What does the Freedom Charter deal with, apart from racial equality?

Q2 Why did Mandela abandon non-violence in 1960?

Q3 How did the Black Consciousness movement affect the young people of Soweto?

REMEMBER! Cover the answers if you want to.

ANSWERS

A1 The Freedom Charter, agreed in 1955, proposed a completely different state from the apartheid state being created by the Nationalist Party in power. It dealt with basic human rights, such as the right to a fair trial, free speech, freedom of movement and so on. It also dealt with economic and social fairness, such as state control of industries, better housing, education and health care.

Of course, non-white South Africans were suffering most from unfairness, but it offered more than just racial equality.

A2 The ANC was committed to non-violence. Its President, Chief Albert Luthuli, was awarded the Nobel Peace Prize in 1961 for non-violent protest against apartheid. However, Nelson Mandela abandoned non-violence in 1960 following the Sharpeville shootings. He, and many other young ANC activists, felt that non-violence was getting nowhere. Protests were met with violence and mass arrests. Even the world disapproval of the Sharpeville shootings seemed to have no effect on the South African government.

A3 Steve Biko was a leading figure in the Black Consciousness movement of the early 1970s. He was a powerful writer and speaker who was killed by the South African police in 1977. He encouraged black people, especially young blacks, to stand up for themselves, not to accept the inferior status they were given by white South Africans.

When the government tried to impose the Afrikaans language on all schools in 1976, students aged from ten to twenty rioted in protest. It is hard to be precise about how much the Black Consciousness movement affected these young people, but it would seem to have been important.

TUTORIALS

T1 *The Freedom Charter is a socialist document, in many ways. It not only offers justice and human rights, as this answer says, but it proposes a welfare state and state ownership of much of the economy as a way of achieving justice. In this way you can see the influence of the South African Communist Party on the Charter and perhaps the Labour government of 1945–51 in Britain.*

T2 *If you have studied non-violence in India, led by Gandhi, or in the USA in the 1960s, led by Martin Luther King, you will know that both campaigns met huge amounts of violence but the governments they were dealing with believed in the rule of law. This did not seem to be true of the South African government. The police were prepared to use violence, mass arrests, censorship, bannings and did not care about world disapproval. These factors affected Mandela's decision to form Umkhonto we Sizwe.*

T3 *The Soweto pupil rioters showed huge courage in facing the police and making their objections known. In doing so they made it clear that apartheid was never going to be willingly accepted by the non-white population, but could only be imposed on them by force. This was important in the developing opposition to apartheid: up to then the government had seemed able to crush opposition inside South Africa and successfully defy international opposition. From 1976 it was clear that there would be internal strife as long as apartheid existed.*

APARTHEID SURVIVES, 1960–80

HOW DID THE REST OF THE WORLD REACT TO APARTHEID?

The United Nations

The UN (see chapter 11) criticised apartheid from 1952. Sanctions were imposed in 1962 and South Africa was expelled from the UN in 1974.

The British Commonwealth

After the Second World War Britain began to dismantle its Empire. Many countries, especially in Africa, became independent (see Fig. 9.5). In 1960 the British Prime Minister Harold Macmillan visited South Africa and warned the government that a 'wind of change' was sweeping through Africa. He meant that, all over Africa, white colonial rulers were handing over power to the Africans. In the face of hostile criticism from other Commonwealth members, South Africa left the Commonwealth in 1961.

Organisation for African Unity (OAU)

The newly independent countries of Africa (see Fig. 9.5), formed the OAU in 1963. They were bitterly hostile to apartheid. The Lusaka Manifesto, 1969, declared their intention of overthrowing apartheid, by force if necessary.

HOW DID APARTHEID SURVIVE?

Despite the apparent hostility of the world, South Africa survived and, indeed, prospered, up to about 1980.

Minerals

All the nations of the world wanted South Africa's mineral wealth. It was not just gold and diamonds, but chromium, manganese, cobalt, platinum and aluminium, minerals without which a modern economy could not operate. Britain, West Germany, Japan and the USA invested heavily in South African mining.

South Africa's prosperity also brought other investors. Manufacturers liked to place factories in South Africa because of the low wages paid to black workers. These investors put pressure on their governments not to boycott South African trade.

The Cold War

Throughout this period the world was divided into two hostile power blocs (see chapter 10). The South African government was fiercely anti-Communist. The West feared that if white rule in South Africa ended, a new government might be more friendly to the USSR. This would mean all South Africa's wealth falling into Soviet hands. South Africa also protected the route taken by oil tankers from the Middle East to Europe and the USA. They dare not let it fall under Soviet control.

Geography

The geography of Africa was on South Africa's side (see Fig. 9.5), creating a line of 'buffer' states between South Africa and hostile black-ruled states to the north.

Figure 9.5
Africa in the 1960s and 1970s

- Angola and Mozambique. While Britain, France and Belgium had given independence to their colonies in Africa, Portugal had not. This left Angola and Mozambique still under white colonial rule.

- Botswana had become independent of Britain in 1966 but was a poor country, utterly reliant on South African economic support.

- South-West Africa – Namibia – was formerly a German colony, taken away from Germany at the Treaty of Versailles and handed over to South Africa as a League of Nations mandate (see chapter 3). Under the mandate, South Africa was supposed to help Namibia towards independence. In fact it was simply absorbed into South Africa and the apartheid system. In 1969 the UN ordered South Africa to hand Namibia back. South Africa refused and soon its army was involved in civil war there against a black independence movement – SWAPO (the South-West African People's Organisation).

- Rhodesia – Zimbabwe. The white settlers in the British colony of Rhodesia refused to accept independence under African rule and made a Unilateral Declaration of Independence in 1965. Britain and the UN declared sanctions against Rhodesia but South Africa helped prop up the illegal white government. All Rhodesia's supplies came in through South Africa or Mozambique. South African police helped the white Rhodesians fight the black nationalist movement.

LIFE IN SOUTH AFRICA

The government

The country was prospering and they were prepared to defy the world. They put money into refineries to convert their plentiful coal into oil, in order to beat sanctions. They could afford to build up their armed forces and make their own weapons. They even secretly developed nuclear weapons.

The whites

With good salaries, big houses, swimming-pools, cars and cheap black servants, many white South Africans lived well. Poor whites enjoyed the status and protection of apartheid laws. The sunny climate encouraged an outdoor, 'Californian' life-style. Segregated housing meant that whites and blacks hardly ever mixed. They were rather cut off from the rest of the world: they did not travel abroad much, there was no television until 1976 and heavy government censorship. This did not worry most people. Men were fanatical about sport, especially rugby. Women's equality lagged behind Europe and the USA.

There were white critics of apartheid:

- the Progressive Party;
- the Anglican Church, which elected Desmond Tutu as the first black Archbishop of Cape Town;
- the Black Sash organisation – white women who supported black women in the townships.

The blacks

A few educated black Africans and successful black businesspeople did well. Some prosperous black suburbs grew up. Wages for skilled black workers rose rapidly as government and employers wanted to create groups of better-off blacks. This new black middle class liked black Caribbean and US music, and soccer.

But for most black South Africans life was hard. Many worked as maids or garden 'boys' for white families, living tucked away in the gardens of white houses. Many still lived in the all-male compounds of the mining companies, away from their families for long periods. Others lived in the huge townships, in bad housing, overcrowded, poor, often unemployed, terrorised by violent gangs – the tsotsis. Over the years, more and more blacks were forcibly removed from their homes under the Group Areas Act (see p.186) because whites wanted their land. They were removed to barren patches of land, with little or no amenities and no jobs. Their only chance of a job was to commute to the nearest city, where they could work but were not allowed to live. This could mean spending up to six hours a day on a bus.

◀ **EXTRA POINTS**

1. When South Africa left the Commonwealth in 1961 many Afrikaners were pleased. It was a reversal of the 1902 peace treaty at the end of the Boer War, in which they had been forced to join the British Empire and accept the sovereignty of the British monarch.

2. Anti-apartheid groups in Britain tried to prevent all-white South African teams playing rugby or cricket here. Throughout the 1960s they disrupted games, but the British government was reluctant to use effective sanctions. South Africa would not admit teams from other countries which included non-white players.

3. The white South Africans saw themselves as different from white settlers in other parts of Africa. Elsewhere, British, French or Belgian settlers had a 'home country' in Europe to go to if they wanted to leave after independence. The Afrikaners had long since cut themselves off from the Netherlands, which they did not regard as home at all. They claimed they had 'nowhere else to go' and so clung on to their position.

Check yourself

QUESTIONS

Q1
a) Which organisations in the world outside South Africa tried to bring apartheid to an end?
b) Why did they fail for so long?

Q2 How important was the outside world to South Africa?

Q3 Look back to the 'theory' of apartheid (p.186). How far was it working by 1980?

REMEMBER! Cover the answers if you want to.

ANSWERS

A1
(a) The United Nations, the British government, the Organisation for African Unity.
(b) They failed because whatever means they tried did not work. Being disapproved of by Britain and the UN cut no ice with the Nationalists in power. They believed they were right and everyone else was wrong.

Sanctions did not work because many governments and companies found it too valuable to continue to trade with South Africa. Western governments, locked in a Cold War with the USSR, did not want to see the white government overthrown for fear that forces favourable to the USSR would take over. The West would then lose control of South Africa's resources and their important oil-tanker route round the Cape would be threatened.

The government could not be removed by military attack as all South Africa's neighbours were friendly countries. OAU countries were too weak to take on the powerful South African army.

A2 To some rural Afrikaners the outside world was unimportant. They had ignored it for years and would go on doing so. However, South Africa was no longer a farming economy, but a modern business and commercial economy. The country had to sell its goods abroad in order to buy things. In the 1960s and 1970s the world wanted to buy the minerals South Africa had to sell, so the country was deeply locked into world trade and prosperous white South Africans were used to foreign imports.

TUTORIALS

T1 *During this time ANC leaders in exile, notably Oliver Tambo, tried to win support for their cause. Most Western governments, particularly Britain, were not very sympathetic and did as little as possible. They called the ANC 'terrorists' and preferred to believe South African propaganda about them. Some argued that it was better to keep business contacts with South Africa, to try to persuade them to change their ways. Vorster (Prime Minister of South Africa, 1966–78) was good at sweet-talking Western visitors into thinking that things would get better.*

T2 *Its white population was used to a high standard of living, importing goods, like cars, clothes, electrical and other consumer goods. If ever trade worsened, they would feel the pinch. Some old-fashioned Afrikaners were deeply influenced by the laager state of mind (see p.182). They were quite prepared to defy the rest of the world for ever. This was not really practical for the country by this time.*

ANSWER

A3 The separation of races had been achieved, to such an extent that South African children hardly ever met up with children of a different racial group. However, there was no sign that South Africa's black population were growing to accept the situation. The Soweto riots and the continuing support for the ANC made this clear.

TUTORIAL

T3 *Further, the whole idea that black people were rural, farming people and so could be confined to the black homelands, was not happening. In fact, the trend was the reverse: in 1950 half of all black South Africans lived in towns and cities; by 1980 it was two-thirds (and these were just the official figures – lots more blacks lived in urban areas illegally). Apartheid had achieved a prosperous, white-run state, but it had no future.*

THE END OF APARTHEID

WHY DID APARTHEID END?

There were several long-term reasons.

Population

The population of South Africa was growing, but the different racial groups were growing differently. Back in 1946, 21 per cent of the population was white and 69 per cent black. By 1980, blacks made up 76 per cent of the population and whites only 13 per cent. They were clearly a tiny minority. Nor were the blacks staying in rural areas, as the builders of apartheid had intended. An increasing proportion now lived in towns and cities.

Economy

Business people were finding that apartheid and a modern business economy did not mix. As businesses expanded, they wanted to employ more people, but apartheid made it hard for black people to live in towns. In fact, they were being removed from towns. Businesses also began to want better educated employees and criticised the limited and underfunded black education apartheid provided.

Sanctions

In the early 1980s sanctions were still ineffective. At this time the British Prime Minister was Margaret Thatcher and Ronald Reagan was President of the USA. Both were strongly anti-Communist and opposed tough sanctions on South Africa. They knew that sanctions would hit their own trade with South Africa and argued that South African blacks would be hurt more by sanctions. They were not deterred by appeals from black leaders, like Archbishop Desmond Tutu, that sanctions were necessary. Sporting links between South Africa and other countries had been ended and sport-loving South Africans regretted this. Some ordinary people boycotted South African goods. However, neither of these pressures were going to bring down apartheid.

The end of the buffer states

In 1975 there was a revolution in Portugal and both Mozambique and Angola were given independence. The long civil war in Rhodesia ended with independence in 1980 under black rule. The country changed its name to Zimbabwe.

There were now hostile countries on South Africa's borders (see Fig. 9.5). They provided bases for ANC and PAC guerrillas who could now plant bombs in South African cities.

South Africa seemed on the brink of a terrible civil war, perhaps accompanied by invasion by black states to the north.

P.W. BOTHA AND 'TOTAL ONSLAUGHT, TOTAL STRATEGY'

The Prime Minister from 1978 to 1989 was P. W. Botha. He strengthened the links between the Army, big business and the Nationalist Party. He called his response to the situation: 'Total onslaught, total strategy'.

Total Onslaught

Army leaders worked closely with the government to keep order inside the country and crush its external enemies. The South African Army was built up until it was 500,000 strong by 1980. A further 130,000 were trained as a Citizen Force to resist invasion. The army raided guerrilla bases across the borders. It kept Namibia in a state of civil war by helping rebels. South African agents assassinated ANC and PAC leaders in foreign countries. Letter bombs were also sent. They waged a secret 'dirty' war.

They saw this war as part of the Cold War, fighting against Communism in Africa.

Total Strategy

This was a programme of reforms, intended to win the support of business people and Asians, coloureds and some blacks.

- The Mixed Marriages Act was repealed and so was segregation in some bars, theatres and restaurants.
- Blacks were allowed more freedom to move around to take jobs. The Pass laws were relaxed, then abolished in 1986.
- Black trade unions were allowed, 1979.
- Restricting some jobs for whites only was stopped, 1979.
- More money was put into black secondary education: three times more black people took up the opportunity.
- Under a new constitution, 1983, there were to be elections to a three chamber parliament, for whites (178 members), Asians (45) and coloureds (75).
- There were to be elected black councillors in the black townships.

These small-scale reforms only brought home to black South Africans that they had no real civil or political rights.

It is impossible to say what would have happened if the reforms of 'Total Strategy' had not been introduced, but their effect was to bring South Africa to the edge of chaos, from which the only peaceful way out was to abandon apartheid.

Short-term reasons for the end of apartheid:

- Black trade unions used the relaxation of the law to increase their strength and hold massive strikes. In 1986 1.5 million workers went on strike. These were clearly political strikes, accompanying the violent outbreaks on the streets.
- Black secondary school students formed strong student organisations.
- The growth of numbers of black people in the towns and the absence of Pass Laws made it easier for ANC guerrillas to slip into the country undetected. ANC guerrillas in Umkhonto we Sizwe caused explosions in shopping centres.

- Asians and coloureds were not impressed with the new constitution. Only about 20 per cent of them voted in the elections. The new black councillors in the townships were regarded as puppets of the whites and were often corrupt.

- More and more black people were able to live in towns. This made living conditions in the black townships even worse.

- In 1983 the United Democratic Front (UDF) was formed. Its leaders were churchmen, like Desmond Tutu and Allan Boesak, and ANC leaders like Winnie Mandela and Albertina Sisulu. The UDF was multiracial and based on the principles of the Freedom Charter (see p.191). It criticised the new constitution, with its continuing racial divisions and exclusion of the black population.

- The ANC leader in exile, Oliver Tambo, called on the South African people to make the country ungovernable. By the end of the 1980s they had succeeded.

- **Violence**
  All these grievances exploded in huge outbreaks of violence in the black townships and schools from 1984 onwards. The South African police used force to put them down, but never really regained control in some areas. A state of emergency was declared which covered almost the whole country by 1986. It was like an uprising.

  Some of the violence was between blacks, sometimes using 'necklace' killings, in which the victims were burnt alive by hanging a petrol-soaked car tyre round their necks. Targets of black violence were the better off, black councillors and black policemen. Soon it was clear that the South African police were encouraging black-on-black violence to distract them from attacking the white government.

- **Economic problems**
  The riots, including police violence on unarmed demonstrators, was seen on televison throughout the world. Although the South African government censored media coverage later, the damage had been done. Anti-apartheid demonstrations and boycotts increased. Companies who had invested in South Africa came under pressure at shareholders' meetings. For example, in 1985 Barclays Bank sold its South African operation. In the USA particularly, black politicians and businesspeople put pressure on international companies, like Shell, to pull out of South Africa. By the late 1980s more and more companies were doing so.

  Inflation, high taxes, absence of imported goods from the shops, began to hurt the white community.

- Some whites felt that Botha's reforms were to blame and split off from the Nationalist Party. The Conservative Party began to gain support by calling for a total return of apartheid. In 1987 they won 37 per cent of the Afrikaner vote. P. W. Botha's policies were clearly failing. He was succeeded in 1989 by F. W. de Klerk.

F.W. DE KLERK AND THE END OF APARTHEID

In his first speech, February 1989, de Klerk called for radical changes:

- Un-banning of the ANC, PAC and the Communist Party
- Release of Nelson Mandela
- A new constitution based on equal rights for all.

201

Why did de Klerk call for radical change?

- Worldwide Communism was collapsing (see p.248). The Cold War was ending and perhaps there was no Communist threat to South Africa.

- The economic situation was getting worse (see above).

- Secret talks had been held between National Party leaders and ANC leaders in exile, some of them in country houses in Britain. Nationalists discovered, perhaps to their surprise, that ANC leaders were reasonable, intelligent men who could be trusted.

- By 1989 much of the country was ungovernable, except through tough police methods. Violence was escalating each month. Four thousand people had been killed since 1985 and 50,000 were in prison.

- Some people have argued that de Klerk made a mistake: he thought the ANC would split, that Mandela, now aged 70, would want to retire quietly, that the National Party could share power. If so, he reckoned without the extraordinary personality and political determination of Nelson Mandela and the rest of the ANC leadership.

THE LAST FOUR YEARS OF WHITE RULE

The return of the ANC

In October 1989 Walter Sisulu was released. Nelson Mandela insisted that he would only agree to release if he was allowed to take part in politics. De Klerk agreed this in February 1990. On his release Mandela promised:
'I stand before you as the humble servant of you all, the people. I place the remaining years of my life in your hands.'

He went to meet the rest of the ANC leadership in Zambia to reassure them he was still fit and capable. He was elected Deputy Leader to Oliver Tambo, who had kept the ANC alive in long difficult years of exile, and who was now ill. By the end of 1990 the ANC had called off the guerrilla war and the exiles had returned.

Apartheid is dismantled

De Klerk then repealed most of the apartheid laws:
End of segregated hospitals, 1990; Separate Amenities Act repealed, 1990; Group Areas Act repealed, 1991; Land Act repealed, 1991; Population Registration Act repealed, 1991; all other racially-based laws repealed, 1993.

Talks begin

The Convention for a Democratic South Africa (CODESA) began in 1991 to work out a new constitution.

Violence continues

The background to these constructive developments was escalating violence. Between 1990 and 1994, 60,000 people were killed in political violence, more than the number who died in the Boer War.

What were the causes of the violence?

- ANC members were impatient for change. They felt the Nationalists were deliberately delaying talks so as to cling on to power and hope that the ANC split. Mandela needed all his force of personality to hold his supporters together.

- Chief Buthelezi and the Inkatha Freedom Party. Chief Buthelezi was a puzzling character. He had been a member of the ANC Youth

Wing, but had accepted the position of Chief Minister in one of the apartheid 'homelands', KwaZulu. He called for the release of Nelson Mandela but had links with the National government. He set up the Inkatha Freedom Party to campaign for self-government for the Zulu people in a democratic South Africa, claiming that the ANC only represented Xhosas, not Zulus.

● He did not attend the CODESA talks and Inkatha committed acts of violence against ANC members, such as the massacre at Boipatong in 1992, in which thirty-eight people were brutally killed. ANC supporters also attacked Inkatha members.

● It soon became clear that Inkatha was being assisted by the South African police. Some people in the National government were trying to build Buthelezi up as an alternative black leader to Mandela, so weakening the influence of the ANC. However, the violence of Buthelezi's supporters only put off many people and further discredited the National Party.

● Some whites turned to armed extremist groups like the AWB. They threatened civil war if white rule came to an end.

FREE ELECTIONS, APRIL 1994

De Klerk held a referendum among whites in 1991, calling for support for his programme of complete change. He won a big majority, weakening the position of the Conservative Party and the extremists.

A new constitution was agreed in November 1993 and the first fully democratic elections in South Africa's history were held in April 1994 (see Fig 9.6).

Figure 9.6
Voters of all races outside a polling station during the 1994 elections

Results

The ANC won 62.5 per cent of the vote, and seven of the nine provinces. The National Party won 20.5 per cent of the vote and Western Cape province. The Inkatha Freedom Party won 10.5 per cent of the vote and Natal province.

Nelson Mandela became President of the new South Africa, de Klerk became Deputy and Buthelezi a Minister. Mandela called it 'a small miracle'.

EXTRA POINTS ▶

1. Trade unions were very important in the years when the ANC was banned. In 1985 the Confederation of South African Trade Unions (COSATU), led by Cyril Ramaphosa. He also played a large part in the CODESA talks.

2. The AWB (Afrikaner Weerstands Beweging – Afrikaner Resistance Group) was an extreme, neo-Nazi, white supremacist group. They were armed and seemed to pose a threat to law and order

3. The CODESA talks were not easy. In May 1992 the ANC pulled out because the National Party was only talking about power-sharing, not real democracy. The ANC also insisted that the National government were using Inkatha and the police to incite violence against ANC supporters, such as at Boipatong. They began a campaign of civil disobedience and strikes which brought the country to a standstill. Talks resumed in March 1993. The ANC agreed on a period of power-sharing leading to full democracy.

Check yourself

QUESTIONS

Q1 How did (a) population changes, and (b) changes in states to the north affect apartheid?

Q2 Look at the list of measures that made up P. W. Botha's 'Total Strategy'. Which were intended to win over business people and which to win over Asians, coloureds and some blacks?

Q3 Why did 'Total Strategy' fail?

Q4 Nelson Mandela wrote, in 1990: 'Whites are fellow South Africans and we want them to feel safe and to know that we appreciate the contribution they have made towards the development of this country.' Why were these views important?

Q5 Why couldn't the picture, Figure 9.6, have been taken at any other date than April 1994?

REMEMBER! Cover the answers if you want to.

ANSWERS

A1
(a) The black population was growing faster than the whites, so the whites were in a smaller and smaller minority. Also the proportion of blacks living in towns was rising, not falling as the original architects of apartheid had intended.

(b) The states to the north of South Africa, Mozambique, Angola and Rhodesia (Zimbabwe) were ruled by whites until the late 1970s. This meant that other African states, sworn to overthrow apartheid, were kept at bay. From 1980 hostile forces could be built up right on South Africa's borders.

TUTORIALS

T1
(a) *The statistics are worth looking at: in 1946 blacks outnumbered whites by only just over three to one. By 1980 it was nearly six to one. Some whites began to argue that they would not be able to hold down such a huge majority for much longer.*

(b) *After 1980 ANC (Umkhonto we Sizwe) and PAC guerrillas set up bases just outside South Africa. In the long term, the black nations of Africa might launch a military attack on South Africa. The events in the three buffer states had a profound effet on South Africa's external security.*

A2 Business people: relaxation of the Pass Laws; removal of whites-only job restrictions; trade unions; more black secondary education.

Asians, coloureds and some blacks: Mixed Marriages Act and segregation in public places; 1983 constitution; elected black councillors.

A3 It was too little, too late. The opponents of apartheid saw the concessions of 'Total Strategy' as a sign that apartheid was weakening. They were also not going to be bought off with a few concessions which left the whites still in complete control of South Africa.

A4 Mandela was holding out a hand of friendship to white South Africans. Their fear was that they would be swept aside when black majority rule came in. Their proud claim was that they had built up the country, invested their lives and money in it. Mandela was acknowledging this.

A5 This was the first ever election in South Africa's history when whites and blacks, everyone of voting age, could vote, with each vote equal.

T2 *There is some overlap. P. W. Botha wanted to create a black middle class, who, he hoped, would have too much to lose in the form of good houses, jobs and possessions to throw in their lot with the anti-apartheid forces. So everything that allowed blacks to get better jobs and education was also intended to win over these people.*

T3 *It also loosened the grip of apartheid on the lives of black people so they were able to move about more freely, protest more freely through trade unions and the UDF. Total Strategy also unleashed violence on a massive scale, which the government simply did not have the force to contain.*

T4 *This is a remarkable statement. Only a few months before he had been released from twenty-six years of a humiliating prison sentence and here he is offering to acknowledge their contribution and wanting them to 'feel safe'. Mandela's absence of revengefulness did a great deal to win over white opinion to change.*

T5 *They are all voting together, too. For the decades of apartheid there had been separate post offices, hospitals, waiting-rooms, train compartments and government offices. Now white and black were using the same polling station.*

EXAM PRACTICE

Sample Student's Answers & Examiner's Comments

---

1 Read this source and answer the questions which follow:

'I am not a Communist and have never been a member of the Communist Party.... It is true that there has often been close co-operation between the ANC and Communist Party. But co-operation is merely proof of a common goal ... not complete community of interest.'

Nelson Mandela, speaking at his trial at Rivonia in 1964

(a) Why was Mandela on trial? (4)

Nelson Mandela was on trial for opposing apartheid and trying to overthrow the government using violent means. He and his organisation —Umkhonto we Sizwe — had caused explosions which brought down power cables.

3/4

EXAMINER'S COMMENTS

MARK SCHEME

Level 1	General comments, e.g. he was opposed to apartheid	**1–2 marks**
Level 2	Knowledge of the specific accusations	**3–4 marks**

This answer goes nearly all the way in the right direction. However, the charge was not just that the explosions had taken place, but that they were part of an organised plan to overthrow the government and the whole system.

(b) Why was he making such a strong point about his relations with the Communist Party? (4)

He was anxious to clear himself of the charge of Communism because the South African government regarded any opposition to apartheid as motivated by Communism. In fact the Freedom Charter had been drawn up in 1955 by the ANC and other organisations, including the Communist Party. He wanted to make it clear that there was more to opposition to apartheid than just a Soviet plot.

4/4

EXAMINER'S COMMENTS

MARK SCHEME

Level 1	Wanted to show he was not a Communist	**1–2 marks**
Level 2	Wanted to show that opposition was not restricted to Communism but was more broadly-based	**3–4 marks**

The last sentence gets the full marks here. It was a brave stand he was making. It was easy for the government to dismiss all opposition as just motivated by Communism, which they – and many people in the Western world at that time – regarded as totally evil. (For more on this attitude, see chapter 10.)

2 Why were several countries unwilling to impose sanctions on South Africa? (8)

The UN imposed sanctions on South Africa in 1962. This meant that other nations should not trade with South Africa. The aim was to provoke an economic crisis which would cause the government to change its policies. However, several countries did not apply sanctions fully, or even at all.

Some traded with South Africa. They needed the specialised metals —chromium, manganese, cobalt, platinum and aluminium — which South Africa could provide. There were also many outside companies with branches in South Africa and doing very well. They were unwilling to lose this trade.

Some countries were afraid that if the National government in South Africa were overthrown, it would be replaced by a pro-Soviet one. Thus all these vital supplies would fall into Soviet hands. It would also give the USSR a base in South Africa which could threaten the oil-tanker route from the Middle East to Europe and the USA.

5/8

EXAMINER'S COMMENTS

MARK SCHEME

Level 1	Suggests these countries supported apartheid	1–2 marks
Level 2	Gives simple reason(s) for opposition to sanctions	3–5 marks
Level 3	Explains complex reasons, including those who opposed apartheid but doubted that sanctions were the best way to do this.	6–8 marks

The answer gives the two main reasons why some world leaders of the 1980s, like President Reagan and Mrs Thatcher, were against sanctions. It is well-detailed, and so gets the top marks in its level, Level 2.

However, there were those who wanted to change the system but doubted whether sanctions was the way to do it. Some wanted to keep up business connections with South Africa, arguing that they needed to keep talking with South Africans, to change their minds.

Another argument, often from the same people, was a doubt that sanctions would work. They pointed out that sanctions would hit black workers at least as much as the white government, probably more.

Questions to Answer
The answers to Questions 3 and 4 can be found on pp.274 and 275

3 Did apartheid fall because of outside pressure or internal protest? (15)

4 Percentage of South Africans living in towns:

	Whites	Africans
1951	78	27
1991	91	58

(a) Explain the reasons for these changes. (5)

(b) Why did these changes present a problem for the policy of apartheid? (5)

CHAPTER 10

THE COLD WAR

THE ORIGINS OF THE COLD WAR

Soldiers from the USA and the USSR were wartime allies in the struggle against Hitler (see Fig. 10.1). Yet within a year of the end of the war the two **superpowers** were locked in a new struggle, a **Cold War**, which lasted for forty-five years.

Figure 10.1
US and Soviet soldiers meet in Germany, May 1945

Superpower

The most dominant countries in world politics up to 1945 were European: Britain, France and Germany. By 1945 these countries were in ruins or crippled by the Second World War. The world was now dominated by two new countries, the USA and the USSR.

As we shall see, they were very different from each other. The USSR was the largest country in the world, with the biggest army. The USA was the richest country in the world, with the atom bomb. These two were far ahead of their rivals, and their power extended over the whole world. They were therefore called superpowers.

Cold War

This term was first used in 1947. It was a war carried out by every possible means short of the US and USSR actually fighting each other. Sometimes, as you will see, the Cold War nearly became a real – 'hot' – war, but one side or the other always held back.

- **An arms race** (see p.224)
  Both sides spent large amounts of money on building up stockpiles of weapons, particularly nuclear weapons. Soon they had enough weapons between them to destroy all life on earth. This is why the Cold War is so important.

- **Rivalry**
  They were rivals in the space race: the USSR launched the first satellite, in 1957; the USA made the first moon landing, in 1969. They were also rivals in sport.

- **Propaganda**
  Each side broadcast propaganda to their own people and to the rest of the world.

- **Spying**
  Each side had a huge network of spies to find out what the other was up to. The USA had the CIA (Central Intelligence Agency); the USSR had the KGB.

- **Control**
  Each side controlled the countries nearby. Any attempt by one of these countries to break free and follow their own line was crushed, for example, the USSR in Hungary, 1956 and Czechoslovakia, 1968 (see p.242 and 243), Afghanistan, 1979 and Poland, 1980–81 (see p.244); the USA in Cuba, 1962 (see p.228), Guatemala, 1954 and Chile, 1973.

- **Substitute wars**
  Both superpowers took part in substitute (or proxy) wars. That is, each helped its allies fight the other superpower or its allies. For example, the USA helped South Korea and USSR helped North Korea in the Korean War, 1950–53 (see p.220); the USSR helped North Vietnam in war against the USA, 1961–73 (see p.232). The USA and the USSR helped rival sides in civil wars in the Congo, 1960 (see p.259) and Namibia. The USA helped Israel and the USSR helped several Arab nations in their conflicts in the Middle East.

WHAT WERE THE LONG-TERM CAUSES OF THE COLD WAR?

Russian fear of the West

Russia had been invaded three times in the twentieth century: in 1914, at the start of the First World War (see p.28), in 1918, in the Civil War (see p.108) and in 1941.

Stalin felt that some Western leaders wanted to see Communism crushed. They remembered that Britain, France and other Western countries sent troops to help the Whites against the new Communist government in 1918. They felt the Western powers had been too slow to join with them against Hitler in the 1930s. In the Second World War, up to twenty million Soviet citizens had been killed, soldiers as well as civilians. Farmland, industries and cities had been devastated. The Red Army had only driven back the German invasion after a long and bitter struggle. They felt the Western countries did not understand how they had suffered and had been too slow to relieve German pressure on the USSR by invading Western Europe.

US and Western fear of Communism

Some people believed that Communists were intent on causing revolutions in other countries. If you have read chapters 5, 6 and 7 you will have seen something of the ways the governments and the economies of the USA and the USSR worked. They were very different.

- **Government**
  The USA had a two-party democracy, with elections for President and Congress.

  The USSR was a one-party state. There were elections, but the Communist Party was the only party allowed. Stalin had ruled as a dictator since 1928.

- **Economy**
  The USA was a *capitalist* country. That is, the land and industry was owned by private individuals who ran them for their own profit. It produced great unfairness, with some people very rich and some very poor, but it also created successful industry and commerce. The average standard of living was higher in the capitalist West.

The USSR was a *Communist* country. That is, the land and industry were owned by the state, which ran them – in theory – for the good of every citizen. There was security of employment, free education and health, but lack of competition and heavy government control led to inefficiency in industry and business. The result was a shortage of goods, lower quality and less innovation; in general, a lower standard of living.

● **Freedom**
There was more political freedom in the USA, for example, more than one party to vote for, a free press which could criticise the government, no secret police, freedom to travel where you wanted, relaxed censorship in the arts and media.

In the USSR, there was strict censorship, criticism of the government could land you in prison, you couldn't travel outside the USSR and the Soviet block.

Both sides felt they were right and claimed that the other was trying to extend its system all over the world.

The end of US isolation

The USA felt that they had been partly to blame for the Second World War by their isolationist policy between the wars (see p.134). They felt they could have done more to stop Hitler earlier and were now determined to use their power to play a big part in world affairs. For many Americans this meant opposing dictatorship and setting up multi-party democracies and capitalist economies everywhere. Many were bitterly opposed to Communism.

President Roosevelt was keen to take up the idea of an international peacekeeping organisation which President Woodrow Wilson had supported in 1919 but which the USA had never joined (see pp.46 and 158). Roosevelt had plans for a new organisation, the United Nations, of which he had high hopes (see chapter 11).

EXTRA POINTS ▶

1. Superpowers. The statistics are:

	USA	USSR
Size	9 million sq.km.	21 million sq. km.
Population	226 million	262 million (1984)
Armed forces	2 million	4.8 million (1984)
Wealth	$2,100 billion	$1,200 billion (1984)

2. Early Communists, like Marx, Lenin and Trotsky, had tried to spread Communism all over the world. Comintern, set up in 1919 was designed to promote this. Stalin, however, had always promoted a policy of 'Socialism in one country' (see chapter 6).

Check yourself

QUESTION

Q1 Use the description of the two different systems in the USA and the USSR to fill in the gaps at (a), (b), (c) and (d) on this table:

	USA	USSR
Government	Two-party democracy	(a)
Economic system	(b)	(c)
Freedom	(d)	Censorship, secret police, restrictions on travel

REMEMBER! Cover the answers if you want to.

ANSWER

A1
a) Only one party allowed, the Communist Party.
b) Capitalism. That is, all economic activity is owned and run by private individuals. They seek to make a profit from supplying what the public wants at a price the public will pay.
c) Communism. The state owns and runs all economic activity. Factories make what the state planners tell them to make, at a price fixed by the state.
d) More personal freedom. Owners of businesses – capitalists – have freedom to run their businesses how they like. People have freedom to travel. The press and TV criticise the government freely. There is less censorship.

TUTORIAL

T1
a) The Communists still called this one-party system democracy. Elections were held, and debate took place inside the Communist Party rather than between parties. This confusion over the meaning of democracy was one of the key misunderstandings of the early days of the Cold War.
b)&c) The description here applies to the USA (b) and the USSR (c). There are other forms of capitalism and Communism.

In several Western European countries, for example, capitalists are not free to do what they like and the state owns some businesses. Other Communist states are not so centralised as the USSR. It was the stifling of personal initiative and freedom which led to the failure of Soviet Communism, as you will see at the end of this chapter.
d) This freedom also includes the freedom to sack workers, to pay low wages and to make other people poor and homeless. State control of economic activity in Communist states prevented these things from happening.

THE COLD WAR BEGINS

The short-term causes of the Cold War arose out of the events of 1945–46 as the war ended and the peace began. The long-term fears and resentments described in the previous section began to appear at two important meetings in 1945.

YALTA, FEBRUARY 1945

Churchill (the British wartime Prime Minister), Roosevelt and Stalin met at Yalta, in the USSR (see Fig. 10.2). It was clear that Germany was about to be defeated and the three victorious allies met to decide how to manage the peace. There were some disagreements, but the three leaders seemed to be able to negotiate to settle them.

Figure 10.2
Churchill, Roosevelt and Stalin at Yalta

- The USSR agreed to join in the war against Japan as soon as Hitler was defeated.

- All three agreed to join the new United Nations.

- They discussed in general terms what should happen in countries liberated from Nazi rule. Vague statements were agreed that 'free' elections would be held and that Eastern Europe should be a Soviet 'sphere of influence'.

- They agreed that Germany should be divided into four zones as their armies advanced. Churchill pressed for a French zone to be added to the other three in order to give another anti-Soviet voice to the armies of occupation. The important capital city of Berlin was similarly divided, even though it was inside the Soviet zone, and so was the country of Austria (see Fig. 10.3). These were not intended to be permanent divisions.

Figure 10.3
Europe in 1945

Map legend:

Occupation zones in Germany and Austria
- American
- British
- French
- Russian

- German border, 1939
- Post-war boundaries
- Iron curtain
- Countries taken by Russia, 1945
- Countries under Russian communist influence
- Communist country but not allied to Stalin

- There was some disagreement over Poland. Stalin wanted to add some Polish territory to the USSR, compensating Poland with land in the east from Germany (see Fig. 10.3 for what this meant). Roosevelt was not keen on this but Churchill was ready to accept it if the USSR accepted British influence in Greece. In the end Roosevelt agreed as the price for Soviet joining the UN. There was, in fact, little the Allies could do about anything in Eastern Europe, as the advancing Red Army occupied it all.

Roosevelt died of cancer in April 1945 and Harry Truman took over as President of the USA. Germany surrendered in May. A Communist government was set up in Poland, without democratic elections. The next meeting was at Potsdam, just outside Berlin.

The USA successfully tested an atomic bomb just before the conference. Stalin's spies had already told him that this was going to happen, but he was annoyed that the USA had not shared their knowledge with their ally, the USSR. This also increased his fear of the USA which could clearly now destroy the USSR if it wished.

POTSDAM, JULY 1945

Churchill was defeated in the British 1945 General Election part way through the conference. Discussions therefore took place between Truman, Stalin and the new Labour Prime Minister Clement Attlee. Truman did not get on with Stalin and the Potsdam conference did not go so well.

● The only agreement was to put twenty-one leading Nazis on trial at Nuremberg for war crimes and to round up and punish Nazis in their respective zones.

● Stalin wanted harsh peace terms for Germany, demanding $20 billion reparations, crippling the country and seizing what was left of its industry. Truman disagreed, remembering the effects of the Versailles Treaty of 1919 on Germany.

● Truman was angry at Soviet actions in Poland imposing a one-party Communist state and their seizure of more land (see Fig. 10.3). Parts of Finland, Poland, Czechoslovakia, Romania as well as all of Lithuania, Latvia and Estonia were now under Soviet rule. The USSR had expanded 480 kilometres westwards, bringing 22 million people under Soviet rule.

THE SOVIET TAKEOVER OF EASTERN EUROPE

Over the next three years all of Eastern Europe came under Soviet control. In Bulgaria, Hungary and Romania Communists took over at once. In Poland and Czechoslovakia they shared power for a while and then non-Communists were thrown out. The last to fall was Czechoslovakia in 1948. The next stage was that local Communist leaders were replaced by pro-Soviet, pro-Stalin Communists. In 1947 'Comiform' (the Communist Information Bureau) put all Communist parties under the control of Moscow. Secret police began their work, putting an end to freedom and their economies were run for the benefit of the USSR. Soon all eight countries shown in Figure 10.3 were little more than provinces of the USSR. They were often called 'satellites' in the West.

Only Tito, in Yugoslavia, managed to keep a Communist government free of Stalin's control.

What was really going on? Here, and at other points in this chapter, different interpretations can be put on events.

INTERPRETATIONS

● Stalin said that these measures were purely defensive. He pointed out that anti-Soviet governments in these countries had helped the German invasion of 1941. He went on: 'What can there be surprising about the fact that the Soviet Union, anxious for its future safety, is trying to see that governments loyal to the Soviet Union should exist in these countries?'

● People in the west were horrified.

  ■ They were angry that undemocratic governments had been set up in these countries, contrary to what they thought Stalin had promised at Yalta. They were opposed to dictatorship.

  ■ They did not believe Stalin was acting purely defensively. There were powerful Communist parties in France and Italy; the Red Army had not gone home. Perhaps they would march into Western Europe next.

THE IRON CURTAIN

As early as May 1945 Churchill had used the phrase 'Iron Curtain' to describe what was happening in Europe. More famously, speaking at Fulton, Missouri, in 1946 he said: 'An iron curtain has descended. Behind that line lie all the states of Central and Eastern Europe. This is not the liberated Europe we fought to build. Nor is it one which allows permanent peace.'

SUMMARY OF SHORT-TERM CAUSES OF THE COLD WAR

- Soviet need for secure borders
- Soviet fear of US atomic weapons
- Soviet fear of US attack
- US resentment of Communist takeover of Eastern Europe
- US fear of Communist move into Western Europe
- US fear of Communist plans to expand all over the world.

Personal relations between the leaders at Yalta and Potsdam played a part in the growing hostility. Roosevelt felt he got on quite well with Stalin and was critical of Churchill's imperialism. Truman was openly hostile to Stalin. Stalin was suspicious of all four of the Western leaders he had to deal with.

 **EXTRA POINT**

Check yourself

QUESTIONS

Q1 Which do you think was the strongest superpower in 1945? Give reasons for your choice.

Q2 List the reasons why Stalin feared the West.

Q3 Why were relations between the Allies at Potsdam worse than they were at Yalta?

Q4 'The Cold War was based on misunderstanding between the USA and the USSR.' How accurate do you think this statement is?

ANSWERS

A1 The USA, because it was by far the richest and had the atom bomb.

A2 Western countries had tried to crush the Bolshevik government by helping the Whites in 1918 in the Civil War. Western powers had refused to let the USSR join the League of Nations until 1934 and treated them as outcasts in the 1930s. Stalin thought some people in the West actually wanted Hitler to attack the USSR rather than Western Europe. Stalin thought the Western Allies had refused to open up a second front so that the USSR had borne the brunt of Hitler's invasion.

A3 There were different people at Potsdam from Yalta: Attlee replaced Churchill; Truman replaced Roosevelt. Roosevelt had got on better with Stalin than Truman did.

Stalin was annoyed and worried by the US atom bomb test, partly because the USA had not shared their nuclear know-how and partly from fear of a US nuclear attack.

Truman was angry about the Soviet takeover of Eastern Europe, setting up puppet governments, ignoring the wishes of the people, and forcing communism on them.

A4 There was misunderstanding. Both sides thought the other was intent on expanding further. Stalin feared that the USA would follow up the hostility which other countries had had towards the USSR since 1917 by using its atomic bomb. Truman thought the Soviet takeover of Eastern Europe was just the first stage in a move to expand Communism all over the world. Both sides claimed they were only acting defensively. Stalin referred to the three attacks on Russia/the USSR this century. USA claimed to have no plans to attack the USSR.

TUTORIALS

T1 *It is clear, with hindsight, that this is right. The USSR was never really in the same league as the USA and the standard of living of its people was far below that of US citizens. However, it was not as clear as this in 1945. The huge Red Army had defeated the German army and lay across half of Europe. Its planes and tanks had proved superior. It is easy to see why they seemed more equal then.*

T2 *All these were partly true: some leading figures in Britain openly preferred Hitler to Stalin, although it was never British government policy to nudge Hitler away from the West towards Russia: he always intended to invade Russia anyway.*

T3 *At Yalta, in February, the war was not over and the Allies still had to work together to defeat Germany. By July, at Potsdam, the war in Europe was over. The statesmen were more concerned to look forward to the peace and new rivalries emerged.*

T4 *It has been pointed out that in 1945 neither side had an effective network of spies looking at the real motives of the other side. If they had, they might have known that Stalin was not intending to go any further west and no one in the US government had plans to bomb the USSR.*

Some US politicians were not so hostile to the USSR as Truman. Some argued, as Roosevelt had done, that each side should agree to differ. However, all this is seen with hindsight: in 1945–46 anything seemed possible.

THE TRUMAN DOCTRINE, CONTAINMENT AND THE BERLIN AIRLIFT

Truman did not at first agree with Churchill's 'Iron Curtain' speech of 1946. However, as events unfolded in Eastern Europe, he began to feel that the USA should be taking a tougher line with the USSR. In 1947 he set up the NSC (National Security Council) and the CIA.

WHAT WAS THE TRUMAN DOCTRINE?

After 1945 there was civil war in Greece between the monarchists, supported by the British, and Greek Communists. In 1947 Britain, going through a very hard time economically, announced that they could not afford to go on helping the monarchists. Truman decided he could not let another country fall to the Communists and sent money to help the monarchists.

More important was his announcement of his reasons, in which he said: 'I believe that it must be the policy of the United States to support free peoples who are resisting attempted subjugation by armed minorities or outside pressure.' This was called the 'Truman Doctrine' and began the policy of **containment**. This meant that the USA was not going to allow any more countries to turn Communist: it was going to 'contain' the expansion of Communism. It was to be a huge commitment.

WHAT WAS THE PURPOSE OF MARSHALL AID?

Truman and his advisers believed that people were turning to Communism only because they were desperate. In 1948 Truman sent his Secretary of State, General George Marshall, to Europe to look at the problem. He found Europe still in dire difficulties. Unlike the First World War, fighting in the Second World War had taken place all over Europe. In the last year of the war retreating Nazis had destroyed everything, ripping up railway tracks and burning towns. Allied bombing raids left massive destruction. Refugees were criss-crossing Europe looking for their homes and families or for safety. Europe owed the USA $11.5 billion. Marshall recommended loans totalling $17 billion so that Europe could recover.

The US Congress was reluctant to agree to such a huge loan. Then came the brutal Communist takeover in Czechoslovakia and Congress voted to find the money for Marshall Aid.

Marshall Aid helped to rebuild Western Europe. Britain alone received $3.1 billion between 1948 and 1952. It was not quite a selfless gesture: Marshall Aid helped US industry by giving them a market for their goods. Stalin refused to accept any, and would not allow any Eastern block country to accept any. He said it was just part of the US plan to undermine Communism and spread capitalism all over the world.

WHY WAS BERLIN A FLASHPOINT IN THE COLD WAR?

At the heart of the problem of reviving Europe was what to do about Germany. The agricultural east was in the Soviet zone while the more industrial west was in the three Allied zones. This split had been agreed at Yalta but they had not allowed for disagreements between the four occupying powers. The German population was swollen by sixteen million refugees from all over Europe. Its economy was in ruins, reduced to barter or using cigarettes as currency. There was not enough food or medical supplies.

Stalin continued to dismantle German factories and take them off to the USSR. As far as he was concerned, Germany and its people could rot.

The Allies felt they could not let the German people starve. On the other hand they could not afford to just hand out food.

INTERPRETATIONS

- The Western Allies decided that the German economy should be allowed to recover so that the German people could work and trade and so earn money to feed themselves. In 1946 the three Allied zones were united in one unit. In 1948 a new currency was introduced to help the German economic revival. The USSR was not consulted over this owing to the mistrust developing between the two sides.

- Stalin feared the revival of Germany. The USSR had suffered terribly at German hands during the war and he now feared that German revival would lead to a combined attack on the USSR. He was furious and in June 1948 closed off all road, rail and canal access to Berlin (see Fig 10.4).

Figure 10.4
Berlin and Germany, 1948–49

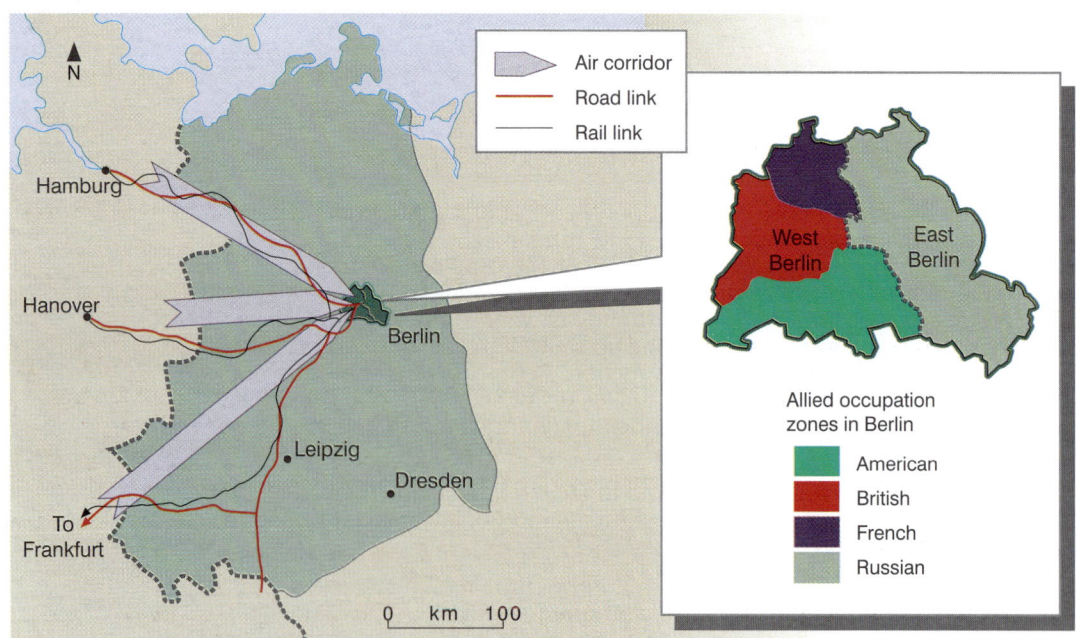

Stalin hoped the blockade would force the Allies out of West Berlin. Truman announced: 'We are going to stay. Period.' 2.1 million citizens lived in the Allied Western zones of Berlin. They needed 4,000 tonnes of supplies a day to exist. How were they to be supplied? Should the Allies send tanks down one of the roads and fight their way through? Should they threaten to bomb the USSR in retaliation?

Either of these alternatives would lead to another war and the Allies chose the least aggressive option: to supply the city by air. For the next ten months – 318 days – food, fuel and medical supplies were flown in. The aeroplanes made a total of 27,000 flights before the USSR opened the land routes again in May 1949.

RESULTS OF THE BERLIN CRISIS

1. Germany remained divided until 1990. In 1949 the Allied zones became West Germany (Federal Republic of Germany); the Soviet zone became East Germany (Democratic Republic of Germany).

2. West Berlin stayed a Western island inside East Germany and a permanent source of tension in the Cold War.

3. The division of Europe – the Iron Curtain – became permanent. By the 1950s watchtowers, barbed wire and mines had turned it into a real barrier. Travel across it was very difficult. Europe was a divided continent as long as the Cold War lasted.

EXTRA POINT

More of Truman's words from his speech explaining the Truman Doctrine quoted above are worth reading as examples of how the US thought about the clash of systems at that time:

'At the present moment nearly every nation must choose between alternative ways of life. The choice is too often not a free one. One way of life is based on the will of the majority, freedom of speech and freedom from political oppression. The second way of life is based on the will of a minority forcibly imposed on the majority. It relies on terror and oppression, a controlled press and radio, fixed elections.'

Check yourself

QUESTIONS

Q1 What two reasons does Truman give in his speech to explain how Communists were taking over?

Q2 'A helping hand to Europe'; 'An attempt to spread US capitalism across the world'. Which of these two views of Marshall Aid do you think is more accurate?

Q3 In what ways is the Berlin Airlift an example of Cold War, not hot war?

REMEMBER! Cover the answers if you want to.

ANSWER

A1 Armed minorities; outside pressure.

TUTORIAL

T1 *Perhaps Truman had Greece in mind for the first, where armed Greek Communists were fighting to take over the country. Britain's inability to go on opposing them was the occasion for Truman making this speech. For 'outside pressure' he would have been thinking of all the countries of Eastern Europe, pressured by the USSR into setting up Communist-controlled governments.*

ANSWERS

A2 It was a helping hand to Europe, but that is not the whole story. It was also motivated by a fear that Communism flourished in conditions of poverty and desperation. A revived Europe would be able to resist Communism better.

A3 The Berlin Airlift is an example of Cold War because the USA and the Allies avoided direct confrontation with the USSR when they might have tried to bust through the Soviet blockade.

TUTORIALS

T2 *This answer is right as far as it goes. There was idealism, a 'helping hand'. There was also a real fear in the West at this time that Western Europe would soon join Eastern Europe in the Communist camp. However, US business did stand to gain, even if Stalin's complaint about the spread of worldwide capitalism was unjustified. They remembered the Wall Street Crash, caused mainly by over-production (see p.146) and realised that the USA had to develop markets in other countries to avoid another depression.*

T3 *The USSR also avoided direct confrontation by not attacking any of the planes in the airlift. They may have thought it was impossible to supply a big city by air, but they did not try to stop it.*

CONTAINMENT AROUND THE WORLD: KOREA

1949 was a bad year for the USA in the Cold War:

- The USSR exploded its own atom bomb. This meant that the USA no longer had a monopoly of nuclear weapons and its whole strategy had to be re-thought (see p.224).

- China became Communist after a long civil war in which the USA had backed the losing side, the Nationalists. They had spent $2 billion and now, despite their efforts, the most populous country in the world was Communist.

Results

McCarthyism

A kind of anti-Communist hysteria gripped the USA. A young senator, Joseph McCarthy, claimed that things were going wrong for the USA because there were Communists in high places in American society and government. He received massive publicity by claiming that he had evidence of fifty-seven Communists in the US State Department.

In the anti-Communist mood of the time no one dared oppose him. Merely to question his charges led to accusations of being a Communist. Many people lost their jobs as a result. Lawyers were afraid to defend those accused.

In 1952 McCarthy was put in charge of the 'Un-American Activities Committee'. He turned his attention to the film industry. Charlie Chaplin was among those accused and some producers and actors could not get work. In 1954 it became clear that he had no evidence and his lies and bullying were revealed.

NSC 68

In 1950 the National Security Council sent Truman a document, NSC 68, telling him about Communist activities in the world beyond Europe. Was containment intended to apply all over the world? Truman soon had to decide.

WHY WAS KOREA A FLASHPOINT IN THE COLD WAR?

At the end of the Second World War the Japanese in the northern half of Korea surrendered to the USSR and those in the southern half to US forces. A Communist system was set up in the north and a capitalist one in the south. The two countries became bitter enemies.

Then, in 1950, north Korean troops invaded the south. By September they had taken most of the country (see Fig. 10.5(i)) Truman sent troops and ships to the area and appealed to the United Nations.

Figure 10.5
The Korean War

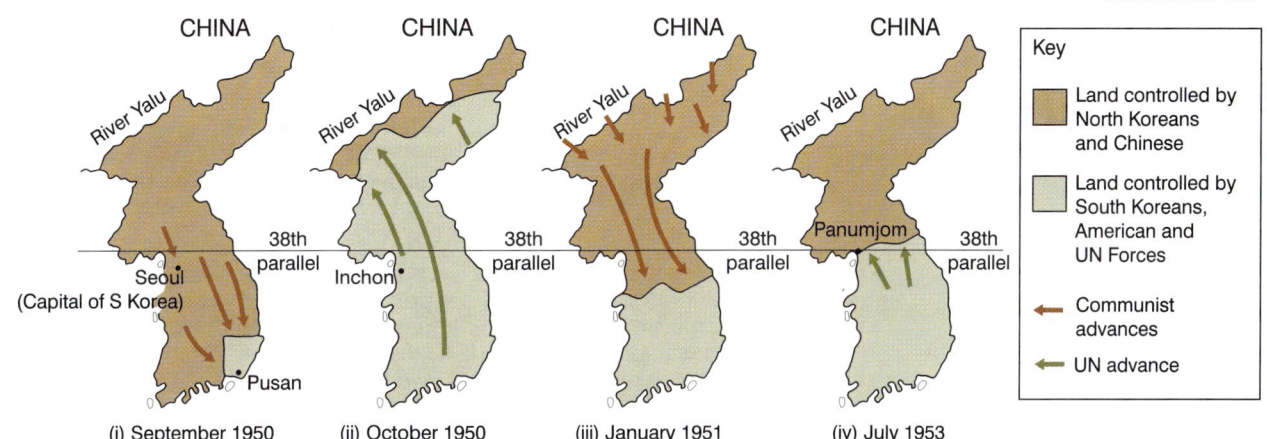

Key	
▨	Land controlled by North Koreans and Chinese
▧	Land controlled by South Koreans, American and UN Forces
←	Communist advances
←	UN advance

(i) September 1950   (ii) October 1950   (iii) January 1951   (iv) July 1953

The 38th parallel was the border between North and South Korea from 1945 to June 1950

The Korean War 1950-1953

INTERPRETATIONS

- This was an international crisis like the Manchurian and Abyssinian crises of the 1930s (see pp.165 and 166). One country was being invaded by another. The US believed that their failure to get involved then and the subsequent failure of the League of Nations had helped to cause the Second World War. They were determined to see that the powers of the UN were used to deal with North Korea.

- This was part of the Cold War. North Korea was an aggressive Communist state. Communists had taken over in China in 1949 and they were now trying to take South Korea. They were also active in other countries in Asia: Indo-China, Malaya, Indonesia, Burma. The US government believed in the 'Domino theory': that is, one country after another would fall to Communism like a line of dominoes. The US must act and containment must be extended all over the world.

Normally the USSR would have used its Security Council veto to stop the UN acting (see chapter 11). However, the USA had refused to allow the new Communist government of China to take over China's place in the UN. The USSR had withdrawn from the UN in protest so the veto was not used. The UN condemned the North Korean invasion and authorised the use of force to stop it.

Eighteen countries, including Britain, sent troops to join the UN force, but the USA provided most of the armed forces as well as the commander, the successful Second World War veteran General MacArthur.

The events of the war can be seen on the map:

- Figure 10.5(ii) UN forces landed at Inchon and South Korean forces moved north. By October the North Korean army had been driven back nearly to the Chinese border. This was already further than the UN resolution had agreed. Chinese leader Mao Zedong warned them to stop. They did not.

- Figure 10.5(iii) 200,000 Chinese troops with Soviet weapons invaded and drove the UN forces back into South Korea by January 1951. MacArthur wanted to extend the war to attack China, using nuclear weapons. He said the USA should put 'Asia first' in the battle against Communism. Truman could see the dangers of this and stuck to containment. In April 1951 Truman, as President and therefore supreme Commander of US forces, sacked MacArthur.

- Figure 10.5(iv) Peace talks began but fighting continued until July 1953. Peace was made with more or less the same boundaries as the two countries had had before the war.

EXTRA POINTS ▶

1. McCarthy's accusations were made just a little more credible because in 1950 two Americans were found guilty of selling US nuclear secrets to the USSR during the war (the USSR was an ally of the USA at that time!). Also some State Department officials had been members of the Communist party twenty or thirty years earlier.

2. Both North and South Korea were undemocratic countries with more or less dictatorial rulers. US support for the ruler of South Korea was based on little more than his opposition to Communism. In this way US Cold War policy led the USA to support governments all over the world which were far from free or democratic.

Check yourself

QUESTIONS

Q1 How did the victory of the Communists in China affect US Cold War policy?

Q2 Why was it so difficult to oppose Senator McCarthy's charges?

Q3 What did Truman and MacArthur disagree about?

REMEMBER! Cover the answers if you want to.

ANSWERS

A1 The victory of Mao Zedong and the Chinese Communists in 1949 affected US Cold War policy in several ways. It made the USA feel it was losing the fight against Communism. This was the climate in which McCarthyism was able to flourish. It made the USA realise that the Cold War was going to be worldwide, not confined to Europe. This led them into the Korean War and, later, into the Vietnam War.

TUTORIALS

T1 At first China just followed the Soviet line but after 1960, when they split from the USSR, Chinese Communism complicated the Cold War issues. It meant that there were now two types of Communism. The Chinese Communists had won the civil war and were undeniably popular. This ran counter to what Truman had said about Communism in his speech about the Truman Doctrine (see p.217). It was hard for the USA to accept that some people could voluntarily want a Communist government.

ANSWERS

A2
In the early 1950s it was a patriotic duty to oppose Communism. McCarthy posed as a great patriot, weeding out these foreign agents. It seemed unpatriotic to oppose him.

He got lots of favourable publicity. If you tried to oppose him, or question him, you got bad publicity. People were frightened to lose their jobs – this was especially true of Hollywood actors, producers and scriptwriters, who were looking for work. Film company bosses refused to hire those people McCarthy had named.

A3
Truman and MacArthur disagreed over US war policy in Korea. MacArthur wanted to tackle the Chinese, who were helping North Korea. He wanted all-out war, perhaps including nuclear weapons, against China. MacArthur felt that there was a real opportunity for the USA to win the Cold War in the East.

Truman felt that to extend the war was going beyond simply containing Communism. The war was also a UN action, not just a US one. To go on to attack China was going far beyond what the UN had agreed.

TUTORIALS

T2
McCarthy's accusations were lies and suggestions, not hard facts. It is easier to show that facts are untrue than to disprove a rumour. He was dealing with attitudes: was it 'Un-American' to be an admirer of the USSR? McCarthy was very popular from 1950–54. Many people made their name supporting him including a lawyer, Richard Nixon and an anti-Communist actor, Ronald Reagan.

T3
Here again we see leaders in the Cold War declaring a limit on how far they are prepared to go. Although the USA had the power, Truman was not prepared to use it aggressively. Note that MacArthur had tremendous support in the USA.

CONTAINMENT AROUND THE WORLD: THE ARMS RACE

From 1952 to 1959 John Foster Dulles was US Secretary of State. He was a Cold War fighter, and as soon as he took up his post, spoke of going beyond containment to 'liberating' countries from Communism. This need not be done by force, he said, but by putting pressure on Communism and by propaganda.

ALLIANCES

In 1949 NATO (North Atlantic Treaty Organisation) was set up. Its twelve members were Britain, France, Belgium, Holland, Luxembourg, Portugal, Denmark, Ireland, Italy, Norway, Canada, USA. It was a military alliance and the USA provided by far the largest part of its forces.

The Cold War was clearly now a world war and Dulles built up a system of global alliances.

- SEATO (South-East Asia Treaty Organisation), 1954: Thailand, Phillipines, Pakistan and USA
- CENTO (Central Treaty Organisation), 1955: Turkey, Iran, Iraq, Pakistan and USA
- The USA also had alliances with Japan (1951) and Australia and New Zealand.

INTERPRETATIONS

- These were defensive alliances, to contain Communism.
- These were aggressive alliances, designed to surround the Communist countries of the world. The USSR was particularly concerned that the alliances allowed the US to set up air bases in member-countries. US bombers or missiles could therefore be stationed on the very borders of the USSR.

THE ARMS RACE

The atom bomb dropped on Hiroshima on 6 August 1945, killed 45,000 people instantly and reduced the city to rubble.

The results of dropping the bomb on Hiroshima – and the second one on Nagasaki – were:

- Massive death and destruction was clearly now possible. The awesome power of the atomic bomb totally changed the idea of war and made international relations more serious.
- The USA had a monopoly of nuclear weapons for the time being. This gave it great superiority, but produced great fear in the USSR.
- The imbalance was so serious that an arms race began between the superpowers. At first the USSR was racing to develop their own bomb. Later this **arms race** continued as each side strove for superiority. By 1987 there were enough nuclear weapons in the world to kill the entire human race several times over.

Key features of the arms race were:

- Each side tried to get ahead of the other, either to produce more bombs or better technology. Neither side dared to fall behind in the arms race or else the other might think it was so far ahead that an attack was worth launching. In fact the USA was almost always ahead in the race, but they did not think so, or were afraid to think so, and the race continued.
- There were several turning-points, where the race changed because of new technology, see below.
- It was massively expensive. Even the USA, the richest country in the world, had to divert money from more worthwhile programmes in order to pay for the arms race. For the USSR, not nearly so rich, the expense was crippling and indeed helped to lead to the collapse of Communism in the 1990s.

Turning-point 1: 1949 The USSR exploded its own atom-bomb.

The USA at once began to develop a much more powerful bomb, the hydrogen bomb. Their first H-bomb test was in 1952. H-bombs were hundreds of times more powerful than the Hiroshima bomb.

Turning-point 2: 1953 The USSR exploded its own H-bomb.

US President Eisenhower realised that it was cheaper to build up nuclear weapons than ordinary explosive bombs. He therefore decided to put the USA so far ahead in numbers of bombs that the USSR would not dare attack for fear of **massive retaliation**; that is, the US counter-attack would be so huge that the USSR dare not act first. Eisenhower also thought the USSR had far more bomber aeroplanes than it actually had. This spurred him on to order lots of big bombers to deliver US H-bombs.

Turning-point 3: 1957 The USSR launched a satellite (the 'sputnik') into space.

If they could launch a satellite, they could launch a missile carrying a nuclear bomb. At once ICBMs (Inter-Continental Ballistic Missiles) made bomber aeroplanes out of date. A new arms race began, to build missiles. In the 1960 presidential election campaign, Kennedy claimed that there was a 'missile gap' – that the USSR had more missiles than the USA. In fact this was not true, but it helped him win the election. When he was in power Kennedy did order more missiles to be built and by 1963 the USA had 550 ICBMs to the USSR's 100.

The USA also had the advantage in siting missiles too. Because of its alliances (see above), these could be sited on the borders of the USSR. At first the USSR could not do this, and its missiles could not reach US cities. This is what made the Cuban missile crisis (see p.228) such a threat to the USA.

Kennedy also dropped 'massive retaliation'. The USA realised that if only a few of these new, powerful missiles got through to bomb US cities there would be huge destruction and loss of life. He therefore tried to build a 'balance of terror': in this way, it was argued, nuclear weapons acted as a **deterrent**; that is, the other side were deterred from starting a war because it would end in their being totally destroyed. This was called '**Mutually Assured Destruction**' or MAD.

Turning-point 4: 1960 US launches missile from submarine.

Submarines could go anywhere, almost undetected, and so be able to launch missiles at any city or military site in the USSR. The race continued and soon the USSR had submarine-launched missiles.

Protest

Public opposition to the nuclear arms race began to grow in the 1950s.

- More information about Hiroshima told of the horrible deaths of those who died at once, and the lingering deaths of those who died afterwards. Hiroshima victims were still dying of radiation sickness many years later. Many people did not want their government to possess such immoral weapons.

- Testing the bombs caused loss of life. We now know that some servicemen were deliberately exposed to radiation. So were some islanders in the Pacific where bombs were tested.

- Some objected to the enormous cost of this huge military expense at a time when their countries were not at war.

- Many felt that possessing nuclear weapons made war more likely, not less. Civilians knew they stood little chance of surviving a nuclear attack, especially on a small island like Britain.

In Britain the Campaign for Nuclear Disarmament (CND) was formed in 1957. By the early 1960s many thousands joined its Easter marches to the government's Atomic Weapons Research Establishment at Aldermaston.

 **EXTRA POINT**

The arms race continued, as new inventions brought about more changes: anti-ballistic missiles, which could knock out incoming enemy missiles were developed. For a while they gave one side an advantage, until MIRVs (Multiple Independent-Targeted Re-entry Vehicle) were developed in the 1970s. These were missiles which carried lots of warheads (bombs). Each was separately targeted, so if just one missile got through, lots of places would be destroyed. And so the race went on.

Check yourself

QUESTIONS

Q1 Look at the two cartoons, Figures 10.6 and 10.7

a) What does cartoon, Figure 10.6, tell you about US views of the USSR?

b) What does the cartoon, Figure 10.7, tell you about Soviet views of: US military power? Air bases? Marshall Aid? US politicians?

c) Use these two cartoons and your own knowledge to explain why the Cold War went on so long.

Figure 10.6 *US cartoon about the USSR*

Figure 10.7 *Soviet cartoon about the USA, 1952. The main caption reads 'Words and Deeds'. It shows a US general sticking a flag in Greece, on the map. Greece had just joined NATO. The US politician holds an olive branch (symbol of peace) and talks of 'Peace, Defence, Disarmament'.*

Q2 Use the account of the arms race to give examples of policy being motivated by: money; US politics; mistakes; military issues.

REMEMBER! Cover the answers if you want to.

ANSWERS

A1

a) The US sees the USSR as a big Russian bear trying to seize the whole world.

b) The USSR sees US military power as big and ugly, moving nearer to the USSR.

The airbases are all pointing at the USSR, threatening it.

The big cartoon soldier has dollars sticking out of his pocket. To the USSR US loans, like Marshall Aid, were just another way of threatening the USSR.

The cartoon shows US politicians as just little creatures, talking away while the soldiers do what they like. Their words like 'Peace', etc. are meaningless.

TUTORIALS

T1

a) *Remember to look hard at these cartoons: nothing is drawn by accident. Perhaps it is important that the bear is about to grab Africa in this cartoon. The bear has the star of the Soviet Army on its cap.*

b) *Note the date: in 1952 nuclear warheads were still being delivered to their targets by big bombers, so having bases near to the enemy was important. NATO is shown as just a way of getting US airbases nearer and nearer to the USSR. Everything in the cartoon is designed to show the USA as big, aggressive, rich, armed, moving ever closer to the USSR. It is saying that the USA says one thing but its armed forces do quite the opposite.*

ANSWERS

c)   Both sides thought the other was trying to take over the world. Both sides claimed to be acting only peacefully, in their own defence. Both sides claimed the other was being aggressive.

A2   Saving money was one of President Eisenhower's reasons for developing US nuclear weapons in the 1950s because they were cheaper than ordinary weapons.

Kennedy's claims of a 'missile gap' helped him win the 1960 presidential election; it was useful to him in making his opponent look as if he was not defending the USA properly.

Both the missile gap under Kennedy, and the bomber gap under Eisenhower were mistakes; neither existed.

There were military reasons for each of the turning-points: the Soviet A-bomb meant the USA had to develop a more powerful bomb, the H-bomb; the change from bomber-aeroplane delivered bombs to missile-delivered warheads were all military issues.

TUTORIALS

c)   *This answer is too closely based just on the cartoons. Note that the question asks you (i) to add some of your own knowledge, and (ii) to explain why the Cold War went on so long.*

Under (i) you could mention the Soviet takeover of Eastern Europe in 1945–48, the growth of NATO, SEATO, CENTO, Korea, Berlin. Under (ii) the point to make is that both sides thought the other was hell-bent on destroying them. They dared not let up for fear of being defeated and so were locked in a spiral of aggression in which the arms race was a big part.

T2   *Eisenhower's decision to build nuclear weapons is a rare example of trying to save money. Mostly the arms race mopped up vast amounts of money. It was Eisenhower himself who complained about the power of the 'military–industrial complex'. Such vast amounts of money were involved that both the companies who built the planes, missiles and bombs, and the armed forces which ordered them and used them had a vested interest in the arms race continuing. Large numbers of jobs were involved too; an end to the arms race would mean huge adjustments to the US and Soviet economies.*

It is open to doubt whether the politicians really thought there were 'gaps' or whether they just used the idea as a stunt. It is possible that advisers from the armed forces persuaded the politicians there was a 'gap' in order to get them to spend more money on weapons.

KHRUSHCHEV, KENNEDY AND CUBA

Khrushchev was premier of the USSR from 1955 to 1964. Stalin died in 1953. There was a power struggle at the top but in 1955 Khrushchev emerged as leader. He was the tough son of a miner who had worked under Stalin.

PEACEFUL CO-EXISTENCE

Khrushchev wanted to improve the standard of living of the ordinary Russian people. He could see that the Cold War was enormously expensive and proposed a policy of 'peaceful co-existence' with the West: rivalry in trade and industry, not weapons. In fact this did not happen and the arms race continued.

DE-STALINISATION

He tried to make Soviet society more free than it had been under Stalin. In a speech to the Twentieth Communist Party Congress in 1956 he denounced Stalin for his intolerance, brutality and abuse of power in killing and imprisoning millions of Soviet citizens (see chapter 6).

THE EASTERN BLOCK

In 1955 he formed the Warsaw Pact, a defensive alliance of the USSR and all Eastern block countries (a NATO of the east). In spite of peaceful co-existence and de-Stalinisation, he was not prepared to let Eastern block countries cut their links with the USSR: he sent tanks to crush the rising in Hungary in 1956 (see p.242).

COLD WAR

U2 spy-plane, 1960

The USA used special U2 spy-planes to fly at high altitude over the USSR taking photographs. In 1960 one was shot down. Khrushchev made a great row about it, claiming it proved that the USA was not sincere in talking about peaceful co-existence. A proposed peace conference in Paris broke up and Cold War hostilities continued.

Berlin Wall, 1961

By this time the contrast between West and East Berlin was enormous. The West's shops were full of goods as part of the economic recovery West Germany was having; East Berlin was still poor and dowdy. 15,000 to 20,000 people left East Germany for the West through Berlin every year, draining the country of its best workers.

Most Russians of Khrushchev's generation still hated Germany because of the war and resented West Germany's prosperity. In 1961 a wall was built all round West Berlin. No one was allowed to cross it and anyone who tried to escape was shot.

Many people expected US President Kennedy to react, as Truman had done in 1948 over the Berlin airlift, but Kennedy did nothing. Khrushchev took this as a sign of Kennedy's weakness.

CUBA, 1962

Why did Cuba become a flashpoint?

The island of Cuba is only 150 kilometres from the US coast (see Fig. 10.8). For many years the USA had supported the corrupt and brutal dictatorship of Batista. US companies owned much of Cuban business and most of Cuba's main export, sugar, was sold to the USA.

Figure 10.8
The Cuban missile crisis

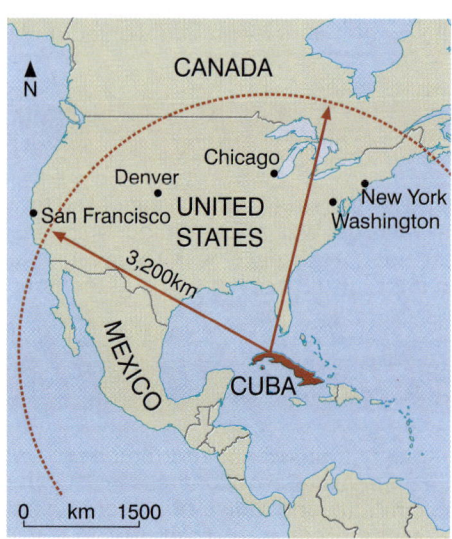

In 1959 Batista was overthrown by a popular rising led by Fidel Castro. Castro said he only wanted to run Cuba independently and meant no harm to the USA. However, he took over US businesses on Cuba and, when the USA refused to buy the sugar crop, sold it to the USSR.

In 1961 the USA backed an attempt by Cuban enemies of Castro to overthrow him. The force landed at the Bay of Pigs and was defeated by Castro's forces. From then on relations grew steadily worse between Castro and the USA and the Cuban army received large amounts of weapons from the USSR. Then came the missile crisis.

On 16 October 1962, a US spy-plane came back from flying over Cuba with photographs showing that Soviet missile bases were being built there (see Fig. 10.9). As the map (Fig. 10.8) shows, Soviet bases on Cuba would put nearly all of the USA within reach of their missiles. US spy-planes also reported that the actual missiles were not yet installed but were at that moment on Soviet ships on their way to Cuba.

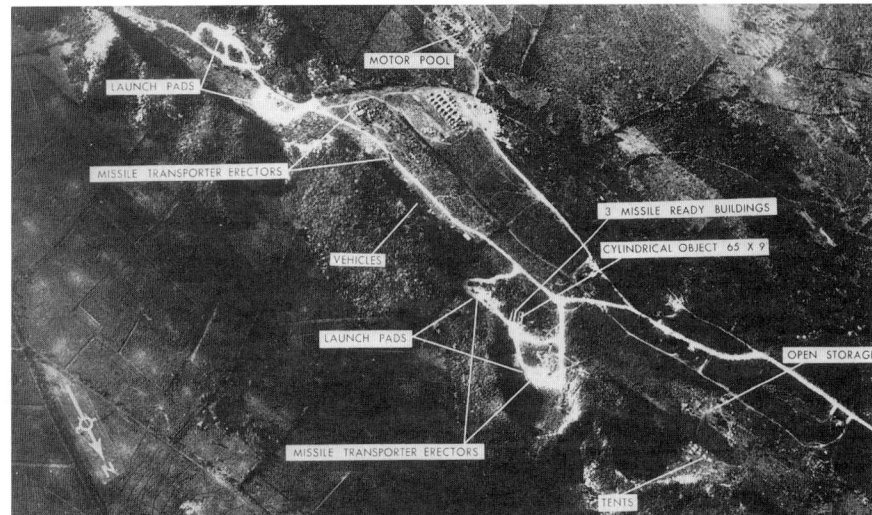

Figure 10.9
US spy-plane photograph of Soviet missile base on Cuba

Why did Khrushchev put missile bases on Cuba?

This was a very provocative thing to do. Why did Khrushchev do it?

- The USA was far ahead of the USSR in long-range missiles. Short-range Soviet missiles on Cuba would make up for this.
- Perhaps he thought he could get away with it. Kennedy had done nothing about the Berlin Wall and had failed over the Bay of Pigs: Khrushchev had a low opinion of Kennedy.
- Perhaps he intended them as a bargaining point: he would remove them in return for some concession by the USA. For example, there were US missiles in Turkey which could hit any city in western USSR in six minutes.

What should Kennedy do?

He could do nothing. US cities were already within reach of Soviet long-range missiles so nothing much had changed. However, this would look weak. Kennedy had already been criticised over his reaction to the Berlin Wall and did not want to lose the support of US public opinion.

He could attack. He could invade Cuba, or bomb the bases, or send troops into Berlin. This was risky. Soviet soldiers would almost certainly be killed, the USSR could retaliate and nuclear war could break out.

He could find a strong but non-violent response. This is what he did. On 20 October he ordered US warships to sea to stop the Soviet ships carrying the missiles reaching Cuba. At the same time he ordered his forces to be ready for nuclear war. The world waited anxiously: it was the closest to nuclear war, and perhaps total annihilation, that the world had come.

Events unfolded day by day:

24 October	Soviet ships stopped
26 October	Letter from Khrushchev to Kennedy offering to think about withdrawing the missiles if Kennedy promised not to attack Cuba.
27 October	Second, tougher, letter from Khrushchev, under pressure from his military advisers, saying he would only withdraw his missiles if US missiles were withdrawn from Turkey.
28 October	Kennedy ignores second letter, agrees to first. Khrushchev orders missile sites to be dismantled and missiles to be sent back to USSR.

Results of Cuban missile crisis

- Both leaders felt they had taken their countries and the world too close to nuclear war. They made efforts to improve relations:
  - Hotline: a telephone link between the White House and the Kremlin, 1963.
  - Test Ban Treaty, 1963: a ban on testing nuclear weapons. This was one of the things the anti-nuclear protestors wanted.
- Kennedy came out of it well. US public opinion felt he had stood up to Khrushchev, but also avoided war.
- Khrushchev did not come out so well. Opinion in the USSR condemned him for putting the missiles there in the first place and then for giving way. The Cuban crisis was a factor in his fall from power in 1964. Later historians are puzzled by his initial decision to place the missiles in Cuba but feel he acted bravely in agreeing to withdraw them rather than pushing Kennedy any further.

EXTRA POINTS ▶

1. Khrushchev was sincere about trying to develop better relations with the West, particularly when he first came to power. Soviet forces withdrew from Austria. He travelled to Western countries and met their leaders.

2. President Kennedy's brother Robert played a big part in the crisis. It was he who suggested answering Khrushchev's first letter. He also secretly told the USSR that the US would withdraw their missiles from Turkey.

3. The Soviet presence on Cuba was large: there were nine missile sites, with capacity for sixty-four missiles. There were also 43,000 Soviet soldiers on the island.

Check yourself

QUESTIONS

Q1 Look at the picture, Figure 10.9 (p.229).

a) How was this picture obtained?
b) Why did this picture alarm President Kennedy and the US government?

Q2 Who won the Cuban missile crisis?

Start your answer to this question by writing a sentence each about Kennedy and Khrushchev. Then decide what factual information you are going to use to support your opinion.

Then write an answer, beginning each paragraph as follows:

'Kennedy could claim that he won because ...'

'However, he had not succeeded in ... '

'Khrushchev could claim that he won because ... '

'However, he had not succeeded in ... '

'My conclusion is... '

ANSWERS

A1
a) This picture was taken by a U2 spy-plane.
b) It alarmed Kennedy and his advisers because it showed that Soviet missile-bases were being erected on Cuba. Soviet missiles launched from Cuba could hit almost every city in the USA.

A2
Kennedy did well out of the crisis because he forced Khrushchev to withdraw his missiles from Cuba.

Khrushchev did well because he got the USA to agree not to attack Cuba.

Kennedy could claim that he won because the Soviet missiles were withdrawn from Cuba. He had discovered that the USSR was building missile sites on Cuba on 16 October 1962. The missiles were not yet in place, but some were already at sea in Soviet ships. He ordered US ships to impose a blackade on Cuba and told his armed forces to be ready for nuclear war. On 28 October Khrushchev agreed to send the missiles home and dismantle the sites.

However, he had not succeeded in removing the pro-Soviet government of Cuba, which stayed there as a permanent propaganda victory for Communism in the Americas. He had also taken the world to the brink of nuclear destruction, although he must share the blame for this with Khrushchev.

Khrushchev could claim that he won because he had kept Cuba as an ally in the Americas. He had made the USA promise not to attack Cuba and it now stood as an example of anti-capitalism to other American countries.

However, he had not succeeded in keeping his missiles in Cuba. If he had, he would have improved the Soviet position in the arms race. They were well behind in numbers of long-range missiles but the use of a base so close to US territory would have allowed the USSR to use short-range missiles, of which it had plenty.

My conclusion is that Kennedy made sure that the USA stayed ahead in the arms race, but that Khrushchev ensured the survival of Castro. The real gain was that both leaders made some moves towards avoiding such serious near-wars in the future by setting up the 'hotline' in 1963 between the White House and the Kremlin, and by banning some nuclear testing.

TUTORIALS

T1
a) *The U2 was the same type of plane which was shot down over the USSR in 1960. It flew very high, over fifteen kilometres up, but could take accurate photographs, as you can see. Nowadays satellites are used to do this kind of spying.*
b) *Soviet missiles on Cuba did not really make that much military difference: US cities were already within range of Soviet long-range missiles. However, they were a great propaganda advance for the USSR. Ever since the 1920s the USA had expected every country in both the Americas to be an ally. Cuba breached this policy, called the 'Monroe Doctrine'. The missiles just made it worse.*

T2
You have written a good short essay here, by combining three stages: ideas + facts + a plan. All three of these elements are necessary for an effective essay-answer. You will have to do this for youself in an exam, of course. notice how the opening sentence of each paragraph, which you were given, helps you organise your answer, as you hang all the little points you want to make under it.

Khrushchev might receive more blame than you have given him for putting the missiles on Cuba in the first place. He did not try to hide them and he should have known it was bound to cause an angry American reaction. However, he might receive more credit for having the courage to back down on 28 October and pull back his missiles. It is easier to be tough than to give way in these situations. Kennedy got lots of praise in the West (which he refused to acknowledge, to his credit), for forcing Khrushchev to back down. However, he did take the world to the edge of nuclear annihilation in order to get his way.

VIETNAM AND THE END OF CONTAINMENT

WHY DID VIETNAM BECOME A FLASHPOINT IN THE COLD WAR?

Vietnam and the French

Vietnam, in South-East Asia, was part of the old French colony called Indo-China. When the Japanese captured it from the French in the Second World War, a Vietnamese resistance organisation, the Vietminh, was formed. Its leader was Ho Chi Minh, a Communist, but it was supported by most Vietnamese. The Vietminh fought a successful guerrilla war against the Japanese and when the Japanese surrendered in 1945, was ready to take power. The French, however, wanted their colony back. The Vietminh then began a new guerrilla war against the French.

HOW DID THE US GET INVOLVED?

The USA at first disapproved of the French, but from 1949 Communist China began to support the Vietminh. The USA, by now deep into their Cold War fear of Communism, began to help the French. Soon they were bearing one-third of the cost of the war.

Figure 10.10
Vietnam after 1954

North Vietnamese supply line (Ho Chi Minh Trail)

Areas under Communist control by 1973

In spite of US support, the French could not win and in 1954 were severely defeated at Dien Bien Phu by the Vietnamese General Giap. At the **Treaty of Geneva, 1954**:

- Indo-China was divided into four countries: Laos, Cambodia, North Vietnam and South Vietnam (see Fig. 10.10).
- Free elections were to be held in the two Vietnams as soon as possible in order to reunite the country.
- No foreign power was to intervene in their affairs.

A Vietminh Communist government took over North Vietnam under Ho Chi Minh. The rulers of South Vietnam were from the landlord class, rich, Christian (while most of the population was Buddhist), undemocratic and often corrupt. Soon war started again. A resistance movement, called the Vietcong, began to attack the South Vietnamese government. It consisted of South Vietnamese Communists, supplied by North Vietnam down the Ho Chi Minh trail (see Fig. 10.10). The USSR began to send weapons to North Vietnam.

The USA sent CIA 'advisers' and weapons to South Vietnam. They opposed holding elections in South Vietnam because they feared that the Vietcong would win. By 1962 President Kennedy had increased the number of US advisers to 16,500 and spent $3 billion. In spite of this, more than half South Vietnam was in Vietcong hands and the unpopular South Vietnamese government was collapsing.

HOW DID THE USA JOIN IN THE WAR?

President Johnson committed the USA to the Vietnam war. On his election in 1964 he declared: 'I am not going to be the President who saw South-East Asia go the way China went.' US policy was still based on 'containment' and on the 'Domino Theory' (see Fig. 10.11), that Communism was taking over the world country by country, like a line of dominoes falling.

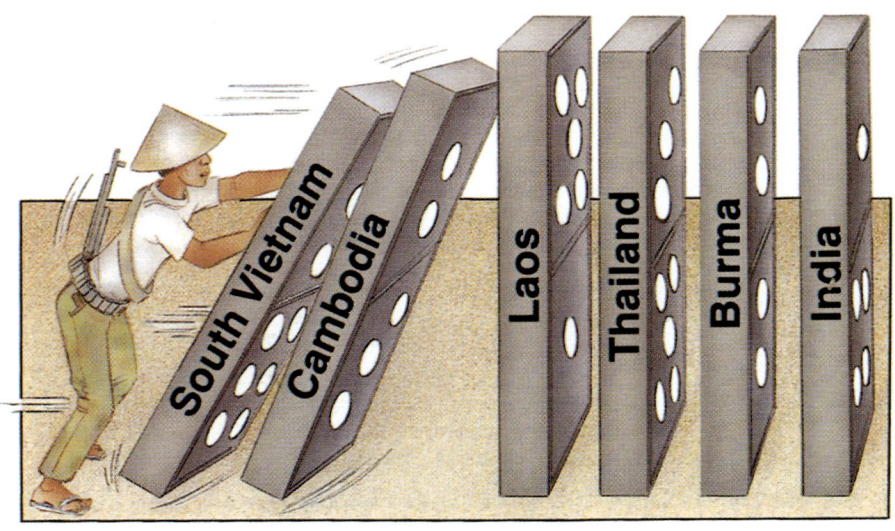

Figure 10.11
The Domino Theory

- Congress passed the Tonkin Resolution in 1964, allowing Johnson to take what military action he thought necessary.
- In 1965 he began Operation Rolling Thunder, a massive bombing campaign against North Vietnam.
- He sent in US forces. By 1969 there were half a million US soldiers in Vietnam.

Yet the USA could not win the war.

WHY DID THE USA LOSE THE VIETNAM WAR?

Guerrilla war

After over twenty years of fighting a guerrilla war against the Japanese, the French, the South Vietnamese and now the Americans, the North Vietnamese were experts in guerrilla warfare. They also learnt from the successful guerrilla war waged by Mao Zedong in China.

- They used their knowledge of the land, its jungles, mountains and paddy fields. They could travel about easily and stay hidden by day. They moved about the jungle trails by night. Supplies were carried on bicycles. Guerrilla soldiers lived rough, sometimes in underground hideouts.

- They had the support of the Vietnamese peasants – or, in some cases, forced them to give support. Wearing ordinary clothes, they could mingle with the villagers undetected. Mao Zedong had described the same tactics in China: 'The people are the water and we are the fish.'

- They specialised in ambushes, surprise attacks on isolated groups of US soldiers. Occasionally they massed their soldiers for a big attack, but only if they were sure of winning.

US morale

It was very difficult to counter this kind of guerrilla warfare. US troops did not know the landscape. Unlike the Vietcong soldiers, most of them were inexperienced raw recruits. While US soldiers were highly visible among the Vietnamese people, they never knew who was an innocent peasant going about his or her daily life and who was a Vietcong guerrilla about to lob a grenade at them. The Vietcong had no fixed positions to be captured. The danger of ambush was wearing on the nerves and the morale of US troops was low. This was not the glorious war in defence of freedom which they had expected to fight.

US tactics

- Bombing. One thing the USA did possess was technological superiority. They used it to launch massive bombing raids on North Vietnam and Vietcong-held areas of South Vietnam. More bombs were dropped on North Vietnam in three years than were used by all sides in the Second World War. Inevitably South Vietnamese civilians were killed too, and their villages destroyed.

  The bombing was extended into Cambodia and Laos too, as the Vietcong were using them as bases. The effect was to stir up opposition to the USA in those countries and turn their people to support the Communists.

- Defoliants. The US developed chemical defoliant sprays, like Agent Orange, to remove the leaves from jungle trees. This was to deprive the Vietcong of cover, but defoliants also affected the peasants' crops.

- Napalm. These were bombs containing an inflammable jelly which sticks to human beings. Again, inevitably, civilians were sometimes horribly burnt and killed.

- Search and destroy. The hardest thing for US troops to deal with was identifying who the enemy were. In 'search and destroy' tactics, soldiers were sent into areas where all the villagers had been ordered to leave. They were told that anyone left there must be a Vietcong. However, mistakes were made and innocent villagers were also killed.

- 'Hearts and minds'. This was supposed to be a war of ideals, of freedom versus Communism. Each side was trying to win the 'hearts and minds', as the US government put it, of the South Vietnamese people. Clearly US tactics prevented them from winning the battle for 'hearts and minds' any more than the military conflict.

Public opinion in the USA

- Cost. By 1969 the war was costing $30 billion a year. It was also costing 300 US lives a week. Yet the USA was not winning.

- The TV war. The war was covered by TV so that war pictures were seen in every home every night. People saw villagers' huts being burnt; they saw Vietcong suspects being tortured; they saw US soldiers dying. Reporters revealed even more shaming deeds, such as events at My Lai, see below.

- Protest. A strong anti-war movement began, in the USA and across the world, including among US allies in Europe.

The My Lai massacre, 1968

My Lai is a village in South Vietnam. In 1968 a company of soldiers was sent on a 'search and destroy' mission into the village. They had been told that all the villagers would be at market and that it was a Vietcong headquarters. They killed three to four hundred villagers, including women, children and old men, and burnt their houses.

A year later a soldier told the press what had happened. Reporters followed it up and one of the officers, William Calley, was put on trial for murder. He was found guilty and sentenced to twenty years of which he served only five. Many people felt he was only the scapegoat for what had happened and that such events had often happened in the war.

THE USA PULLS OUT

- In 1968, in spite of the massive US presence in Vietnam, the Vietcong launched the Tet Offensive, capturing many towns in South Vietnam. Clearly the USA could not win this war.

- In 1968 President Johnson announced he would not be standing for President again and called a halt to the bombing.

- His successor, President Nixon, tried to find a way of getting out of the war without the USA losing face. He came up with 'Vietnamisation': opposition to the Communists would be handed over to the South Vietnam government, helped by US money, but 'the boys would come home'.

- Peace talks with North Vietnam began in Paris and ended in 1973.

- In fact the war continued and Saigon, capital of South Vietnam fell in 1975. Vietnam was united under Communist government.

RESULTS OF THE WAR

- Containment had failed. A policy devised for Europe in the 1940s was clearly not right for Asia in the 1960s.

- Communism had advanced. This had not happened, as Truman had said in 1947: 'by armed minorities or outside pressure' (see p.217), but by the wish of the people of Vietnam.

235

- Communism had also made progress in Laos and Cambodia as a direct result of US actions.
- The USA had presented its Cold War strategy as a moral crusade against the evil of Communism. After their actions in Vietnam: the atrocities, the napalming, the chemical warfare, their support for an unpopular and undemocratic government, the USA had lost its moral superiority.

EXTRA POINTS ▶

1. Low morale, and the difficulties of fighting a guerrilla war in unfamiliar territory, among unfamiliar people, produced a sort of racism among many soldiers. They ceased to distinguish between Vietnamese and regarded all of them as potential enemies. In this situation ordinary Americans could carry out massacres like My Lai and the battle to win 'hearts and minds' could never be won.

2. The chief negotiators at the Paris peace talks were Henry Kissinger, for the USA, and Le Duc Tho, for North Vietnam. They were awarded the Nobel Peace Prize for their efforts.

Check yourself

QUESTIONS

Q1 Source 1

'For Hanoi (capital of North Vietnam), the immediate aim is the conquest of the south. But for Beijing (capital of China) however, Hanoi's victory would only be the first step towards eventual Chinese rule over the two Vietnams and South-East Asia'

Robert MacNamara, US Defence Secretary, 1964

a) What does the speaker in Source 1 think is happening in Vietnam?
b) Use this source and your own knowledge to describe what is meant by the 'Domino Theory'.

Q2 Source 2

'In sending US troops to South Vietnam, the US imperialists have met a people's war. The people's war has succeeded in gathering all the people to fight their attackers in all ways and with all kinds of weapons.'

North Vietnamese General Giap, 1967

a) Who was General Giap?
b) Use this source to explain what he means by 'a people's war'.

Q3 Use both sources and your own knowledge to explain why the USA lost the war for the 'hearts and minds' of the Vietnamese people.

ANSWERS

A1

a) This American thinks that although North Vietnam sees the war as just a war to conquer South Vietnam, to China it was a war to take over both Vietnams and then all of South-East Asia.

b) The Domino Theory was an American idea that the little countries of South-East Asia would become Communist one by one. That is, a Communist victory in one would only lead them to move on to the next. Source 1 sees this expansion of Communism as all coming from China.

A2

a) General Giap was the North Vietnamese commander. A genius at guerrilla warfare, he had defeated the French, the South Vietnamese and the Americans.

b) By a 'people's war', General Giap meant a war in which all the people are involved. This was essential for the kind of guerrilla war he was waging, because his soldiers depended on the support of the people to hide them, supply them, keep them informed etc.

A3

The USA failed to win the 'hearts and minds' of the Vietnamese people because of how they carried out the war. Faced with opponents, the Vietcong, using guerrilla warfare, US commanders used mass bombing, chemical warfare and destroyed villages. They were also supporting a corrupt government which did not have the support of the people.

TUTORIALS

T1

(a)&(b) This source is a brief outline of US motives for pouring so much money and so many US lives into Vietnam: it was the point where Communism was to stopped in Asia, the Vietnam domino was not to be allowed to fall. In fact, North Vietnam got far more supplies from the USSR than from China. Relations between the two were never good and China invaded Vietnam briefly in 1979.

T2

(a)&(b) Giap's kind of war was the same as Mao Zedong had fought in China from the 1930s until his eventual victory in 1949. Both were 'people's wars' and in both cases Communist forces defeated much stronger but conventional opposition armies because of their support from the people. In both cases this support was partly because of national feeling, partly because the Communists promised to give the peasants more land.

T3

The war in Vietnam was really all about the hearts and minds of the Vietnamese people because it was supposed to be about beliefs and ideas, not power. The USA believed that their form of capitalist democracy was better than Communism and that people, given a real free choice, would choose it. Their failure in Vietnam was therefore not just a blow to US power but it undermined the whole basis of their Cold War ideology.

In Europe, in the 1940s, the USSR did take over countries and force Communism on them. This was the basis of the US sense of outrage at what the USSR was doing and the policy of 'containment'. By the 1960s, on the other side of the world, containment had simply come to mean resisting Communism wherever it cropped up, even if, unlike in Eastern Europe, it had popular support, and even if it meant supporting undemocratic, corrupt and unpopular governments.

DÉTENTE

Détente means an easing of tension. What did this mean in the Cold War?

- A halt to the arms race
- Not interfering in each other's affairs
- Meetings of leaders (called 'Summit' meetings)
- Contacts between citizens on each side, in sport, the arts, science etc.

WHY DID DÉTENTE HAPPEN?

For both superpowers:

- **Cost**
  The arms race was tremendously expensive, and getting more expensive all the time. Both the USA and the USSR could see that there were better things that they could spend their money on.

- **Danger of war**
  The Cuban missile crisis (see p.228) had brought the world to the edge of nuclear destruction. It could happen again while relations between the two superpowers were so strained. War could happen by accident: a missile could be launched in error. There was also the danger of other countries acquiring nuclear weapons, apart from USA, USSR, Britain and France. Israel, China, South Africa and India were developing nuclear weapons. The more countries which had them, the more the likelihood of nuclear war.

- **Opposition**
  There was opposition to nuclear weapons, mainly in the West, but also in the Communist block.

For the USA

- **To keep USSR and China apart**
  While the Cold War was on, there was a danger that the USSR and China could join forces against the USA. They had fallen out with each other in 1960. The USA promoted détente, particularly with China, to keep them apart.

- **The aftermath of Vietnam**
  The USA was rethinking its Cold War strategy after their defeat in Vietnam. A 'live-and-let-live' attitude was replacing their earlier readiness to get involved in anything and everything across the world.

For the USSR

- The cost of the arms race, of maintaining huge conventional armed forces and supporting allies across the world, was more than they wanted to spend.
- Fear of the USA and China combining against them.

For China

- To find a powerful ally against the USSR
- To trade more with the West and so improve its economy.

WHO SUPPORTED DÉTENTE?

In the USA: Presidents Nixon (1968–74) and Carter (1976–80).
In the USSR: President Brezhnev (1964–82).

WHEN WAS DÉTENTE?

In some ways the first example of détente was the 'hotline', established in 1963 after the Cuban missile crisis. The main years, however, were from the late 1960s to 1980.

Main events

1968 Nuclear Non-Proliferation Treaty
USA, USSR and Britain agreed not to supply any other countries with nuclear technology. Unfortunately France, China, Israel and South Africa refused to sign the treaty.

1971
Table-tennis players from the USA went to play in China. This was the first contact of any sort between the two countries since Mao and the Communists came to power in 1949.

China joined the United Nations later in 1971 (see chapter 11).

1972
US President Nixon visited Mao Zedong in China (see Fig. 10.12)

Figure 10.12
Nixon and Mao Zedong in China 1972

SALT (Strategic Arms Limitation Talks) between USA and USSR ended in a treaty to limit the numbers of long-range missiles each side had.

1975
Helsinki agreement between Carter, Brezhnev and thirty-five other countries. Each side recognises the boundaries of countries in Europe reached in 1945. At Carter's insistence, each side agrees to observe human rights.

US and Soviet astronauts met up in space.

1979
SALT 2, covering other sorts of nuclear weapons as well as long-range missiles, was prepared after long and difficult negotiation. Then the USSR invaded Afghanistan and the USA refused to sign the Treaty.

LIMITS OF DÉTENTE

- The arms race still went on. Despite the minor, hard-worn over restrictions of SALT, both sides had large stockpiles of weapons. They put a good deal of effort in getting round the SALT restrictions. There was also the problem of **verification**: how did you tell what weapons the other side actually had?

- Wars still happened. For example, the 1973 war in the Middle East, with the USA supplying Israel and the USSR supplying Egypt and Syria.

- Human rights violations continued. The USSR made little effort to observe the terms of the Helsinki Agreement.

- In 1980 this period of détente came to an end as Ronald Reagan became President of the USA and returned to Cold War attitudes and policies.

EXTRA POINTS ▶

SALT: Calling a halt to the arms race was very difficult. By the 1970s there were many kinds of nuclear weapons, some launched from land, from from submarines, some long-range, some medium-range, some with multiple warheads, and so on. How did you equate one side's lead in one type with another side's lead in another?

And how was any agreement to be verified? Neither side was ready to have generals from the other side travelling round their secret bases looking at their missiles.

Check yourself

QUESTIONS

Q1 Source 1

'We shall pay any price, bear any burden, meet any hardship, support any friend, oppose any foe, to assure the survival and success of liberty.'

President Kennedy, speaking in 1961

Source 2

'America cannot, and will not, conceive all the plans, design all the programmes, execute all the decisions and undertake all the defence of free nations around the world'.

President Nixon, speaking in 1972

(a) What are the differences between the policies in these two speeches?
(b) Why had US policy changed in the eleven years between these two speeches?

Q2 Why did the USA make such an effort to improve relations with China in the 1970s?

Q3 What did détente achieve?

ANSWERS

A1
a) In source 1, Kennedy is commiting the USA to unlimited intervention in the world. In source 2, Nixon is saying that there were limits on what the USA would do now.

b) The main thing that had happened was the Vietnam war. US intervention in this war, using massive amounts of resources and men arises from Kennedy's declaration in source 1. However, mere commitment to 'pay any price, etc' had not brought the US victory. Not only had they been defeated, but their judgement of the situation had been wrong. In Vietnam, Communism was popular and the government the USA was fighting to prop up was undemocratic, corrupt and unpopular. Three hundred US soldiers were dying each week at the height of the war in 1968.

In future, as Nixon says, the USA will not be so ready to assume that it should take the lead and jump in.

A2 The USA made an effort to make friends with China in the 1970s partly to drive a wedge between China and the USSR and prevent them making friends. Partly also because China was a powerful influence in the Far East, where the USA had big interests.

A3 There was some slowing down in the arms race; tension between the two sides lessened, so ordinary people may have felt less in danger of nuclear war.

TUTORIALS

T1
a) *The two speeches are like mirror-images of each other. Probably Nixon had Kennedy's famous speech in mind when he made his own, deliberately opposite, speech.*

b) *Whether you consider the cost, in money, or in lives, the atrocities, the defeat, the loss of 'moral high ground', Vietnam was very difficult for the USA to handle.*

T2 *Another reason for friendship with China might be to open up trade opportunities with such a vast country. Further, China was very powerful, with the world's largest population and the world's biggest army. Some were arguing that it was a third superpower. It could not be ignored.*

T3 *In fact, spending on arms continued to rise throughout the détente years. Apart from an improved mood of conciliation it is hard to see what all the effort put into détente achieved.*

THE USSR IN EASTERN EUROPE

Much earlier in this chapter (p.214), you read about the Soviet takeover of Eastern Europe in 1945. For forty-four years after they were occupied by the Red Army as it pursued the retreating Nazis into Germany, these countries were utterly controlled by the USSR. On several occasions attempts were made to break free, but they all ended by being crushed.

As Europe began to recover after the war, the people of Eastern Europe compared themselves with the people of Western Europe. They saw that people in Western Europe had:

- More freedom, for example, more than one party to vote for, a free press which could criticise the government, no secret police, freedom to travel where you wanted, relaxed censorship in the arts and media.

- Higher standard of living

In this section we look at the three most serious attempts to change things, in Hungary, Czechoslovakia and Poland. As you read about these events, look for:

- things that were the same in each of the three countries before the protest;

- things that were different;

- which of the two kinds of demands above did the rebels want most;

- how did each protest try to learn from the one before?

WHAT DID THE PEOPLE OF HUNGARY WANT IN 1956?

Hungary had been hostile to the USSR before the war. The Communist Party had never been popular and in the first elections after the war it only gained 17 per cent of the vote. Nevertheless Stalin insisted on it taking part in government and then the other parties were eased out. By 1948 Hungary was ruled by a Communist dictator, Rakosi. He was hated because:

- He was slavishly pro-Soviet. He did exactly what Stalin told him. The Red Army continued to occupy Hungary.

- Industry. Hungary is a prosperous agricultural country but under COMECON (Stalin's system of uniting all the economies of Eastern Europe together) it had to develop industry, mainly to serve the needs of the USSR. The Stalinist system of Five Year Plans was introduced. Workers' hours were long and pay low.

- Agriculture. Collective farms, also on the Soviet model, were forced on the Hungarian peasants. They did not co-operate and there were food shortages.

- Standard of living. The standard of living actually fell by 5 per cent between 1949 and 1955.

- Secret police. There were 100,000 in the secret police, the hated AVOs. 200,000 Hungarians were in prison and torture was common.

Khrushchev's speech to the Twentieth Communist Party Congress in 1955, denouncing Stalin (see p.227) brought a ray of hope in Eastern Europe. There were anti-Soviet demonstrations in Germany and Poland. Soviet troops were sent in to crush them. Many people were killed.

In Hungary Rakosi was forced to resign following massive demonstrations. He was replaced by Nagy, a much more popular Communist. However, Nagy was no longer in control of events. On the streets of Budapest people attacked and killed AVOs. They demanded free elections, with other parties apart from the Communists allowed to take part; they demanded that the Red Army should leave and that Hungary should leave the Warsaw Pact (see p.228), and become part of the group of neutral nations. Some Hungarians seem to have taken US anti-Communist propaganda at face value, and expected the USA to support them.

Khrushchev decided that he could not have Hungary pulling out of the Soviet block and sent in a thousand tanks to crush the revolt (see Fig. 10.13). There was bitter fighting in the streets and 30,000 Hungarians were killed. 180,000 fled the country. Another Communist, Kadar, took over the country. Many Hungarians felt betrayed by the West.

Figure 10.13
Soviet tank commander advances angrily on Western cameraman, Budapest, 1956

WHAT DID THE PEOPLE OF CZECHOSLOVAKIA WANT IN 1968?

Czechoslovakia before the war was a much more developed democracy and manufacturing economy than Hungary. Nevertheless, the situation twenty years after the war was much the same as in Hungary in 1956 (and indeed throughout Eastern Europe). That is:

- Stalinist rule under Novotny
- Soviet control of the economy
- Strict censorship
- Stagnant economy and a low standard of living.

Socialism with a human face

Then, in 1968, a different group of Communists led by Alexander Dubcek removed Novotny and took over the government. They put forward alternative plans. In order to achieve more growth and competitiveness in the economy, there should be more freedom. More economic freedom needed more political freedom. They called it 'Socialism wth a human face'.

They reduced censorship, allowed more free discussion on TV and in the newspapers, weakened the powers of the secret police. Writers and artists supported them. It was an exciting time in Czechoslovakia, called the 'Prague Spring'.

They were careful to stress that they were Communists, that they did not intend allowing other parties to take part in politics and had no intention of leaving the Warsaw Pact or Comecon.

Soviet leader Leonid Brezhnev did not like it, but did not act at once. He threatened Dubcek and Czechoslovakia. Huge Soviet tank manoeuvres were held on their borders. Eventually the other Communist leaders of Eastern Europe feared for their own positions if 'Socialism with a human face' spread, and tanks were sent in to crush the Prague Spring. The Czech people reacted with passive resistance but Dubcek was removed and gradually the old system was restored.

Again the West did nothing. Western leaders were trying to get détente going and did not want direct confrontation with the USSR.

Brezhnev announced that:

- no member of the Soviet block was allowed to leave the Warsaw Pact;
- no multi-party systems would be tolerated.

These two principles became known as the Brezhnev Doctrine.

WHAT DID THE PEOPLE OF POLAND WANT IN 1980?

Protest in Poland had almost always purely economic: demanding higher wages, or lower prices, or the right to 'free' trade unions. (There were official trade unions but these were controlled by the government and the Communist Party. Strikes were forbidden by law.)

The government had usually met their demands. Polish workers in fact did quite well in the 1970s, but by 1980 depression had set in.

In July 1980 Lech Walesa, an electrician in the shipyards at Gdansk, led a strike for higher wages. He also set up a free trade union, called Solidarity. By January 1981 Solidarity had 9.4 million members, 60 per cent of all non-agricultural workers in Poland. It had been recognised by the government and was campaigning for all kinds of workers' rights, including the right to join the free unions and to strike.

Why didn't the government crush Solidarity?

- It had massive support, including many Communists.
- It had lots of members in vital Polish industries.
- Walesa was careful not to criticise the Communist Party or make any proposals for political change.
- Walesa and Solidarity had close links with the powerful and popular Roman Catholic Church.
- Half of all journalists, writers and film-makers had joined it.
- Walesa was well-known in the West, subject of TV interviews and a media figure.

The Solidarity protest lasted longer than the revolts in Hungary and Czechoslovakia. However, it was too much of a threat to the authority of the government to be allowed to continue. Poland was in chaos, with massive inflation and unofficial strikes. Walesa could not hold Solidarity together. Splits occurred and some members called for changes which were against the Brezhnev Doctrine.

Early in 1981 General Jaruzelski, head of the Army, became Prime Minister of Poland. In December 1981 he arrested Walesa and 10,000 Solidarity leaders. Solidarity was suspended. 150,000 members were hauled in by the police for 'cautionary talks'.

Poland remained in a state of unrest for the next few years. By 1986 Solidarity was reviving and Walesa was again a leading figure. But by then events all over Eastern Europe were changing fast (see p.248).

EXTRA POINTS ▶

1. Nagy, the Communist who took over Hungary in the 1956 revolt, had been Minister of Agriculture after the war. He had ordered the sharing out of land among Hungary's 640,000 peasants. This had made him very popular, but there was no place for him under Rakosi.

2. The man who put forward the ideas for economic reform in Czechoslovakia in 1967 was called Otto Sik. He proposed that

factories and businesses should run their own affairs, instead of being controlled by the state planning office. They should each have boards of management, with elected worker representatives. He realised that economic freedom and political freedom were linked: people will not have enterprising attitudes and ideas to make businesses prosper unless they have freedom to think for themselves. It was these ideas which led to the 'Prague Spring' of 1968. Twenty years later they appealed to Mikhail Gorbachev when he was trying to convert the USSR to 'Communism with a human face' (see p.248).

Check yourself

QUESTIONS

Q1 At the beginning of this section you read that people in Eastern Europe felt that they had less freedom and a worse standard of living than people in Western Europe. Which of these two motives was uppermost in the three protests described here?

Q2 Did the Czech protesters break the Brezhnev Doctrine?

Q3 In what ways did each revolt try to learn from the one before?

REMEMBER! Cover the answers if you want to.

ANSWERS

A1 The Hungarian revolt was about personal freedom; the Czech revolt was more about standards of living, while the Polish, Solidarity, protest was entirely economic.

A2 The Brezhnev Doctrine said that no Warsaw Pact member should have multi-party government or leave the Warsaw Pact. The 'Prague Spring' protest in Czechoslovakia did not demand either of these things.

A3 The Czechs learnt that they should not try to introduce multi-party democracy or try to leave the Warsaw Pact and become neutral. These were seen as the two factors which had led Khrushchev to send the tanks into Hungary in 1956. The Czechs emphasised that they were all loyal Communists and would remain so.

The Poles carefully avoided making any political protest at all, trying to avoid the Czechs' problems.

TUTORIALS

T1 *None of them was as clear-cut as this. The Hungarian revolt of 1956 was motivated by resentment over low standards of living, although their demands were mainly political. In Czechoslovakia the two elements were combined. The Solidarity protest seems purely economic, but lack of political freedom drove the protest to take the form it did.*

T2 *The Czech reformers indeed set out specifically to avoid breaking these two principles. The problem, for Brezhnev and the other hardline Communist leaders of Eastern Europe, was that their reforms looked as if they might lead eventually to more radical changes.*

T3 *What Brezhnev and his allies most feared was change and popular protest. Whatever they said, they were bound to see it as a threat and try to crush it. Solidarity lasted longest because its appeal was to the material well-being of the working classes – the very group the Communist Party was supposed to look after.*

THE END OF THE COLD WAR

The Cold War was over by the end of the 1980s, yet the decade began with a new arms race.

REAGAN'S ARMS RACE

The new arms race was almost entirely due to Ronald Reagan, President of the USA, 1980–88. Reagan was a determined anti-Communist, an ex-actor who had made his name in the McCarthy era (see p.220). He criticised his predecessors for their détente policies, which had allowed the USA to fall behind in the arms race. He was encouraged in his new arms race by Mrs Thatcher, Prime Minister of Britain, 1979–90.

- He dropped the détente language of friendshp with the USSR. He returned to the 1950s language of a moral crusade against Communism, calling it the 'evil empire'.

- He increased US arms spending from $178 billion in 1981 to $367 billion in 1986.

- He developed lots of new weapons: the neutron bomb, which killed people by radiation but left buildings intact; the MX bomb; Cruise missiles; the 'Star Wars' defence system, in which laser satellites in space would destroy all incoming missiles from the USSR. The USSR responded to this arms race with new weapons of its own, like the SS-20 missile. New weapons and a new arms race seemed to make nuclear war more likely.

- The deployment of Cruise missiles at US bases in Europe led to a huge revival of anti-nuclear protest. CND membership increased. Women protesters set up peace camps, especially at the US base at Greenham Common in Berkshire.

- START (Strategic Arms Reduction Talks) between USA and USSR in 1985 failed.

- The USA boycotted the Moscow Olympics in 1980 and the USSR boycotted the Los Angeles Olympics in 1984

GORBACHEV

In 1985 the USSR had a new leader, Mikhail Gorbachev. He was only fifty-four in 1985 (Reagan was seventy-four). He was charming, intelligent, with an equally charming and intelligent wife, Raisa. He was a lifelong Communist, but was determined to bring about radical reforms in the USSR.

GORBACHEV'S REASONS FOR REFORM

Standard of living

The people of the USSR continued to have a low standard of living. Although the USSR is rich in raw materials and with fertile agriculture, they could not seem to make simple household goods that worked, or to supply the shops with food.

The Brezhnev years

Brezhnev had ruled the USSR for a long time, from 1964–82. He was followed by two more old men (Andropov, 1982–83, and Chernenko, 1983–85). Little had changed in the USSR since Stalin's days. But people did not work hard, as they had under Stalin, because there was no point. Alcoholism was rife. So was corruption. Party members had too many privileges, including their own shops, where food and imported luxuries were on sale, and *dachas* – country cottages where they retired to at weekends and holidays.

Cost of war and weapons

The USSR was locked into:

- the arms race, which probably took 25 per cent of its spending, compared to 7 per cent of that of the USA;
- a war in Afghanistan, which began in 1979 but which the USSR could not win. It was the USSR's Vietnam.

Lack of freedom

There was no freedom of speech, so that no discussion of the problems of the USSR could take place. Intellectuals sent round *samizdat* – self-published, or duplicated newssheets or other writing, but this was illegal. Government secrecy was a habit. For example, parents had difficulty finding out what had happened to their sons who were killed fighting in Afghanistan. So strict and secretive was government control of censorship that when the Chernobyl nuclear accident took place in 1986 no news was released until Western observers noticed it. The result was greatly increased loss of life in the USSR.

Another aspect of lack of freedom was that managers of factories, farms and other economic enterprises had no freedom to take their own decisions. Everything was decided in Moscow. This was the main reason for the lack of economic success.

The environment

Lack of a free press to criticise the government, and lack of government self-control had led many parts of the USSR to have some of the worst pollution and environmental disasters in the world. Apart from Chernobyl, the Aral Sea had disappeared because of river diversions; Lake Baikal and many of Russia's great rivers were terribly polluted.

Gorbachev could see that all these problems were linked. If he was going to improve people's standard of living he had to change the way the economy worked. This meant getting out of expensive and unnecessary military expenditure. It meant more freedom to create a more enterprising economy. It meant more freedom of the press and debate to make industry more responsible.

He had to tackle the Cold War, Eastern Europe, and all aspects of life inside the USSR. He was trying to change forty years of Cold War and seventy years of Communism. It was a huge gamble.

The Cold War

Gorbachev met Reagan in 1986 at Reykjavik and in 1987 at Washington. They declared their friendship and Gorbachev offered to make such concessions in the arms race that Reagan could only agree.

- 1987: INF (Intermediate Nuclear Force) Treaty. Both sides agreed to remove all medium-range missiles from Europe within three years.
- 1991: START (Strategic Arms Reduction Treaty). This promised further reductions in long-range nuclear missiles at once and more over the next twelve years (see Fig. 10.14).

Soviet forces left Afghanistan, removing a major cause of US–Soviet tension and an unpopular and expensive war.

Eastern Europe

Gorbachev realised that Eastern Europe was not as essential to the security of the USSR as it had seemed to Stalin in 1945. He had ended the Cold War, and anyway, by the 1980s missiles could attack the USSR from any direction, without the 'buffer' of Eastern Europe.

Figure 10.14
Soviet missiles being dismantled

He also wanted the changes he was bringing to the USSR (see below) to benefit the peoples of Eastern Europe too. The old Stalinist rulers of the Eastern European countries were horrified, but Gorbachev told them that he would no longer send Soviet troops to support them. The Soviet empire in Eastern Europe rapidly collapsed.

- **May, 1989**
  Free elections in Poland lead to victory for Solidarity. Lech Walesa becomes Prime Minister.

- **June, 1989**
  Hungarian border guards dismantle the 'Iron Curtain' border with Austria, allowing free movement. Thousands of Eastern Europeans, especially East Germans, cross to the West.

- **October, 1989**
  Huge demonstrations in East Germany.

- **November, 1989**
  Demonstrators march to the Berlin Wall. Guards throw down their weapons. Berlin Wall demolished.

  Czechoslovakia sets up multi-party state.

- **December, 1989**
  Anti-Communist demonstrations in Hungary, Bulgaria and Romania. Ceaucescu, Communist dictator of Romania, executed.

- **March, 1990**
  Germany reunited

The USSR

All these events made Gorbachev immensely popular in the West and in Eastern Europe. He was not so popular inside the USSR where his policies were not working so well.

In most of Eastern Europe, which had been Communist only since the late 1940s, democracy and capitalism were soon restored. It was much more difficult in the USSR, which had been Communist since 1917, and which had little experience of democracy and a backward economy even then.

Gorbachev had proposed two new policies:

- *glasnost* – openness, more democracy, freedom of speech;
- *perestroika* – restructuring, introducing a free market in which goods were produced which people wanted at prices they were prepared to pay, not produced and priced by government department.

In fact, *glasnost* undermined the success of *perestroika*. That is, the only people who could make the economy work were removed by the free elections. By 1990 the USSR was suffering from rising prices, falling value of wages, crime and black marketeering.

Powerful anti-Russian nationalist feelings were released. In 1990 Latvia left the USSR. The other three Baltic states soon followed. By 1991 the USSR had collapsed, leaving fifteen new independent states. They formed a loose grouping called the Commonwealth of Independent States (CIS) but this was not at all what Gorbachev wanted.

Russia was by far the most powerful of these new states and its Prime Minister was Gorbachev's enemy, Boris Yeltsin. In 1992, the old Communists tried to seize power. They failed, but Gorbachev was forced to resign. Yeltsin declared the Communist Party illegal. He also brought in many other changes, including changing the name of the city of Leningrad back to St Petersburg.

With the arms race over, independent countries in Eastern Europe and the USSR collapsed, the Cold War was definitely over.

EXTRA POINTS

1. Andropov, ruler of the USSR briefly, 1982–83, was a reformer, but did not have time to put his reforms into practice. Gorbachev was his deputy.

2. A sign of how the Cold War distorted the Soviet economy was pointed out by Gorbachev: their scientists could launch a rocket to put an astronaut in space with pinpoint accuracy, but the USSR did not seem to be able to make good, cheap fridges. Although Communism was supposed to provide for the needs of working people, the Soviet state had become better at weapons technology.

3. Although the INF Treaty and the START reduced the numbers of nuclear weapons, there are still thousands of them. Since the breakup of the USSR, these have become the possession of many of the states which make up the CIS. There are now therefore more nuclear states than there were during the Cold War, which some see as possibly a dangerous situation.

Check yourself

QUESTIONS

Q1 How did Gorbachev and Reagan end the arms race so rapidly?

Q2 How were *glasnost* and *perestroika* designed to solve the problems of the USSR?

Q3 Why was Gorbachev so popular in the West?

ANSWERS

A1
The arms race ended in two arms reduction treaties following the Gorbachev/Reagan talks in Reykjavik in 1986. The INF Treaty, 1987, reduced medium-range missiles; START, 1991, reduced several kinds of missiles, including long-range missiles. In both cases Gorbachev offered more reductions than Reagan. This willingness on his part to make big concessions meant the treaties were quickly negotiated.

A2
Perestroika was restructuring. This meant dismantling the whole apparatus of state control of the Soviet economy which Stalin had set up in the Five-Year Plans. He wanted a free market economy, in which production levels and prices (both of which had been set by the government before) would be decided simply by what goods factories could make at a price the customers would pay.

In order that this economic freedom could flourish, there had to be political freedom, openness – *glasnost*. This meant free elections, free speech and a free press.

A3
The end of the Cold War was popular in the West as it removed the threat of another major war which had been hanging over people's lives since 1945. Gorbachev was seen as a hero who had rejected the USSR's past and was trying to give it a Western system.

TUTORIALS

T1
The speed with which Reagan and Gorbachev reached agreement contrasts with the long drawn out SALT negotiations of the détente period in the 1970s. At that time, both sides may have wanted arms reduction, but neither was willing to see a deal which gave any advantage to the other side.

In the INF Treaty, the USSR gave up 3,000 warheads, the USA 800. In START, the USSR gave up 5,000 warheads and the USA 3,500. These were big concessions on Gorbachev's part, but he thought it was worth it because if the Cold War came to an end he would have more money to spend on changes in the USSR.

T2
The fact that Communism was dismantling itself and choosing to turn the USSR into a capitalist state was seen by many as the West having 'won' the Cold War.

The idea of a free society, with a free market, like in the West, may have been a good one. The problem was getting from a highly-controlled state economy to a free market one, with a population which had no experience of it. The problems of the change are still making life in the CIS very difficult. Not surprisingly, many people in the late 1990s now look back on the Communist era with some affection.

T3
In Eastern Europe, which had never really accepted Communism, the changes were also popular. It was the hero's welcome which Gorbachev received in East Germany in 1989 which led them to realise that the old system was on the way out.

EXAM PRACTICE

Sample Student's Answers & Examiner's Comments

---

1 What was the Iron Curtain? (4)

The Iron Curtain was Winston Churchill's description for the division of Europe between the East, which the USSR controlled and the West. Lithuania, Latvia, Estonia, Poland, Czechoslovakia, Hungary, Romania, Bulgaria and perhaps Yugoslavia were behind the Iron Curtain.

4/6

EXAMINER'S COMMENTS

MARK SCHEME

Level 1	Describes Iron Curtain as split	1–2 marks
Level 2	Details of split: countries etc.	3–4 marks
Level 3	Describes Iron Curtain as Western term, implying dislike or resentment of what USSR was up to	5–6 marks

The details in this answer are impressive – hence 4/6 – but the element that is missing is Churchill's worry about what was happening behind it. A 'curtain' hides something, and Churchill was sure that the USSR had something to hide.

---

2 How did the Cuban missile crisis change relations between the superpowers? (6)

After the Cuban missile crisis of 1962, the hotline was set up in 1963, between the White House, residence of the President of the USA, and the Kremlin, where the leader of the USSR worked.

There was also a Test Ban Treaty in 1963. Both sides agreed to ban nuclear tests in the atmosphere.

2/6

EXAMINER'S COMMENTS

MARK SCHEME

Level 1	Describes hotline and Test-Ban Treaty	1–2 marks
Level 2	Explains these two agreements as part of results of Cuban crisis	3–4 marks
Level 3	Sets an explanation in context of wider effects of Cuban missile crisis on Cold War	5–6 marks

This is clearly a thin answer: the facts are there but with no context. The Cuban missile crisis had been tense because there was no clear way for Kennedy and Khrushchev to talk together. There was a real need for each to explain and discuss exactly what the other was really up to.

The arms race was serious in the years up to 1962 as well. Kennedy had complained of a 'missile gap' between the USA and the USSR. This did not exist, but increased testing led to increased levels of radioactivity all over the world, and hence the treaty.

The answer could end by saying that the crisis had scared both Kennedy and Khrushchev with how close they could come to war. They did achieve a kind of détente. However, wider tensions and disagreements between them meant that the Cold War lasted for another twenty-six years.

3 Why was Germany such a cause of tension between the USA and the USSR in the years 1945–49? (15)

In 1945 the USA and the USSR were united in defeating Nazi Germany. At Yalta, in February, 1945, they agreed to divide Germany into four zones, for the Soviets, the USA, Britain and France. The capital city of Berlin was to be similarly divided, though it was inside the Soviet zone. At Potsdam in July 1945, they agreed to put leading Nazis on trial. The discovery of the concentration camps and the Holocaust made both sides equally bitter against Germany.

By 1946, however, their policies began to diverge. There was total chaos in Germany and much of Europe. Economic life had been shattered in the last year of the war by retreating armies and bombing raids. Many people were starving. In Germany the problem was made worse by the arrival of 16 million refugees, Germans from all over Europe. People bartered for food, or used cigarettes as currency.

Eventually the Allies decided that some economic revival should take place in Germany: the alternatives were to let the people starve to death, or to supply them with handouts. The first of these was not acceptable and they could not afford the second. In 1946 the three Allied zones were united and in 1948 a new currency was introduced so that Germany could take advantage of Marshall Aid.

The USSR was angry. They blocked all routes into Berlin. The Allies decided to supply Berlin entirely by air — the Berlin airlift, which lasted for 318 days, until May 1949.

Although the Berlin situation did not result in war, it was a permanent cause of grievance between the USA and the USSR. The two parts of Germany became two separate countries in 1949 and remained so until 1990.

Germany was such a cause of tension between the super-powers because they had agreed to rule it together at the Yalta Conference, and so were closely linked in running the country. It was therefore where the two systems, the two sides met, and became the first flashpoint of the Cold War.

12/15

EXAMINER'S COMMENTS

MARK SCHEME

Level 1	General account of hostility, with some incidents	**1–5 marks**
Level 2	Describes some of the events of 1945–49, with some understanding of reasons for tension	**6–10 marks**
Level 3	Shows why tension over Germany in particular, using good selection of detail in support.	**11–15 marks**

This is clearly quite a good essay. The good points are: it has a good sense of chronology. Even though it only has to cover five years, there were huge changes in this time and the essay explains these well. Secondly, it selects detail well. This does not have to be a full account of the Cold War in Europe. Only those events relevant to Germany are mentioned. Thirdly, it presents a simple but effective conclusion, summing up the period.

What is missing is a real understanding of the Soviet point of view. Stalin, and everyone in the USSR had gone through hell in the Second World War – they call it 'The Great Patriotic War'. Their cities were destroyed, their people were killed. Those areas occupied by Germany were savagely treated. Only if this is realised – and there were many in the West in the 1940s who did not realise it, does Stalin's lack of pity for the Germans become clear. This is not explained in the essay. Their rivalries and fears were particularly focused on Germany as the sharpest source of tension between the superpowers in the first few years after the war.

Question to Answer

The answer to Question 4 can be found on p.276

4 SOURCE A: A US soldier, speaking in 1969, describes the war in Vietnam:

'The same village you'd gone in to give them medical treatment ... you could go through that village later and get shot at. Go back in and you would not find anybody. We were trying to work with these people. You didn't trust them any more. You didn't trust anybody.'

SOURCE B:

Figure 10.15 *US soldier setting fire to a Vietnamese villager's hut.*

(a) Read Source A.
Use your own knowledge to explain what Source A tells you about the Vietnam war. (5)

(b) Look at Source B.
How does Source A help to explain what is happening in Source B? (6)

(c) 'The US lost the Vietnam War because they used the wrong tactics.'
Use these sources and your own knowledge to say how accurate you think this statement is. (10)

WHY WAS THE UNITED NATIONS STARTED?

During the Second World War Allied leaders met several times to discuss what they were fighting for, what they wanted the world to be like after the war and how to prevent war in the future. US President Roosevelt and British Prime Minister Churchill met in mid-Atlantic in 1941. They were very clear that they were fighting against the undemocratic and violent politics of Hitler and the Nazis. Together, they drew up the Atlantic Charter. This described 'Four Freedoms':

- Freedom from want
- Freedom of speech
- Freedom from fear
- Freedom of religion.

They believed that wars start when people do not have these freedoms. It would be necessary to set up an international organisation to promote these ideals across the world after the war: a United Nations Organisation. Like US President Woodrow Wilson in 1917, they believed that the best way of making a country behave reasonably was to put it under pressure from all other nations in the world, through an international organisation.

The **Declaration of the United Nations** was drawn up in 1942. They tried to learn some lessons from what had gone wrong in the inter-war years. If you have read about the inter-war years you will be able to tell why these points were written in:

- No part of a country can be taken away from it without the free consent of its people.
- All citizens should have the right to choose the form of government under which they live.
- All countries to have equal rights of access to world trade.
- All countries should work together to run the world economy and eliminate poverty.
- All people should live peacefully together and be able to travel freely where they wish.
- Worldwide disarmament.

In chapter 8 you can read how the League of Nations was set up in 1919 after the First World War. It had failed to prevent the Second World War. Why did they return to the idea of an international organisation?

- They now had clear principles on which the UN would be based.
- They decided that the League failed because of problems in the way it was set up and organised. The UN would learn from the mistakes of the League.
- International pressure from lots of countries was still the best way of solving disputes.

Roosevelt was particularly keen on the idea of a UNO. It was discussed at a series of meetings:

1943 Moscow. USA, USSR, Britain and China agree to support the idea of a United Nations.
1944 Dumbarton Oaks. Representatives of the Allies meet to discuss how the UN is to work.
1945 February, Yalta. Roosevelt, Churchill and Stalin agree to the plans.
1945 June, San Francisco.   Leaders of fifty-one countries sign the Charter of the United Nations.
1946 London. First meeting of the UN.
1952 New York. Permanent headquarters set up.

HOW DOES IT WORK?

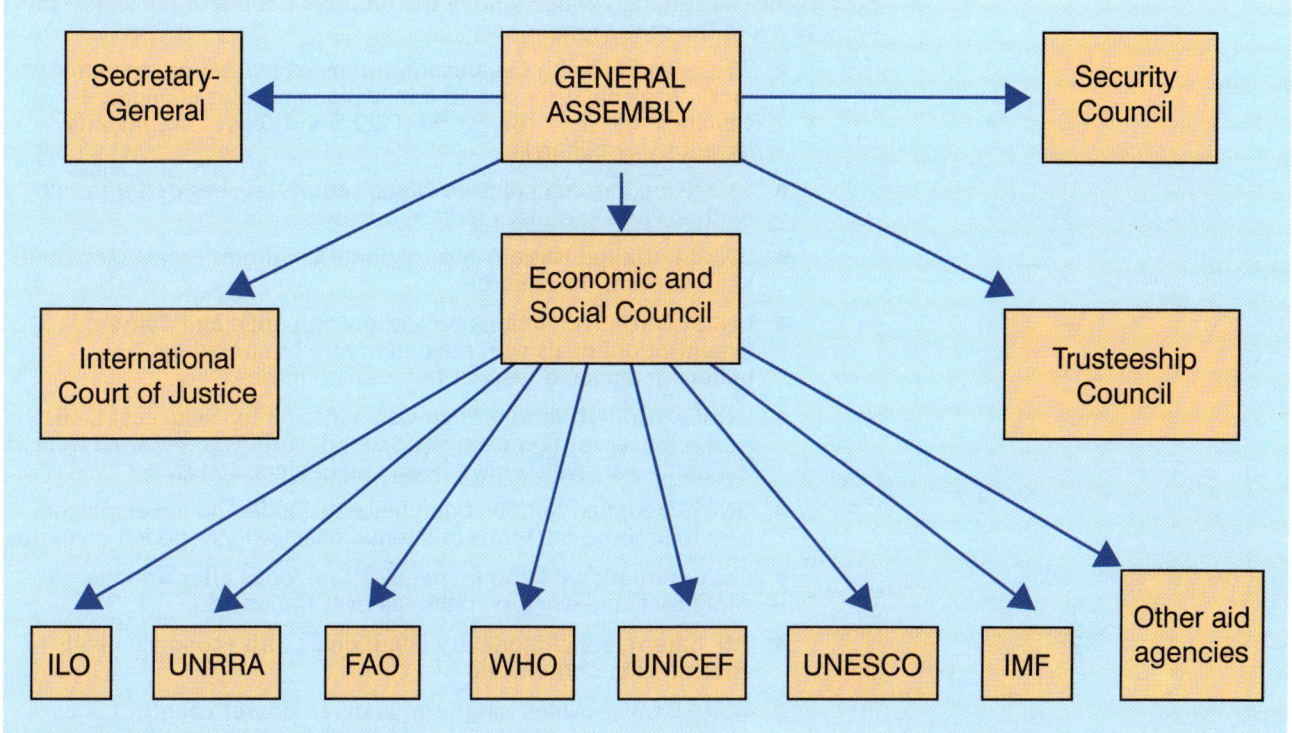

Figure 11.1
The United Nations

The General Assembly

Every country in the world can be a member. Each country, however large or small, has one vote. Resolutions need a two-thirds majority to succeed. All other parts of the UN are responsible to the General Assembly.

The Security Council

From the first, the permanent members have been: USA, USSR, Britain, China and France. Each of the permanent members has the right of veto; that is, they can vote against any action of the Security Council and so block it.

From six to ten other countries are members of the Security Council, for two years, in turn.

The Security Council meets regularly and can act rapidly.
It can recommend:

- working with countries to find a solution to problems that have arisen;
- economic sanctions against a country;
- a UN military force to be sent to keep the peace in an area of conflict. The UN force, wearing light blue helmets, is made up of soldiers from armies of any of the members of the UN.

The Secretary-General

The head of the UN. The Secretary-General has no loyalty to any other country or organisation so can speak for the UN, travel round the world to see what is happening and recommend what, if anything, the UN should do.

International Court of Justice

Fifteen judges from member countries hear cases. Meets at The Hague, in the Netherlands.

Social and Economic Council

Co-ordinates the work of the UN agencies. These agencies each deal with one aspect of life or cause of a problem, on a worldwide basis. By tackling poverty, disease and ignorance among the ordinary people of the world, they hope to avoid the root causes of war.

- WHO (World Health Organisation) runs education programmes to tackle hygiene, disease and family planning. Has eliminated smallpox, but not other worldwide killer diseases like malaria, dysentery or bilharzia.
- FAO (Food and Agriculture Organisation) teaches better farming methods and organises help in famines.
- UNICEF (United Nations International Children's Emergency Fund) helps the world's children.
- UNESCO (United Nations Education, Scientific and Cultural Organisation) deals with education and so spreading understanding and respect between countries.
- UNHCR (United Nations High Comminssion for Refugees) deals with refugees, at first from the Second World War, but then from all the many wars which have been fought since 1945.
- UNCTAD (United Nations Conference on Trade And Development) tries to improve the terms of international trade for poorer countries.
- ILO (International Labour Organisation) looks after working conditions and workers' rights all over the world.
- IMF (International Monetary Fund) deals with economic needs of governments of the world
- World Bank provides long-term loans to poorer countries.

HOW DID THE UN ATTEMPT TO IMPROVE ON THE LEAGUE OF NATIONS?

(This list should be read alongside the summary of the problems of the League of Nations on p.167.)

1. All nations should belong.
2. No nation can veto Assembly resolutions.
3. Security Council to meet more regularly and act faster than the Council of the League.
4. The Secretary-General can make sure the UN acts promptly and correctly in the interests of peace, not the interests of a few members.
5. The UN can use armed force.

EXTRA POINTS ▶

1. China was added to the permanent members of the Security Council at the request of the USA and France at the request of Britain.
2. The Secretary-Generals have been:

   Trygve Lie (Norway) 1946–53
   Dag Hammarskjöld (Sweden) 1953–61
   U Thant (Burma) 1961–71
   Kurt Waldheim (Austria) 1971–81
   Perez de Cuellar (Peru) 1981–91
   Boutros Boutros Ghali (Egypt) 1991–96
   Kofi Annan (Ghana) 1997–

Check yourself

QUESTIONS

Q1 Why were the 'Four Freedoms' important:

a) As war aims?
b) As the basis of an international peacekeeping organisation?

Q2 Why was the USA so keen to play a big part in the UN?

Q3 Look at the five ways in which the UN tried to improve on the League given above. How did they make the UN stronger?

REMEMBER! Cover the answers if you want to.

ANSWERS

A1

a) The Four Freedoms (freedom from want, freedom of speech, freedom from fear, freedom of religion), were drawn up by US President Franklin D. Roosevelt and British wartime Prime Minister Winston Churchill in 1941 as the basis of the Atlantic Charter. It was important to lay out why they opposed Hitler, in order to convince other nations that their war was right. The 'Four Freedoms' were all denied to people living in Nazi Germany.

b) They were gradually incorporated into the Charter of the UN, signed in San Francisco in 1945. The UN was intended to keep world peace and those who supported the UN believed that wars start when people do not have one or more of these things.

A2 The USA was keen to play a big part in the UN because the original plan for an international peacekeeping organisation, the League of Nations, was an American one. Woodrow Wilson proposed it in his Fourteen Points of 1918, but the USA never joined. Many people in the USA thought that their failure to join was one of the reasons why the League failed to prevent the Second World War. Roosevelt was therefore keen to get things right this time.

TUTORIALS

T1 These are two good answers; both start by laying out the facts, accurately but briefly. With names, dates and places out of the way, you have the chance to comment on the events and so answer the question.

a) Note that at the time the Atlantic Charter was signed the USA was not at war, although Roosevelt was already supplying Britain with weapons under 'Lend–Lease' and less than four months later the USA was forced into the war by the Japanese attack on Pearl Harbor.

b) It was the need to deal with poverty, disease, etc. that led to the UN putting importance on its many agencies.

T2 Notice how the answer starts by picking up the wording of the question – a good ploy to get you on the right lines.

There was a wider issue of US isolationism between the wars and a realisation that in 1945 it was by far the most powerful nation in the world. Under Roosevelt the USA was determined to use this power and influence for peace.

ANSWER

1. This meant that no nation could ignore the League because it was not a member.
2. This meant that decisions of lots of nations could not be blocked by only one.
3. This meant that the Security Council could react faster to events.
4. This new post, Secretary-General, also gave the UN power to react fast and get involved.
5. This, of course, gave the UN new authority.

TUTORIAL

It is worth thinking of the overall effect of these five new and different powers together.

The two-thirds majority in the Assembly made decision-making more likely. The Secretary-General, independent of any one nation, ensured that the policies of the UN did not get entangled with the policies of single countries, especially powerful ones. Together with the frequent meetings of the Security Council, the Secretary-General made sure the UN responded rapidly and forcefully to a crisis. (Slowness of response had been one of the main failings of the League of Nations.) A military force gave the UN real power – it could not be ignored, as the League often was.

THE UNITED NATIONS FROM 1945–70

THE UN AND THE COLD WAR

As you can read in chapter 10, international affairs after the war were dominated by the Cold War, the hostility, short of actual war, between the USA and the USSR. This hostility was not at all what those who had founded the UN had expected or planned for.

- The USSR felt the UN was dominated by the West. Of the first fifty-one member-nations, twenty-three were American. With its Western European allies, this gave the USA an in-built majority in the Assembly. The USA and its allies already had a four-to-one majority in the Security Council. The USSR responded by repeatedly using its power of veto to block the UN from taking action.

- China. In 1949 the Chinese Communists won their long civil war and became the government of China. The Nationalists retreated to the island of Formosa (Taiwan). Yet the USA refused to let Communist China take their seat in the General Assembly and the Security Council. The Nationalists continued to represent China at the UN until 1972.

- 'Uniting for Peace', 1950. The General Assembly decided that when an important issue was blocked in the Security Council, it could be dealt with by the General Assembly. This was an important shift of power in the UN.

KEEPING PEACEFUL BORDERS

In several places in the world, a UN peacekeeping force was sent in, made up of soldiers from the nations of the UN, to keep two warring sides apart. In these actions the UN is a kind of world police force.

- In the Middle East, 1957–67, following the Suez Crisis, guarding the Israel–Egypt border.

- In Cyprus in 1964, keeping Greeks and Turks apart.

- In Kashmir in 1965, keeping India and Pakistan apart.

USING MILITARY FORCE

The power to send a UN armed force to take control in a crisis, on the orders of the Security Council, was one of the new powers of the UN which the League of Nations did not have. It was used twice in this period:

Korea 1950–53

This is really part of the story of the Cold War and details of what happened can be found in chapter 10. It was, nevertheless, technically a UN war.

North Korea was charged with aggression against South Korea. Normally the USSR would have used its Security Council veto to stop the UN taking any action, but at this moment it was boycotting the UN because of the USA's refusal to admit Communist China. Therefore North Korea was condemned and a UN force landed at Inchon, in South Korea, to drive them out. Although eighteen nations took part, the USA provided the great majority of the forces, including the commander, General MacArthur. They treated it as a US action, sometimes only telling the UN what was going to happen after they had decided.

Probably the USA would have got involved even if the UN had not. However, it allowed the UN to show how much its armed forces were an improvement on the weaker League of Nations, as this famous cartoon shows.

Figure 11.2
Cartoon from 1950. President Truman leads the armed figure of the United Nations over the ghost of the League.

Congo 1960–64

This country was a colony called Belgian Congo. Belgian rule in the Congo had two features:

- Paternalist. The Belgians provided primary education, but did not consider it necessary to provide much secondary education as they had no intention of giving any responsible jobs to Congolese Africans. In 1960 just seventeen Congolese had a university degree. Medicine and hospitals were provided, but all trained doctors were Europeans. Roman Catholic missionaries spread Christianity and criticised the Africans' own religious beliefs.

● Capitalist. The Congo had been opened up by private mining companies. In the south-east, in the province of Katanga, copper mines produced good profits for the mining company, the *Union Minière*. Belgian settlers lived well, as white settlers did in many parts of Africa at that time. Africans were encouraged to leave their villages to work in the mines, but lived in crowded compounds. They had no chance of any managerial job in mining, although by the 1950s trade unions were allowed and became a focus for discontent.

Independence, 1960

In 1959 protest demonstrations took place in several places. The Belgian government did not have the forces, or the wish, to keep such a large country under control. They had seen France get into huge trouble over trying to cling on to its colonies in Indo-China and Algeria. They therefore, much to the surprise of the opposition, offered independence almost at once, in 1960.

The first Prime Minister was Patrice Lumumba. Within days of independence the country was in chaos.

● Soldiers mutinied and attacked Belgian civilians. The Belgian government sent its army in to protect them.

● Katanga declared independence, under Moise Tshombe, with the support of the *Union Minière* who paid for white mercenary soldiers to come in to keep order.

Katanga was the richest province and Lumumba needed its revenue to run the country. He called on the UN for armed help to force Katanga to rejoin the rest of the country. UN Secretary-General Dag Hammarskjöld refused to do this, but he did try to negotiate with Tshombe.

Lumumba did not like this and called for Soviet help. The USSR was only too happy to get involved. In return the USA, Western countries and European business interests backed Tshombe and Katangan independence. Army leader General Mobutu then seized power, arrested Lumumba and sent him to Katanga. As Mobutu had no doubt expected, Lumumba was shot soon after his arrival.

UN action in Congo

This violence and the involvement of superpowers and European colonial powers was just what African countries most disliked about the way international relations worked in Africa. They called on the UN to act on behalf of peace and the interests of the people of the Congo.

An international force of 20,000 UN soldiers was sent. General Mobutu handed back power to elected politicians. Secretary-General Dag Hammarskjöld persuaded the white mercenaries in Katanga to hand over their weapons to UN soldiers. However, he was killed in 1961 when his plane mysteriously crashed while he was on his way to further talks with Tshombe. The new Secretary-General, U Thant, also tried to negotiate with Tshombe, but in 1962 the UN army had to be used to force Katanga to rejoin the Congo. Tshombe fled to Europe.

The United Nations also sent in their agencies, particularly the WHO and the FAO, to protect the health and food supplies to the people of Congo in this chaotic situation.

UN troops were withdrawn in 1964. There seemed to be stable government, law and order, and Katanga was no longer seeking independence. It had been a long campaign, but the UN had emerged with some credit, especially among its new members, the newly independent states in Africa and Asia.

The UN and international crises

The United Nations played little or no part in several of the major crises of the first twenty-five years after the Second World War. The Berlin airlift, the Suez Crisis, the Hungarian Revolt, the Cuban Missile Crisis, the Prague Spring in Czechoslovakia, the Vietnam War, were all dealt with outside the UN. This was either because one of the Security Council members used their veto, or because they were regarded as 'internal affairs' of the countries concerned: the UN had no powers to intervene in the internal affairs of nations. Clearly, there were weaknesses in the UN's position as the world's police.

 **EXTRA POINTS**

1. The countries providing the soldiers for the 20,000 'blue beret' UN forces in the Congo were: India, Ghana, Ireland, Canada and Nigeria.

2. Unfortunately, UN withdrawal in 1964 was the signal for trouble to restart in the Congo. Tshombe returned from Europe and took over, but was himself replaced by General Mobutu who seized power in 1965. He changed the name of the country to Zaire and remained in power until 1997.

Check yourself

QUESTIONS

Q1 In what ways did the Cold War make it difficult for the UN to operate?

Q2 Why did the UN get involved in Korea?

Q3 Why did the UN get involved in the Congo?

Q4 Was the UN operation in the Congo a success?

REMEMBER! Cover the answers if you want to.

ANSWERS

A1 The Cold War meant that the USSR and the USA were suspicious of each other's actions. As the USA and its allies had a majority in the UN in the early years, this led to repeated use of their veto by the USSR in the Security Council.

A2 The UN got involved in Korea in 1950 because North Korea had invaded South Korea. North Korea was an ally of the USSR but the USSR was boycotting the UN at the time because of the refusal of the USA and its allies to admit Communist China as the real government of China. The USA was therefore able to push through the idea of sending a UN force to Korea without the USSR's veto.

TUTORIALS

T1 *The UN had been founded on the assumption among the victorious allies that their wartime co-operation would continue. It had no real way of dealing with deadlock in the Security Council. This is why 'Uniting for Peace' was introduced in the General Assembly in 1950.*

T2 *The North Korean invasion was an act of armed aggression – just the kind of thing the UN was designed to stop. It seemed like the Japanese invasion of Manchuria in 1931 and the Italian invasion of Abyssinia in 1935. The USA was determined to use the UN. However, it was also, of course, part of US Cold War antagonism to Communist advances around the world.*

ANSWERS

A3 The UN got involved in Congo in 1960 because the Prime Minister of the newly-independent state of Congo, Patrice Lumumba, asked it to. Congo had been given independence by Belgium in 1960 without adequate preparation. Within days of independence the country was in difficulties. The government could not stop the army from mutinying and could not prevent the rich province of Katanga from declaring itself independent, with a black ruler, Tshombe, but supported by white mercenary soldiers.

A4 In many ways the UN action in the Congo was a success. Civil war and superpower involvement were largely prevented. The UN kept the country together, using mainly peaceful methods to disarm Katangese soldiers. Democratic government was restored. The UN also gave aid in the form of food and medical support. UN presence lasted for four years.

TUTORIALS

T3 *There were other factors to the situation in the Congo: several Western nations supported Katanga; Lumumba also called far Soviet help when the UN did not do just as he asked. This was when the very active Secretary-General of the time, Dag Hammaskjöld, took the intitiative. He feared that the Congo could get sucked into civil war, with superpower involvement.*

T4 *Unfortunately, soon after the UN troops left the Congo, General Mobutu seized power in an army coup and ruled for the next thirty-two years. Democracy was not permanently established. The action in the Congo, 1960–64, thus shows the strength and the weakness of UN intervention: it can be very effective, but if the conditions for peaceful, democratic government are not there, in the country, then the UN cannot stay there for ever.*

HOW HAS THE UNITED NATIONS CHANGED SINCE 1970?

MEMBERSHIP

The General Assembly

There are now 184 members of the UN, more than three times as many as in 1945. Most of these new members have been African and Asian countries which gained their independence in the 1960s and 1970s.

Results of changes in membership:

- The majority of members are now 'Less Developed Countries' (LDCs), the poorer countries of the world. The UN has become the voice of the LDCs. This has meant the agencies have become even more important. It has meant that the General Assembly is often critical of the policies of richer nations.

- Where does this change leave the richer nations, who founded the UN and which still pay most of its bills? For much of this time it has meant that the richer nations have paid less attention to the UN.

The Security Council

Questions have arisen about the membership of the Security Council. Are the five permanent members of the Security Council the five most important countries in the world as they were in 1945? What about Germany and Japan, now economically more important than Britain or France? Why no member from Africa? Should Russia occupy the seat which used to belong to the USSR?

PAYING FOR THE UN

Paying for the work of the UN has become a real problem. There have been scandals within the UN civil service. Members have been put off by the huge salaries some UN officials earn, while claiming to speak for the poorest people in the world. In the case of UNESCO, for example, the USA, Britain and several Western nations have left the organisation completely because they have disapproved of its policies and how it was run. The USA regularly refused to pay some of its contribution.

UN IN ACTION

While the Cold War continued and the nature of the UN changed, it took less part in international affairs. Continuing wars in the Middle East, the war in Afghanistan, the Iran–Iraq war, the Falklands War, were all dealt with outside the UN.

Then came the end of the Cold War and a new resolution to use the UN to deal with crises.

- **The Gulf War, 1991**
  When the state of Kuwait in the Gulf was invaded by Iraq, the response came through the UN. Although, as in Korea, most of the forces were from the USA, it was a joint action.

- **Yugoslavia, 1991**
  Yugoslavia was a new country, created at the end of the First World War out of the remains of the Austro–Hungarian Empire. It included disparate and hostile peoples, with different languages, religions and histories. After the Second World War, the former partisan Communist, Tito, held it together by the force of his personality and reputation. This unity continued for a while after his death in 1980. However, in the tremendous changes in Eastern Europe in 1989–90, Yugoslavia began to break up. Some provinces became independent countries, but civil war broke out in others. There was terrible ethnic violence against civilians. The UN sent in a peacekeeping force, but it was prevented from acting decisively because it was technically an internal war in which they could not intervene.

Check yourself

QUESTIONS

Q1 What have been the results of the changes in the membership of the UN since 1970?

Q2 How has the end of the Cold War affected the work of the UN?

REMEMBER! Cover the answers if you want to.

ANSWERS

A1 There are now many more members of the UN than there were in 1945 and most of the new members are former colonies. This means that the General Assembly has become the voice of anti-imperial and poorer countries. The aid agencies have become more important.

A2 The end of the Cold War has meant that the USA and the USSR have been more prepared to co-operate and work through the UN.

TUTORIALS

T1 *This shift in the interest of members has led the superpowers to pay less attention to the UN than they (particularly the USA) did in its first twenty-five years.*

T2 *The USA and the USSR agreed on UN action to stop the Iraqi invasion of Kuwait; they have agreed, up to a point, on UN action in Yugoslavia.*

EXAM PRACTICE

Sample Student's Answers & Examiner's Comments

1 Write a sentence to explain what the General Assembly of the United Nations is. (2)

The General Assembly of the United Nations is the Parliament of the UN. Each nation is a member, with one vote. Decisions have to have a two-thirds majority.

2/2

EXAMINER'S COMMENTS

MARK SCHEME

Level 1   Correctly describes position of
General Assembly   **1 mark**

Level 2   Makes one point about how the
General Assembly works   **2 marks**

There is obviously lots more you could say about the General Assembly: comparisons with the League, changes over time, 'Uniting for peace' etc. However, there are only two marks for this question and the student has sensibly chosen to make a couple of basic points and to leave it at that – quite enough for both marks.

> **2** How succesful has the UN been at keeping peace since 1945? (15)
>
> At first sight the UN has failed to keep the peace very well. There have been wars in the Middle East, Vietnam, Africa, Afghanistan, the Falklands and many other places. Civil wars have caused distress and hardship to many civilians.
>
> However, the UN has kept the peace in several places, such as Cyprus, 1964, where Greeks and Turks both claim the island; Kashmir, 1965, disputed between India and Pakistan, and in the Middle East, from 1957–67. It reacted fast to the North Korean invasion of South Korea. Its best performance was in the Congo, where civil war and foreign involvement seemed likely to pull the country apart. (8/15)

EXAMINER'S COMMENTS

MARK SCHEME

Level 1 Answer in generalisations, with few accurate descriptions of events **1–5 marks**

Level 2 Some description of events, either of wars, or peacekeeping, or both. **6–10 marks**

Level 3 Analysis of role of UN as peacekeeper and peacemaker, using accurate recalled information to support points made. **11–15 marks**

This is a short, descriptive answer. It is correct as far as it goes, but has no real analysis: it therefore only receives a moderate mark within Level 2.

The problem in this question is quite a difficult one: what might have happened if there had been no UN? History does not deal with things that did not happen, and a war which was avoided is not very exciting news.

As with the League of Nations, powerful countries often chose to ignore the UN at moments of crisis – as the USA did over Vietnam, Britain did over the Falklands and the USSR did over Afghanistan. Security Council members and their allies could prevent the UN from acting by using their veto, as the USSR did over Hungary in 1956 and Czechoslovakia in 1968.

The UN works to strict rules. Peacekeeping forces could only stay in a country as long as they are invited. In 1967 UN forces were withdrawn from the Arab–Israeli borders just before the June 1967 war broke out, and there was nothing to stop them going.

They can, it seems *keep* the peace quite effectively, but are up against problems when it comes to peacemaking between nations who seem determined to go to war.

As the history of the League shows, real power lies with nation-states. The UN is stronger, but not strong enough really to live up to its nickname of 'the world's policeman'.

Question to Answer
The answer to Question 3 can be found on p.277

3 Look at Figure 11.2 (p.259).

(a) Use your own knowledge to explain what this cartoon is saying. (6)

(b) What is the attitude of cartoonist to the UN here? (5)

CHAPTER 2   THE FIRST WORLD WAR

Answer to Questions on p. 44

3   The main reason why there was no change in sixteen months is that the generals could not think of a better tactic. Machine-guns were accurate and deadly and could fire eight bullets a second. Casualties were heavy, as Source A describes, but commanders still sent men 'over the top', as Source B shows. They believed that they could get through the enemy lines if only they had enough men to overwhelm the defences. This kind of warfare was entirely new, so the commanders had to work out how to deal with it and did not do this until 1918.   [3/6]

Examiner's Comments

This answer is satisfactory as far as it goes. It describes the situation on the Western Front in general terms, using some additional information. However, as this question calls for 'your own knowledge' there are specific things which could be said. For example, Sir John French, the author of Source A, was replaced in December 1915 by Sir Douglas Haig. Haig may not have agreed with French that heavy casuaties made this method of attacking 'impossible'. Also, the British attack at the Battle of the Somme was made in order to help the French army, hard-pressed at Verdun. Haig had to attack. Nor can you assume that these two sources prove that nothing had changed. Haig thought he had the answer by using heavy artillery in more massive barrages than French had been able to use. The Battle of the Somme may not have been exactly like the battles of 1915, even though the results were no better.

4   Because so many men were away at the war women had to take on lots of jobs they did not usually do. They worked in factories, on the land and on buses. They made guns and filled shells with high explosive. They worked as nurses. They were not paid the same as men for the same work and did not receive the same injury payment if they were injured at work. Some of the work they did, such as farming, was very hard and some, like working in munitions factories, was dangerous. Nearly three million women were working in industry by 1918 and nearly one million in munitions. Many women actually left their jobs as servants to take on these new jobs. Altogether there were over two million more women working in 1918 than in 1914. Women usually had to give their jobs back after the war, when the men came home. Some women over thirty were given the vote in 1918 in recognition of their war effort.   [6/15]

Examiner's Comments

Everything the student has written in this short essay is correct. So why does it get such a poor mark?

In short: because it doesn't answer the question. It is clear from the number of marks available and from the breadth of the topic that you are expected to write an essay. An essay is not just a big pile of all the facts you can remember. It is an organised piece of writing in which you try to answer the different aspects of the question. This will involve using the information you know, but arranged so that it supports the point you are trying to make. There are several examples of essay answers, with Examiner's Comments, in this book (see chapters 4, 5, 6, 8, 9, 10 and 11).

In this case, the question is about the impact of *change*. In order to explain what impact the wartime situation had, you need to say something about the position of women in Britain in 1914. They really were treated as second-class citizens, home-builders, wives and mothers. They had no chance of making a career or even of getting a well-paid job. Their views on issues outside the home were not listened to. Even in the home they were expected to give way to their husband.

All this should go in an opening paragraph: it is a sign of its poor organisation that the answer above has no separate paragraphs.

Then say something about how all this changed. This is what the answer above covers. However, it could be better organised into sections on why women's work was needed, what they did and how men (employers and trade unions) reacted.

Then come the last two paragraphs in which you deal with the two aspects of women's position mentioned: social and economic.

Socially, women had more freedom: they had money of their own; they often left home to work; they found new skills they did not know they had. Even though most women lost their jobs when the war ended, this growth in confidence did not disappear. Women behaved with more freedom after the war. Economically, the change was short-lived. During the war they benefitted; afterwards they had to return to wages lower than men's and being excluded from many good jobs.

CHAPTER 3 THE PEACE TREATIES

Answer to Questions on p. 58

3 a) It tells us that some people in Britain were afraid that there would be war by 1940. They are blaming the three statesmen who had drawn up the Treaty of Versailles for this. [3/4]

Examiner's Comments

Cartoons are always difficult to work on. You have to study every part of them and look for meanings. In this case the other point to add to the good answer above is that the cartoonist seems to be blaming Clemenceau most of all, but that all three seem to be quite unaware of the harm they have done.

It is very interesting that this cartoon was published in 1919. In early 1919 most people in Britain were calling for harsh terms for Germany. Now, less than a year later, someone is saying that they fear that the statesmen have got it wrong. Whoever it drew the cartoon was amazingly accurate in the prediction: only one year out, as the Second World War started in 1939.

b) They felt this because the terms were so tough on Germany that they would want a war of revenge by 1940. German public opinion was angry about several aspects of the Treaty: loss of teritory, loss of armed forces, loss of colonies, having to accept blame for the war, the burden of reparations. They also resented the fact that they were not negotiating as equals but accepting dictated terms as a defeated power.

Of course, no one could have foreseen Hitler, who made the prediction in the cartoon come true. If it had not been for him Germany might have got over her resentment as the years went by. [4/6]

Examiner's Comments

The answer is based on the angry reaction of the German people. But some people in Britain were also saying that the terms were bad for every country in Europe and that the Allies had made mistakes at Versailles. It is not just a question of the danger of revenge.

The last paragraph of the answer makes a good additional point. We know that the prediction came true: but what would they have thought in Britain in 1919?

Lastly, it is worth making the point with any source like this that it may not have been typical. One cartoon cannot sum up all British feelings, and many may still have felt it was right to punish Geremany.

CHAPTER 4   WEIMAR AND NAZI GERMANY, 1918–1945

Answer to Questions on p. 93

4   As the worldwide depression hit Germany in 1929 unemployment began to rise until it reached six million in 1933, as the graph shows. The Nazis did not have much support in 1929, with only twelve seats in the Reichstag. By 1932 they were the biggest single party.

To many Germans, the Depression came as just the last of a series of crises which the Weimar government could not deal with. There had been the humiliating peace treaty in 1919, the French invasion and hyper-inflation of 1923, and now this. To a people who were not very keen on democratic government anyway, this was too much. Although the depression was not the fault of the Weimar government, they seemed unable to do anything about it.

Many German people were desperate, and turned to extremist parties. The Communists promised a workers' revolution and increased their vote, but the Nazis increased theirs most of all. Hitler had always said that the Weimar government would not work. He promised to make Germany great again, solve unemployment and give the country strong leadership. This was just what many Germans felt they needed and voted for him.   [6/8]

Examiner's Comments

This is quite a good answer because it does make some comments about the inability of the Weimar governments to deal with the Depression. It therefore adds something more than just the idea that the German people turned to the Nazis in a crisis.

However, it is not very explicit about the key words 'How far...' The Nazis were far from being passive, after all. They campaigned furiously, helped by money from industrialists scared by the rise of Communism. Hitler's moving speeches, Nazi posters, marches, the uniformed SA all gave a powerful impression of people who knew what they were doing and had answers to Germany's problems.

Another factor which could have been explored a little more is the failure of Hindenburg and the politicians to keep alive democratic structures. From about 1930 Germany was ruled by decree. Right throughout society there was a feeling that democracy had failed. This made Hitler sound less unreasonable than he might have done in a strong democracy.

5   a)   The boys are in the Hitler Youth. They are doing this for fun and excitement at a camp. The Hitler Youth went on lots of camps and outdoor activities to build up strong young people.   [2/4]

Examiner's Comments

Another key element in the Hitler Youth was preparation for war. Hitler wanted them to learn to overcome fear, so that they would be better soldiers. One way of doing this was to do dangerous things like the one shown in the picture.

b)   The Hitler and the Nazis paid special attention to young people as they were the future of the 'Thousand Year Reich'. They took care to train them so that they would be just 'good servants of the state', as the question says.

At school the curriculum was altered so that it was filled with Nazi propaganda. In History they learnt only about Germany, its victories and successes. In biology they learnt about the superiority of the German race and the inferiority of others. PE was expanded so that young people were kept fit.

Most young people had to join one of the youth movements: the Pimpfen from 6–10, the Young Girls or Young German Folk from 10–14, then the League of German Girls or the Hitler Youth for boys. Here they got even more propaganda talks and films. They were prepared for their future as Nazi citizens: boys to be soldiers, girls to be mothers of future good German citizens. [7/10]

Examiner's Comments

This is a good answer as far as it goes. It is factually correct, detailed and well-organised. However, it takes Nazi intentions at face value and assumes they succeeded. It is always advisable in these questions not simply to agree with the statement. You are asked to 'comment on the accuracy of the statement', which says that young people 'became nothing but servants of the state'. Was Hitler 100 per cent successful? There is another side to be put.

To a large extent they *did* succeed: most young people were enthusiastic Nazis. Many did become just servants of the Nazi state. They joined the army and fought and died for Nazism. Some even became racist killers in the SS.

But recent evidence shows that many young people found the atmosphere of Nazi Germany stifling. They particularly resented the time they had to spend in youth movement meetings and the boring and repetitive propoganda. Some young people wanted to 'do their own thing', whatever it was, and the Nazis did not want this. Intellectual young people wanted to study: Nazism did not really want people to study too much. After all, all decisions were taken by the Party leaders. Many did not like the gruelling activities, the long marches and outdoor life. Some even went so far as to join alternatives such as 'swing' groups and the groups the Nazis called 'Edelweiss Pirates'.

CHAPTER 5   THE RUSSIAN REVOLUTION 1900–1924

Answers to Questions on p. 115

3 a) The Duma was the Russian Parliament which the Tsar had agreed to. [2/3]

Examiner's Comments

The second part of the answer is rather vague. Mention could have been made of the 1905 Revolution, which led to the setting up of the Duma, and the Tsar's considerable hostility to it.

b) This source is from the Tsarina's diary, so will be just her personal views. She thinks the protesters are all hooligans and does not take them seriously. [3/6]

Examiner's Comments

If ever there was a source-question where the attribution has to be taken note of, this is it. This is not a newspaper report or foreign observer, who might be expected to try to describe what is going on; this is the Tsarina Alexandra, wife of Tsar Nicholas and effectively ruler of Russia while her husband is away at the war. This is a particularly dramatic example, but do remember that the attribution should always be taken into consideration.

This answer almost falls into the dangerous 'It's biased therefore it's no use' category. It may well be a highly biased description of events, but it has some use. For top levels, rise above the bias of the author to say what you can conclude from the source. In this case, clearly there was unrest in the streets, food shortages, strikes and some Duma support for the protests: however Alexandra describes them cannot hide these facts.

4 When the Bolsheviks tried to seize power from the Provisional Government in July they failed, many were arrested and Lenin had to shave his beard off and flee abroad. Only four months later they succeeded in their efforts and replaced the Provisional Government. How could this rapid change come about?

In July, Kerensky, the Provisional Government's most dynamic member and Prime Minister, was able to rely on the army to stay loyal to him. The Bolsheviks could only hold street demonstrations and so were easily crushed by Kerensky's armed troops.

By November the army was no longer reliable. They were fed up with the Provisional Government's determination to continue the war. Hardly any were prepared to take up their weapons for Kerensky by November. Furthermore, the Bolsheviks were much better organised by November. Enthused by Lenin, organised by Trotsky, they were now armed and Red Guards seized key positions in the city of Petrograd: post offices, railway stations, bridges over the river, the battleship Aurora. This was not a popular rising, it was a seizure of power by one small armed group.

[10/12]

Examiner's Comments

This is a hard question: as hard as anything you are likely to find at GCSE. It demands an understanding, not of one, but of two separate events. At the top levels, it requires a comparison of the two, and the answer given does get near to this: it looks at the loyalties of the army and the different approaches of the Bolsheviks on each occasion.

The other aspect which should have been covered was an explanation of *why* the army had a different attitude in November from July.

In July the attacks on the Eastern Front ordered by the Provisional Government had already ended in failure, but the impact of these latest defeats had not really been felt in the army. Gradually desertions and mutiny led to the crumbling away of army loyalty. More and more soldiers' elected their own representatives to the Bolshevik-controlled Soviets. Some went off home to join in the growing number of peasant land seizures.

Kornilov's attempted coup revealed only the powerlessness of the Provisional Government: it was Bolshevik railway workers who held him off, not the army. Kerensky's decision to arm anyone who was prepared to fight against Kornilov was brave, but it merely put weapons into the hands of the most determined anti-Tsarists, the Bolsheviks. It only needed Lenin and Trotsky to persuade them to turn these weapons against the Provisional Government.

CHAPTER 6 STALIN AND RUSSIA

Answer to Question on p. 133

3 The immense changes which Stalin made to the lives of the people of the USSR brought hardship to many of them. In the new industrial cities they had to work hard, often under dangerous conditions, to meet the production figures expected under the Five-Year Plans. Housing in the cities was in short supply: many families had to live in one room. There were shortages of food and consumer goods. Standards of living were below those in western Europe and the USA.

In agriculture, collectivisation brought hardship, especially for the kulaks and their families. Even for those who were not badly treated, there was famine by the mid-1930s.

Those who suffered under his dictatorship ran into millions. Historians are unsure whether the figure for those arrested amounts to ten million or twenty million. Perhaps a million were killed outright, many died in the labour camps and the rest were kept there under terrible conditions.

These figures do not include their famillies, who grieved at home.

However it is not true that, as the question says, there was 'nothing but hardship'. Standards of living in Russia under the Tsars were lower than elsewhere and many ordinary Soviet citizens actually experienced an improvement under Stalin. This was all the more likely to be so if you were a loyal Party member or a manager, because families in these groups got better food, housing and access to shortage items. Health care and education were better under Stalin and facilities for leisure activities were among the best in the world. If you were prepared to keep quiet and just get on with leading your life, things were not too bad. [9/12]

Examiner's Comments

This is a good answer, well within Grade C. It is balanced and well-supported by factual information, which has been selected to fit the points the writer is making. It follows a simple, sensible and effective plan for this kind of essay-question: make the points which support one side of the argument, then switch tack and put the other side.

An A, or even A* Grade answer might go into some of the complications of how the people really thought of Stalin. He was popular, especially after his leadership of the USSR in the Second World War, in which he led them through terrible hardships to eventual victory. Was this just because people were taught to worship him? Was it just the 'personality cult'? Before the revolution the Tsar was always known as 'the father of his people'. Perhaps Stalin was seen as 'the father of his people' in a way that Nicholas II failed to be.

CHAPTER 7 THE USA, 1919–1941

Answers to Questions on p. 157

3 The picture is more useful. It shows you clearly how much space they had, what their shack was made of, what they wore, etc.

The problem with the extract from *The Grapes of Wrath* is that it is from a novel: the man is made up, the situation is made up. It may be based on what really happened, but we would have to check it all first. The extract describes the man's problems, but not as powerfully as in the picture. [3/7]

Examiner's Comments

This answer makes the common mistake of assuming that photographs are always what they seem. This one might well be accurate, but you have to show as much caution in using photos as you are applying to the novel. After all, it might be posed, using actors. It might not be typical: down the road may be some much nicer houses, or the photographer could have chosen the worst.

If you are as careful about checking both of them the difference is not so great. However, the last sentence of the answer is true, there is a power in the photograph which a short extract cannot match (although, it should be said, the full length novel is certainly powerful).

4 Although it was US President Woodrow Wilson who had suggested the idea of a League of Nations to prevent wars in the future, the USA never joined. This was because the US Senate refused to agree to the Treaty of Versailles which included the League.

The mood of the USA by 1919 was hostile towards any links with other countries, especially the countries of Europe. This was, in fact, traditional US policy. The USA had been formed by breaking away from Britain in the eighteenth century. Many of its people had left Europe for a better life in the New World, glad to see the back of Europe. They were also counting the cost of US deaths in the First World War: 100,000. For all these reasons, they did not want to join in any foreign alliances or agreements and rejected the Treaty. [7/10]

Examiner's Comments

This answer starts well, clearing up the point that US membership of the League depended on their signing the Treaty. It then goes on to offer a general account of the mood of isolationism.

However, the two points are not quite linked: how did a general feeling of turning their back on Europe lead to a rejection of the Treaty? We need to know that it was not up to President Wilson to agree the Treaty, but, under the US constitution, it had to be passed by the Senate. Here some isolationist senators blocked it. Even then, Wilson could have managed to get something through by making compromises, but he refused, and all was lost.

The League was particularly worrying to isolationists because they feared it could pull the USA into all sorts of foreign wars which they did not want.

CHAPTER 8   INTERNATIONAL RELATIONS 1919–1939

Answer to Question on p. 180

4 The failure of the League of Nations contributed a great deal to the outbreak of the Second World War. It was set up in 1919 to keep the world at peace. It was to work by bringing all nations together to talk about their grievances and solve them peaceably. Yet only twenty years later war broke out again. It never included all the major powers, so was weaker than it should have been. The USA never joined, so the most powerful country in the world took no part in forcing those who wanted to cause war to back down. This was most true in the case of the Japanese invasion of Manchuria in 1931, where US sanctions could have brought Japan into line. Japan and Germany left in 1933; Italy left in 1935. The USSR only joined in 1934.

The League was supposed to preserve and enforce the terms of the Treaty of Versailles. This meant that it was hated by the countries defeated in 1919 and made it difficult for nations, like Britain, who thought the terms of those treaties could be changed over time.

It was successful in solving some disputes, usually those involving smaller and law-abiding countries, as over the Åalund Islands in 1923, involving Sweden and Finland. Its work with refugees and in other agencies contributed to a peaceful, less angry world.

However it was not able to resolve big disputes, involving big aggressive nations. It did not stop the Japanese invasion of Manchuria, nor the Italian invasion of Abyssinia, 1935. It did not use military sanctions and its efforts to use economic sanctions were ineffective. This was mainly because the bigger trading nations, which would bear the brunt of a sanctions policy, were either not in the League or afraid of the consequences for their own economies.

This clash of League-interest versus self-interest on the part of Britain and France greatly weakened the League and made determined action against aggressive nations difficult to enforce. It also meant that disarmament was never achieved. This meant that by the time Hitler began to break international rules, over his reoccupation of the Rhineland, 1936 and the Anschluss, 1938, the League was in no position to stop him.   [8/12]

Examiner's Comments

This is a very good answer to the question 'How did the weaknesses of the League of Nations contribute to the war?' However, this is a 'How much?' question – it asks you to take an item, in this case the weaknesses of the League, and weigh it against other factors.

Other factors which should have been mentioned are:

● the Depression, which weakened economies and made nations more self-interested. It also helped the rise of dictators to power, rulers who were determined to promote their own country at all costs.

● Hitler himself. The League expected world rulers to prefer peace to war. Hitler had no such preferences.

● Communism and Stalin. The reactions of many countries in western, and especially eastern, Europe to the Russian Revolution prevented united action against an aggressor. By 1939 it led Stalin, feeling isolated, to the Nazi–Soviet Pact, which opened the door to Hitler's invasion of Poland, and so to war.

CHAPTER 9   **SOUTH AFRICA**

Answers to Questions on p. 207

3   Apartheid collapsed for a mixture of reasons, some to do with outside pressures, some to do with internal protest.

Outside pressure did begin to have an effect by the late 1980s. Some companies were beginning to pull out of South Africa. International boycotts were weakening South Africa's exports. The result was a decline in national income. White South Africans were feeling the squeeze.

The collapse of white colonial rule in Mozambique, Angola and Zimbabwe also brought external threats nearer. Invasion from the north looked a possibility.

Internal protest reached a peak in the late 1980s, with massive riots in the black townships. The police responded with violence and mass arrests. The country seemed to be becoming ungovernable.

It was these considerations which led de Klerk to make his dramatic promises of reform in 1989. Of the two, outside pressures were probably more important: South Africa could not survive without foreign friends and trading partners.   [12/15]

Examiner's Comments

This is a good summary of both sides, ending with a simple, but fair judgement. In fact, the two factors are not water-tight compartments. It was the worldwide television pictures of violence in the townships and between police and rioters, which re-vitalised international opposition to apartheid and stepped up pressure for change. All the arguments of the 1970s and 1980s, about keeping in contact with South Africa in order to bring gradual reform, were seen to have failed utterly.

We do not know how the balance between internal and external factors affected de Klerk's thinking, so there is no 'right' answer to this question. If South Africa had still had foreign support, it might have been able to crush the internal revolt, as it crushed the Soweto riots in 1976, so it is probably these external factors which tipped the scales.

4 a) Over the years 1951 to 1991 South Africa had become a much more urban and industrial country. Mining had been important from the late nineteenth century, and still was, but in the second half of the twentieth century manufacturing and commerce also boomed. This meant more people went to the towns to live, blacks as well as whites.   [3/5]

Examiner's Comments

Some points are missing from this answer which would stop it from getting top marks: it comments on blacks and whites together, but the figures are quite different. Over three-quarters of whites lived in towns anyway in 1951, and this rose to nine out of ten. The rise for black people, however, is much more dramatic: doubling, from only just over a quarter to well over half.

Secondly, farming had also changed. All over the world mechanisation was replacing human labour in farming. South Africa was no different. There just were no longer the jobs in farming that there had been in the past.

Lastly, one must question the figures. Just because figures look reliable and not as obviously biased as personal evidence does not mean they are always right. We know that the National Party tried to classify as many black people as possible as rural-dwellers and used the Pass Laws to restrict their movement. The figures may therefore show a much higher number of blacks living in rural areas than was actually the case.

b) The ideal of apartheid, as expounded by Malan and Verwoerd in the years after the National Party came to power in 1948, was that the towns would become more and more exclusively white, while blacks lived in the countryside. It was part of the crazy ideas of racial superiority which the designers of apartheid held that black people were not 'fitted' for urban life.

These figure show this theory being undermined by economic realities. Businesses wanted more workers, and were prepared to employ blacks as well as whites; attempts to declare areas in towns 'white only' made this more difficult. Black workers were thus sentenced to overcrowded townships or long commuter journeys by bus.   [5/5]

Examiner's Comments

This is better: it gets to the root of the problem apartheid was facing by the late 1980s. Together with the black population rise being so much greater than that of the white population, it was part of the growing realisation among many whites that apartheid could never work. The situation behind the figures also produced the mass irritation and opposition which exploded in the riots of 1985 onwards.

CHAPTER 10   THE COLD WAR

Answer to Question p. 253

4 a) This source tells you what it was like for US soldiers in the Vietnam War. They were trying to help the villagers with medical aid as part of the US policy to win the 'hearts and minds' of the Vietnamese people.

But the villagers were also hiding the Vietcong, who shoot at him when he is unprepared. The soldier finds it hard to accept that the people he was trying to help were trying to kill him. He cannot distinguish between an innocent villager and a Vietcong guerrilla. He ends up trusting no one.

The Vietcong were soldiers from North Vietnam, or Communists from South Vietnam. They had become experts in guerrilla warfare in the long years they had spent in fighting the Japanese, in the Second World War, then the French, who had re-claimed their colony in 1945. As guerrilla soldiers they hid among the Vietnamese people and ambushed the Americans when they were not expecting it.   [5/5]

Examiner's Comments

A good answer, which combines good selection of details from the source with good use of knowledge.

The most straightforward way of tackling these questions which combine comprehending the source with remembering what you can of events is to do one thing, then another. To try to do both, the comprehension and the remembering, will lead to you missing points out and will also produce a jumble in the answer.

Here the answer picks up what the soldier is doing, and helps us understand that this was an important part of US policy. It then goes on to explain what happens to the soldier and how he feels as a result. Remembered knowledge helps us see what the Vietcong were up to.

b) The remark at the end of Source A 'you didn't trust anybody' helps us understand what is going on here. The soldier has lost any sense of wanting to help the Vietnamese people and is taking revenge. He may have been shot at from this village soon after he was giving medical care to the villagers. This leads him to set light to the huts.   [3/6]

Examiner's Comments

This may be right. However, Source B may not just be an act of desperate revenge, as it appears. Setting fire to villages was often done after the villagers had been removed to a safe village somewhere else. If the huts were then destroyed the Vietcong would have nowhere to hide. This 'search and destroy' policy, as it was called, was very controversial and may have brought about events such as the My Lai Massacre of 1968 (see p. 234). It was however, deliberate policy as a way of countering guerrilla tactics.

c) US tactics in the Vietnam War included burning villages, using chemical defoliant to strip leaves off jungle trees and massive bombing. These were their attempts to deal with an enemy quite unlike the enemies the US had fought in the Second World War or Korea.

However, they were in Vietnam to prevent South Vietnam becoming Communist. It was part of their Cold War policy of 'containment' dating back to the Truman Doctrine of 1947. They believed that if South Vietnam fell, then another country would follow, then another and so on, like a line of dominoes. Preventing South Vietnam becoming Communist meant winning over the 'hearts and minds' of the South

Vietnamese people. Some US policies, like free medical aid described in Source A, might have done this. But this made US soldiers easy targets in the villages, as Source A describes. They therefore turned to the tactics listed above as a way of winning the guerrilla war. But these tactics did nothing to win over the hearts and minds of the South Vietnamese. The statement is therefore correct, but it may be that the USA could not win this war whatever tactics they had used.   [8/10]

Examiner's Comments

A carefully-organised answer in which a good plan pays off. It starts by listing US anti-guerrilla tactics. Then it moves to the wider issue of why they were fighting and what they were doing there. This leads on to a good use of Source A to explain how tactics varied. Then comes the conclusion in which the answer returns to the main question: it is always a good idea to do this to see that you have answered the question rather than been distracted into writing something else that interests you.

The last point needs developing, however: there were other reasons for US defeat than simply using wrong tactics. The Vietcong were popular and the South Vietnamese government were unpopular. The whole US intervention was therefore on shaky foundations. Indeed, with the Vietcong supported by the experienced North Vietnamese, and both being plentifully supplied by the USSR, it is doubtful if any tactics could have given the USA victory in this situation. Their defeat was at least as much due to the successful guerrilla tactics of their enemy as to their own 'wrong tactics'.

CHAPTER 11   THE UNITED NATIONS

Answers to Questions on p. 266

3 a) The cartoonist is saying that the UN is stronger than the League, which died because it failed to deal with 'wanton aggression'. It is armed now, which the League never was. The date, 1950, is important, because that was when the UN first used its power to call on military force to deal with an act of aggression. In that year UN forces (mainly US forces, but with soldiers from seventeen other countries, including Britain) landed in South Korea to repel a North Korean invasion.   [3/6]

Examiner's Comments

Remember that a cartoonist spends many hours getting a cartoon exactly right. It may look simple, but every item has its place. In this case, the answer has missed two points:

First, President Truman is the man galloping along with the new, vigourous UN, holding her hand: i.e. the USA is helping the UN succeed where the League failed by taking strong action in Korea.

Second, don't forget to look at the caption. This one, 'History doesn't repeat itself', emphasises the comparison with the events of the 1930s.

b) The cartoonist seems to approve of the action of the USA, Truman and the UN. He regards the League as having failed because it was incapable of dealing with aggression by one power against another and approves of the UN using force in Korea.   [4/5]

Examiner's Comments

This is a good, knowlegeable and thoughtful answer. Cartoons often tell you a lot about attitudes of mind among people generally.

This cartoon is very revealing about the attitudes of many people at the time (the cartoonist is in fact British) about what they regarded as the failures of the League, and the reasons for them. These views were what lay behind the determination of the backers of the UN, especially the USA, to give the UN 'teeth'. In fact, although the North Korean invasion of South Korea was an act of wanton aggression, the USA was only too glad to oppose it as they were involved in the Cold War against Communism. The Korean War was really an extension of the Cold War from Europe into the Far East.

Nor, in fact, was the Korean War like the Japanese invasion of Manchuria or the Italian invasion of Abyssinia, the two events on which the League foundered and which led people to regard it as a failure. Those cases were much harder to deal with as the aggressors on both occasions were members of the Council of the League.

Published by HarperCollinsPublishers Ltd
77–85 Fulham Palace Road
London W6 8JB

www.CollinsEducation.com
On-line support for schools and colleges

© HarperCollinsPublishers Ltd 2001

First published 2001
Reprinted 2001

ISBN 0 00 711198 3

Christopher Culpin asserts the moral right to be identified as the author of this work.

British Library Cataloguing in Publication Data

A catalogue record for this book is available from the British Library.

Edited by Kate Woodhouse

Production by Kathryn Botterill

Cover design by Susi Martin-Taylor

Book design by Rupert Purcell and produced by Gecko Limited

Index compiled by Drusilla Calvert

Printed and bound by Scotprint

Acknowledgements
The Author and Publishers are grateful to the following for permission to reproduce photographs:
Bildarchiv Preussischer Kulturbesitz 7, 71, 79, 88
Camera Press 192
Corbis UK 135, 253
Deutscheshistorisches Museum 59
Getty Images 46, 76, 95 (top), 105, 159, 212, 229
Imperial War Museum 25, 27, 33, 43, 44, 45, 53, 67, 174, 208, 242
Peter Newark's Pictures 140, 141, 157
Katz Pictures Ltd   116
David King 95 (bottom), 96, 124, 128, 130
Novosti 8, 11, 97, 112, 113
Popperfoto 1, 85, 187, 239
Frank Spooner 203, 248
Süddeutscher Verlag 52, 93
Topham Picturepoint 3, 23, 151, 171, 183
Trip/A.Tjagny-Rjadno 127
Weimar Archive 64
Wiener Library 12

Illustrations:
Gecko Ltd 14, 21, 25, 29, 63, 54, 181, 196, 221; Jillian Luff 6, 22, 27, 48, 107, 108, 120, 165, 167, 171, 213, 218, 228, 232; Julia Osorno 233

Every effort has been made to contact the holders of copyright material, but if any have been inadvertently overlooked, the Publishers will be pleased to make the necessary arrangements at the first opportunity.

You might also like to visit:
www.fireandwater.com
The book lover's website

INDEX